SMALL-BLOCK CHEVY PERFORMANCE

Modifications and Dyno-Tested Combinations for High Performance Street and Racing Use

DAVE EMANUEL

HPBooks

HPBooks
are published by
The Berkley Publishing Group
200 Madison Avenue
New York, New York 10016

First Edition: November 1996

© 1996 Dave Emanuel
10 9 8 7 6 5 4 3 2 1

Library of Congress Cataloging-in-Publication Data

Emanuel, Dave, 1946-
    Small-block Chevy performance: modifications and dyno-tested
combinations for high performance street and racing use / Dave
Emanuel.—Rev. and updated, 1st ed.
       p.   cm.
    Includes index.
    ISBN 1-55788-253-3
    1. Chevrolet automobile—Motors—Modification—Handbooks, manuals,
etc. 2. Chevrolet automobile—Parts—Handbooks, manuals, etc. 3. Chevrolet
automobile—Performance—Handbooks, manuals, etc.
I. Title
TL215.C48E43   1996
629.25'04—dc20   96-32740
                                                                   CIP

Book Design & Production by Bird Studios
Interior photos by the author unless otherwise noted
Cover photo by Dave Emanuel

NOTICE: The information in this book is true and complete to the best of our knowledge. All recommendations on parts and procedures are made without any guarantees on the part of the author or The Berkley Publishing Group. Tampering with, altering, modifying or removing any emissions-control device is a violation of federal law. Author and publisher disclaim all liability incurred in connection with the use of this information.

ACKNOWLEDGMENTS

One of the things I dislike most about any awards show is that the winners go on ad nauseum thanking everybody they ever spoke to for one thing or another. Now, here I am about to do the very thing I detest. In this instance, however, it's a bit different, because the people I've named contributed significantly to this book. I'm sincerely grateful for their time and effort.

Chuck Maguire, GM Powertrain; Garry Grimes, Grimes Automotive and Marine Machine; Mike and Chad Hedgecock, Eagle Racing Engines; Jim Oddy, Oddy's Automotive; Norm Wizner, Wizner Performance Products; Brad Brand, Random Technology; Howard Stewart, Stewart Components; Randy Dorton, Hendrick Motorsports; Fred Roland, Vibratech Performance; Scooter Brothers, Competition Cams; Harvey Crane, Crane CamDesign; Myron Cottrell, TPI Specialities; Roger Allen, Chevrolet Race Shop; Jack Underwood, GM Powertrain; John Juriga, GM Powertrain; Pete Incaudo, CNC Cylinder Heads, Inc.; Chuck Leeper, Cody Motorsports; Keith Dorton, Automotive Specialists; John Wilson, Joe Gibbs Racing; Dan Vanderley, Vanderly Racing Engines; Jerry Rosenquist, Fel-Pro; Mark Felser, Gor-Den Racing Engines; Mike Osucha, JVR Engineering; Bill Howell, Mathew Howell, Howell Engine Developments.

Of course, it's common practice for most authors to thank the editor, which in this instance is Michael Lutfy. I've never figured that out, because it's kind of like thanking your mother-in-law for being a nag. After all, what editors do most is complain. No matter what you send them, it's either too much, too little, too light or too dark, too square or too round. But I do owe Mike a thank-you because he's mastered the art of nagging without being a nag and his efforts have brought many improvements to *Small-Block Chevy Performance*.

CONTENTS

INTRODUCTION

At the time I began writing the first edition of *Small-Block Chevy Performance* (which was published in 1992), engine technology was relatively stable. The small block hadn't changed appreciably since its introduction in 1955, and even amongst high performance parts manufacturers, departures from traditional small block architecture were rare. Then the roof fell in. Shortly before we were scheduled to go to press, Chevrolet introduced the LT1, and although it shares many components and designs with the first generation engine, there are a number of radical differences. A few of those were noted in the first edition, but coverage of the LT1 has been expanded considerably in this edition. However, from a horsepower production standpoint, an LT1 is still a small-block Chevy so most LT1-specific information has been woven into the text, rather than being treated separately.

Another significant change in this edition is the inclusion of a chapter devoted to short block preparation. As originally conceived, *Small-Block Chevy Performance* was geared towards modifications that could be made without removing the engine from a vehicle. However, I've been shown the error of my ways. Although there is a good deal of short block information available, most of it is either out of date or geared towards a specific type of race engine. Conversely, the information in this edition is current and has relatively broad application.

Even though the information in *Small-Block Chevy Performance* covers a broad base of applications, the details are specific; much of it comes directly from some of the top engine builders in the country. They certainly didn't give away all their secrets, but they were surprisingly candid and did supply a wealth of practical, usable data on parts selection, machining and set-up procedures. So even experienced engine builders will find something useful in the following chapters. While reading through this book, be aware that you may come across sections containing information that doesn't agree with some common practices. Blame that on technology. It continues to change at a rapid pace and many of the procedures and approaches that were "wrong" 20 years ago have become the norm. So in spite of the fact that some "ancient history" is discussed, *Small-Block Chevy Performance* emphasizes current thinking, not 20-year-old technology. ■

A BRIEF HISTORY

THE SMALL-BLOCK CHEVROLET FAMILY

Since its introduction in 1955, the small-block Chevrolet has been celebrated in word, picture, song, dyno test and bank deposit. For over 40 years, it has reigned as the nation's most popular and prolific performance engine, and has served as the mainstay of the performance industry. While the performance aftermarket produces engine components for a variety of GM, Ford and Chrysler engines, most manufacturers produce more parts for the small-block Chevy than all other engines combined.

Much of the small block's popularity and longevity owes to the fact that the engine is like a chameleon—it can adapt to any environment. Way back in 1955, at a time when flathead Ford V-8s and inline six-cylinders were the "hot rod" engines of preference, introduction of the small-block V-8 was viewed as little more than Chevrolet's answer to the 239 cid Ford overhead valve (ohv) V-8. Ford had introduced that engine for the 1954 model year and in so doing struck first in what would become a high performance poker game. Stuck with nothing more exotic than its outdated "stovebolt" ohv inline six, Chevrolet wasn't yet a

Equipped with Rochester mechanical fuel injection, the small-block Chevy was the first production engine to produce one horsepower per cubic inch—back in 1957. By 1962, refinements boosted output to 1.10 horsepower per cubic inch—360 horsepower from 327 cubic inches. In 1964 and '65 (the last year for Rochester fuel injection) horsepower jumped to 375.

player in the game for high performance leadership.

The 265 Small Block

Little did anyone suspect that the situation would reverse itself the very next year. With a bore of 3.75", a stroke of 3.00", an 8.0:1 compression ratio and a Rochester two-barrel carburetor, the 265 cid Chevrolet small block was rated at 162 horsepower at 4400 rpm. Originally, engines that were mated to manual transmissions were equipped with solid lifters while hydraulic lifters were installed in engines that were coupled to the Powerglide two-speed automatic. Ultimately, the mechanical lifters were dropped in favor of hydraulics across the board.

The first major revamping of the original small-block Chevy is the Second Generation LT-1 engine which was introduced in 1992. Rated at 300 net horsepower when installed in a Corvette, (275 to 285 when installed in a Camaro) it is the most powerful small block ever produced by Chevrolet. Unique intake manifold, reverse-flow cooling system and optically triggered distributor all help the small block reach a new horsepower plateau while remaining emissions-legal.

One of the most underrated small blocks was the 302 cid version installed in 1967-1969 Z/28 Camaros. Rated at 290 horsepower, the engine actually produced well over 300 hp in stock trim.

The 283 Small Block

While Ford may have been first with an overhead valve V-8, Chevrolet's version was much more adaptable to increased performance and Chevrolet engineering continued to raise the stakes at the horsepower table. By 1957, small-block displacement had been increased to 283 cid by virtue of a 1/8" overbore (3.875" vs. 3.75"). More importantly, when equipped with Rochester fuel injection, the Chevrolet small block became the first American production engine to produce one horsepower per cubic inch of displacement. With that accomplishment, the small block became the unchallenged leader in performance engines.

Chevrolet Engineering, largely through the efforts of famed Corvette engineer Zora Arkus-Duntov, promulgated a performance orientation through continual refinement of the engine—and by encouraging the then fledgling high performance industry to produce aftermarket products. It wasn't long before high performance intake manifolds, camshafts, headers, pistons and ignition systems were introduced by a number of manufacturers. With such a wide variety of parts to choose from, it was easier to build a high performance Chevrolet than it was to attempt coaxing increased horsepower from any other engine.

The 327 Small Block

Although Chevrolet had introduced a new family of larger 348 cid powerplants in 1958 (known as the "W" engine), the small block still needed to hold its own. In 1962, when the 348 was dropped in favor of the infamous 409, it seemed only reasonable that a larger small block should serve as the base engine. With bore increased to 4.00" and stroke lengthened to 3.25", displacement was raised to 327 cid. The 327 served as an optional engine in full-sized Chevrolets, but was the only engine offered in the Corvette. However, in addition to the 250-hp base engine a Corvette could also be ordered with 300, 340 and 360-hp versions of the 327.

The 302 Small Block

The next factory-initiated alteration to small-block displacement was actually a step down the ladder. In the mid-sixties, Trans-Am road racing became very popular. Displacement was limited to 305 cubic inches so a special engine was required if Chevrolet's Camaro was to be competitive. In the late fifties and early sixties, hot rodders regularly proved the "no substitute for cubic inches" adage by overboring 283 blocks by 1/8" The resulting 301 cid engine with a 4-in. bore and 3-in. stroke was an outstanding performer, so it's not surprising that Chevrolet engineers took the same approach in building an engine suitable for Trans-Am competition. Depending upon your point of view, the 302 cid small block is either a 327 with a 283 crankshaft or a 283 with a 327

Just about the time Rochester fuel injection vanished, emissions-control devices began to appear. But that didn't slow the march of horsepower very much. When the LT 1 option debuted in 1970, it was rated at 370 horsepower and topped with a 780 cfm Holley four barrel.

As installed in mid-year 1970 Z/28's, the 350 cid small block is hard to beat for street performance. Standard equipment includes a high-rise aluminum intake manifold, Holley 780 cfm four-barrel, mechanical lifter cam, 2.02" intake and 1.60" exhaust valves.

cylinder block. Whether a 283 block is bored, or a 327 is destroked, the result is the same—301.59 cubic inches. (Hot rodders dropped the .59 cubic inches and chose 301 as a displacement figure, but Chevrolet rounded off to 302, hence the discrepancy.)

Chevrolet Regular Production Option (RPO) Z/28, as offered for the Camaro during 1967, '68 and '69, included the 302 engine simply as a means of homologating the car for Trans-Am competition. However, the Z/28 proved tremendously more popular than Chevrolet ever anticipated, so a fair number of 302 engines were produced. For the 1967, 1968 and 1969 model years, Z/28 production registered 602, 7,199 and 19,014 units respectively. In 1970, Z/28's were equipped with 350 cid powerplants.

The 307 Small Block

Another unique displacement change occurred in 1968. Performance cars were still selling well, but the public and federal government were becoming increasingly concerned with exhaust emissions. And as cars became heavier, there was a need to increase the displacement of base V-8 engines. Therefore, Chevrolet engineers designed an engine combination that

seemed to satisfy the need for increased torque and better fuel economy. By combining a 327 crankshaft (with 3.25" stroke) with a 283 block (with 3.875" bore) they kept tooling costs to a minimum, yet devised a 307 cid engine that ideally suited their requirements. The increased stroke concentrated torque in the lower speed ranges which was precisely what was needed for a base engine. Concurrently, it was found that the longer stroke/smaller bore combination also made for lower exhaust emissions compared to an engine of similar displacement with a larger bore and shorter stroke.

Although often confused with the 302, the 307 had a completely different character. It was never a factory high performance engine and was available only with a cast-iron crankshaft and two-bolt mains. However, it does have potential as a solid street performer, in terms of maximum power output, but it is inherently inferior to the 4-in. bore/3-in. stroke combination found in a 302.

The 350 Small Block

Displacement increased once again in 1969. By lengthening the stroke of the 327 from 3.25" to 3.48", displacement was stretched to 350 cubic inches. Originally developed with an eye on performance, the 350 has become a "man for all seasons" engine; at one time or another it has been factory installed in everything from a Corvette to a pickup truck to a four-door Caprice.

LT-1—However, the most powerful stock version was RPO LT-1, produced for one year only, in the Corvette in 1970. It produced 370 gross horsepower at 6000 rpm right off the showroom floor. A mechanical

Tuned Port Injection (TPI) first appeared in 1985 and heralded a new era for small-block performance. TPI offers that valuable combination of high performance, low emissions and excellent fuel economy.

lifter cam, Holley four-barrel carb, 11:1 compression ratio and large port cylinder heads with 2.02" intake and 1.60" exhaust valves contributed to the hot performance of the LT-1.

Twenty-two years later, Chevrolet reactivated the LT1 engine code, but this time it was attached to a powerplant with substantially different character (they also eliminated the hyphen). The 1992 LT1 was substantially different from previous incarnations of the small block. Different enough that it's called the Second Generation or Gen II. As originally released in the 1992 Corvette, the LT1 was rated at 300 net horsepower at 5000 rpm, 330 lbs-ft. of torque at 4000 rpm, yet it met all of the current and very stringent exhaust emissions and fuel economy requirements. In fact, it gets better fuel economy than the L-98 Tuned

Port Injection it replaced—even though it produces 50 more net horsepower.

The following year, Chevrolet installed the LT1 engine in Camaros

and Pontiac followed suit with the Firebird. As configured for the "F-body" cars, the engine was rated at 275 horsepower, the 25-horsepower loss resulting from more restrictive intake and exhaust systems. For the 1996 model year, LT1s destined for Camaros and Firebirds received a 10 horsepower boost courtesy of an exhaust system with dual, rather than single catalytic converters.

LT4—Also new for 1996 was the LT4 version of the small block. Essentially an LT1 with 10.8:1 compression ratio, revised cylinder heads, intake manifold and camshaft, it was available as an option only on Corvettes. Rated at 330 horsepower at 5800 rpm and 340 lbs-ft. of torque at 4500 rpm, the LT4 set new horsepower standards for production V-8 engines.

Although Gen II V-8s have claimed the limelight in passenger car powertrains, the First Generation has soldiered on in trucks. For 1996, both the 305 (5-liter) and 350 (5.7-liter) engines were updated with Central Port Injection (CPI) and a Vortec intake manifold/cylinder head

Horsepower of the second generation small block was boosted for the 1996 model year when the LT4 was introduced. Rated at 330 net horsepower, the LT4 is essentially an LT1 with revised cylinder heads, intake manifold and camshaft. Roller rocker arms are also part of the LT4 package.

Small-block Chevys don't always need exotic intake systems to produce mind-boggling power. The engine in this legal Super Stock 1969 Camaro, owned by Paul Forte of Turbo Action Transmissions, is equipped with many of the "wrong" parts for producing power. But even with a stock QuadraJet carburetor and large chamber "smog" heads, this engine (originally rated at 255 horsepower) propels the car to low 11-second quarter-mile times, reaching speeds of over 120 miles per hour.

configuration similar to the one originally introduced on the 4.3-liter V-6. Other improvements include sequential fuel injection, hydraulic roller lifters, 9.4:1 compression ratio, more aggressive cam timing and a whopping 45-horsepower increase compared to the 1995 305 truck engine. (The '96 version is rated at 220 horsepower at 4600 rpm and 285 lbs-ft. of torque at 2800 rpm.)

The 350 employs virtually the same components but comes up with a 50-horsepower increase—from 200 to 250 and 25 lbs-ft. more torque. Output specifications for the 1996 350 Vortec engine are 250 horsepower at 4600 rpm and 335 lbs-ft. of torque at 2800 rpm.

These engines are controlled by a PCM that incorporates controls for the OBD II (On-Board Diagnostics, Second Generation) system so

installation of a Vortec V-8 in a vehicle not originally equipped with one will require a bit of engineering unless the complete original electronic control system is maintained.

The 400 Small Block

When the 350 was introduced, it was believed that the small block Chevy could be expanded no more. After all, with no change in external dimensions, the engine had grown 85 cid—from 265 to 350 cid. How much more could it possibly be stretched? Chevrolet answered that question just one year later when the 400 cid small block was released. Most (but not all) 400 blocks are distinguished by three, rather than two freeze plugs on each side, but the primary distinction is the engine's 4.125" diameter cylinders and 3.75" stroke crankshaft. The 400 cid small block also has the dubious

honor of being the only small block with a connecting rod length other than 5.70" from center-to-center; rods for 400 cid engines measure only 5.565" in length.

The 262 Small Block

During the Seventies, federal emissions regulations became much more stringent and as engineers grappled with designs that would both meet federal standards and offer acceptable performance, new displacements were occasionally devised. In 1975, a 262 cid emissions engine was introduced for some vehicle models. With a 3.671" bore and 3.10" stroke, the 262 has little performance potential.

The 305 Small Block

However, the 305, introduced in 1976, has proven itself entirely suitable for both standard and high performance usage. While its small bore (3.736") long stroke (3.48") combination make it less than ideal for applications requiring maximum power per cubic inch, a 305 can be turned into an excellent street performance engine. With the same stroke as a 350, a 305 offers strong low-speed and mid-range torque for its size and also has the potential to log excellent fuel economy.

The 267 Engine

In 1979, Chevrolet Engineering developed yet another version of the small block. This one had tiny 3.5" cylinders, a 3.48" stroke crankshaft and a displacement of 267 cubic inches. If you've been thinking of modifying a 267 small block, you better find another source of information, because this is the last reference you'll see in this book to the

Of course, when all else fails, a 6-71 supercharger and two four-barrels are sure to be an antidote for boredom. Blown small blocks offer the bone-crushing torque of a big block and you can't beat that blower whine if you want to signal that something powerful is brewing under the hood.

IDENTIFICATION

The continual expansion of the small block was made possible by a couple of dimensions that had seemingly little significance when the 265 was first designed. A distance between cylinder centerlines of 4.400" allows the bore to be expanded to over 4.125", and a deck height of 9.025" (the distance from the crankshaft centerline to the top of the block) will accommodate a stroke of over 3-3/4". These dimensions have also provided unprecedented interchangeability of parts between virtually all small-block engines.

While all this may look good on paper, one of the most commonly encountered problems when modifying a Chevy small block—of any displacement—is that performance never matches expectations. As ridiculous as it may seem, this is often the result of a misunderstanding of engine type and size. As an example, suppose you own a Camaro that doesn't run particularly well. Before spending a lot of money on modifications, make sure the engine wasn't switched by a previous owner. The 350 you think is under the hood could turn out to be anything from a 262 to a 327; many an "all-original" car has been found to be harboring anything but its original engine beneath its hood.

The best way to determine precisely which engine you're dealing with is to obtain a Motor or Chilton auto repair manual which covers the appropriate model year. At the beginning of the Chevrolet section, you'll find a listing of the engine codes which are cross-referenced to year produced and engine displacement. In many instances, the code will also indicate

267—or the 262 for that matter.

The 372 & 383 Small Blocks

Considering all the bore/stroke combinations Chevrolet has produced over the years, it would seem as though there was nothing new left to try. But American hot rodding ingenuity being what it is, that's not the case. Two combinations that are strictly the result of racers looking for something different are the 372 cid and 383 cid small blocks. Both of these displacements are achieved by combining components from the 350 and 400 engines. The 372 cubic inches are achieved by installing a 350 crankshaft in a 400 block. Chevrolet never produced a forged crankshaft for the 400 and that limits maximum rpm potential unless an aftermarket forged crank is used. But streetable 383 cid small blocks will produce well over 430 horsepower. Forged 350 crankshafts are readily

available, so a 372 cid combination offering excellent high rpm power potential can be built for a relatively low cost.

On the other hand, for high performance street applications, a longer stroke, which offers more low-speed and mid-range power, is ideal. A legitimate street engine rarely needs to turn more than 6500 rpm, so the cast-iron 400 crankshaft is fine. However, before it can be installed in a 350 block, the main bearing journals must be machined to a 2.45" diameter (from their original 2.65" diameter). Once that's done, the 3-3/4" stroke crankshaft from a 400 cubic inch engine will drop into place.

This combination makes for a super high performance street engine because the 3-3/4" stroke puts an enormous bulge in the low-speed and mid-range sections of the torque curve—at precisely the rpm levels where a street engine spends most of its life.

Take a 1970-something Nova, add a well-prepared 350 and you've got a killer street/strip machine. This '71 model, the infamous "Lady in Red", is street-driven and bracket-raced by Fran Gaudsmith of Georgia. The car weighs 3200 pounds and was transformed from a 16-second sleeper to a 11.40-second, 120-mph quarter-mile runner through the creative engine building and photographic efforts of infamous automotive journalist Dale Wilson.

whether the engine was originally mated to a standard or automatic transmission and whether it was a base engine or high performance model. HPBooks' *How to Rebuild Small-Block Chevy* is another good source.

ID Codes

Keep in mind that unless you're certain as to the year and model in which a particular engine was installed, the identification code can be misleading. As an example, a "CKB" code indicates a 350 V-8, but this code will be found on a 1974 Camaro engine with 185 horsepower and automatic transmission as well as on a 1977 base 350 engine in a full-sized Chevrolet. "CKB" code was also used to identify engines in 1973 Chevelles (145-hp), 1972 Camaros and 1973 Novas. In all cases, the "CKB" code refers to a 350, but you can't always count on that being true. Engine code "CGC" was used on 1971 245 hp 350s installed in full-sized cars and on 1975 262 cid Nova

engines.

In order to be absolutely sure as to the identity of a particular engine, you have to know the code as well as the year and vehicle model in which the engine was originally installed. If that information isn't available, the year in which the block was manufactured can be determined by checking the number cast into the rear of the block (see photo). Once the year is known, the engine code should accurately solve the identity crisis.

Castings to Avoid

It should also be noted that although most cylinder blocks will serve as a suitable foundation for a high performance small block, some of the earlier castings—and some later ones—should be avoided.

• The oiling system on original 265 cid engines is substandard; 1955-57 blocks are also designed for front engine mounts only so these engines won't drop into a later chassis which accommodates blocks with motor

mounts on the sides.

• Blocks cast before 1962 don't have as much internal crankshaft clearance as their newer counterparts.

• 1967 and earlier engines utilized crankshafts with 2.30-in. diameter main journals and 2.00-in. diameter rod journals; crankshafts for 1968 and later small blocks have 2.45-in. main journals and 2.10-in. rod journals. Obviously, a 2.45-in. journal can be machined to a 2.30-in. diameter, but these dimensions should be known before a lot of money is spent on parts that don't fit. If you're using a crank for one engine and a block from another, make sure they're compatible.

• Some late-model 305 blocks have extremely thin cylinder walls and should be sonic-tested before overboring. Sonic testing is cheap insurance so any block should be tested before a lot of money is spent on machine work.

THE LT1 ENGINE

In 1970, the LT-1 Corvette engine reigned as the ultimate production small block. Rated at 370 horsepower at 6000 rpm and 380 lbs-ft. of torque at 4000 rpm, the original LT-1 also featured a mechanical lifter camshaft, 11:1 compression ratio, Holley four-barrel carburetor, aluminum high-rise intake manifold, 2.02-in. intake and 1.60-in. exhaust valves—all the good stuff. The following year, compression ratio was dropped to 9:1 so the LT-1 could be operated on lower octane low-lead fuel. By 1972, power rating had dropped to 255 net horsepower and by 1973, the LT-1 had vanished from the option list.

But with the introduction of the 1992 Corvette, the LT1 code has risen from the ashes. Rated at 300 net horsepower, the second coming of the LT1 constituted the highest horsepower small block ever produced by Chevrolet. (Until 1996 when the 330-horsepower LT4 was introduced.) Translated into gross ratings, that means at least 376 horsepower—one horsepower more than the 375-hp, 327 cid fuel-injected engine last produced in 1965.

Beginning in 1993, LT1 engines were installed in Camaros, Firebirds and in 1994, in a variety of full-sized passenger cars. The Camaro/Firebird versions were rated at 275 horsepower through 1995 and 285 horsepower beginning in 1996. The version of the engine installed in full-sized cars has cast iron cylinder heads, a milder camshaft and a 260-horsepower rating. Chevrolet even produced a 265-cubic inch version of the engine for use in the full-sized Caprice.

Externally, the LT1 looks pretty much like any other small block, except for the intake manifold and side covers.

The LT1 distributor is driven by a small shaft that fits into the front of the cam sprocket. Leads inside the cap are routed so that plug wires can be "dressed" to each side of the engine with no crossover.

The LT1's unique cam sprocket has a gear on the rear that drives the water pump shaft and the splined hole in the center drives the distributor shaft.

As produced for the 1990s, the LT1 bears little resemblance to its predecessors. Its leading features are a completely new electronic fuel-injection system, reverse-flow cooling system, optically triggered ignition with unique front-mounted distributor, 10.25:1 compression ratio, and a new cylinder block and heads. And while the LT1 produces an astounding 55 horsepower more than the L-98 it replaced, it also delivers better fuel economy and easily meets federal exhaust emissions standards. It's no wonder that Chevrolet's engineering staff is proud of the newest LT1.

Unfortunately, most of the LT1's components are not interchangeable with earlier small blocks, largely because of the changes necessitated by the reverse-flow cooling system. The accompanying photos and captions tell the whole story.

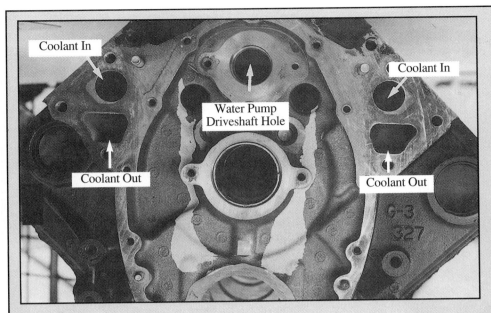

Coolant In

Coolant In

Water Pump Driveshaft Hole

Coolant Out

Coolant Out

New block features two water passages on each side, cored hole for water pump drive assembly, and four-bolt mains (not shown).

The water pump pushes coolant into the block through the top passage. From the block, it flows up into the cylinder heads, then down through the block and returns to the pump through the bottom passage. The thermostat is housed in the water pump and bleed valves are located at several points so air can be bled from the system during filling.

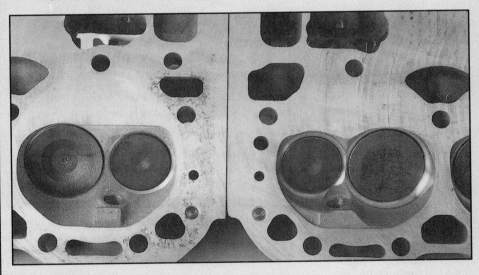

The LT1 cylinder head (right) has revised combustion chamber, and different waterjacket coring to accommodate the reverse-flow cooling system. In an LT1, coolant flows through the head first, then through the block, hence the reverse-flow label.

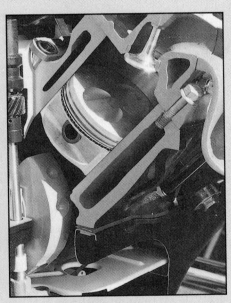

Since the distributor is no longer located in its traditional position, an adapter had to be substituted to drive the oil pump.

A gear on the back of the camshaft sprocket meshes with another one above it to drive the water pump. A collar connects the water pump internal shaft to the one that protrudes from the block.

SHORT BLOCK

2

When the small-block Chevy engine was introduced for the 1955 model year, its 265 cubic-inch displacement didn't raise many eyebrows. Ford, with its 272 cid and 292 cid V-8s won the "bigger is better" battle. But the Chevy came out on top in terms of horsepower per cubic inch—both in standard (162 hp) and optional (195 hp) forms.

Once the small block grew out of its infancy, it quickly increased in size and as a result, a wide variety of displacements, as noted in the previous chapter, are available. For performance applications, the myriad of bore/stroke combinations boil down to three basic types of cylinder blocks, delineated by bore size. The most popular is the 4" bore block as used in 302, 327 and 350-cid engines. A larger variation, which serves as the basis for 400-cid engines, sports a 4-1/8" bore, while at the other end of the scale is the 3-7/8" bore block used for 283 and 307 combinations and the 3-

The small block has come a long way since its introduction in 1955—both in terms of displacement and specific power output. Modified Tuned Port 350s like this one easily put out one horsepower per cubic inch and over 420 lbs-ft. of torque. It takes a properly prepared short block to handle this type of power output over the long term.

3/4" bore casting from which 265 and 305 cid engines are built.

From a basic engine building standpoint, small-block Chevy cylinder blocks are all essentially the same, except for some 4.000" and 4.125" bore blocks which have four-bolt rather than two-bolt main bearing caps. Although the extra bolts are preferred for racing applications, and certainly can't hurt, they aren't necessarily essential for a high performance street engine. Many a 400+ horsepower small block has

been built around a two-bolt main cylinder case. In fact, two-bolt blocks are supposed to be capable of handling up to 500 horsepower.

BLOCK CONSTRUCTION

Of far more importance is cylinder wall integrity. Over the years, quality control has varied considerably and core shift is always a potential problem. Unfortunately, the only way to guarantee cylinder wall thickness is to have a block sonic-tested—which is difficult to do when you're

CID	BORE	STROKE
265	3.750	3.00
283	3.875	3.00
302	4.001	3.00
305	3.736	3.48
307	3.875	3.25
327	4.001	3.25
350	4.001	3.48
400	4.125	3.75

Most high performance street engines are built using a "seasoned" block. When searching for a suitable candidate, the numbers cast into the bellhousing flange identify the casting date. On this block, the date is coded–C049. "C" represents the third month (March), "04" pertains to the 4th day of the month and "9" indicates 1989. This is obviously a late-model block because the 5.7-liter identification is included and that has only been used since the late 80's.

Many times, the decade can't be determined from the casting date, so the code stamped on the front of the block, just in front of the passenger-side cylinder head, must also be used. "CGC" identifies this block as a 350 from a 1971 Chevrolet passenger car. It was originally rated at 245 horsepower and equipped with a 2-barrel carburetor. Prior to 1970, the identification code used on most small blocks contained only two letters.

Attention to detail is the difference between a quality machine shop and a down-and-dirty operation. One of these details is head-bolt hole chamfering. It's a little extra that helps optimize head gasket seal.

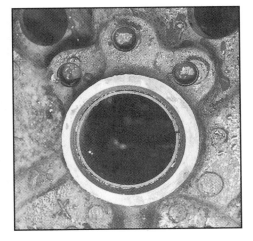

Core shift is always a potential problem because it affects cylinder wall thickness. This block obviously has a core shift problem and is not a candidate for performance use. Note the degree to which the cam bearing bore is offset within the boss.

10% tin and 20% nickel. A single number, either a "010" or "020" represents the amount of nickel and indicates negligible amounts of tin. No numbers, other than the casting numbers that are typically found beneath the timing cover, translates to only minor amounts of tin and nickel being present in the block alloy.

Although an "010"/"020" block is most desirable, it's not always possible to find one that's suitable for high performance use. Again, cylinder wall thickness is the overriding consideration and a block with no tin or nickel and thick cylinder walls is generally preferable to a high nickel block with thin walls.

Truck and older Chevy II blocks are reputed to have thicker than average cylinder walls, but there are no guarantees—sonic testing is the only way to be certain that wall thickness is adequate. But Bow Tie blocks contain considerably more material than their production counterparts, and most engine builders will not bolt

rummaging through a wrecking yard or negotiating at a swap meet. However, core shift is sometimes highly visible. If the cam hole in the front of the block is noticeably offset within the boss, you can bet the block has major league core shift.

Metals

Alloy is also an important consideration. Tin and nickel are two

metals that are commonly alloyed with cast iron to improve durability, hardness and heat dissipation. Many production small blocks have the numbers "010", "020" or both cast into their front face, just above the main bearing bore. (The timing cover must be removed for these numbers to be visible.) If both numbers are present, one above the other, it indicates that the block alloy contains

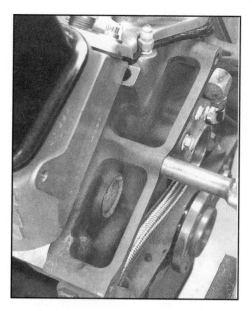

When weight is a problem, machinists get inventive. This NASCAR Winston Cup engine incorporates a block that has had most of its bellhousing flange milled away. Also note the braided line that's connected to the dry sump pump to evacuate oil from the valley area.

a high output engine together unless a Bow Tie block is the foundation of the assembly. According to Garry Grimes of Grimes Automotive Machine, "If you're building a serious engine, you've got to use a Bow Tie block. It not only has thicker cylinder walls, the bottom end is also stronger."

SIMILARITIES & DIFFERENCES

Although there's a great number of similarities amongst the various blocks produced over the years, there are also a number of differences. Beginning with the 1986 model year, Chevrolet began producing blocks with a one-piece rear main seal. There's enough difference between 1985-and-earlier and 1986-and-later blocks that oil pans and crankshafts are not interchangeable unless an adapter is fitted to the block. Since most cast-iron Bow Tie blocks are produced with a one-piece rear main seal, a two-piece rear main seal adapter is commonly installed so pre-'86 oil pans and crankshafts can be installed. (It's interesting to note that while standard Bow Tie blocks are supplied with a one-piece seal, race-prepared cast iron and aluminum Bow Tie blocks feature a two-piece seal.) The adapter that allows the use of crankshafts and oil pans compatible with two-piece rear main seals is available from several aftermarket companies and from GM Performance Parts as part number 10051118.

While 1955 to 1985 production blocks appear to be identical except for bore size, that's not the case. Oil dipsticks have been placed on both the driver's and passenger's side, and a matching oil pan is required to match block dipstick placement. Cast-iron Bow Tie blocks contain undrilled bosses on both sides, so dipstick placement is user selectable.

Back in the days when most people shifted for themselves, all small blocks contained a tapped hole above the oil filter to mount a pivot ball. But as the popularity of automatics increased, the need to drill and tap a pivot ball hole decreased, so some production blocks have only an undrilled boss in the pivot ball hole location. It's no problem to drill and tap a hole, provided the need to do so is discovered before the engine is installed in a vehicle.

Another area to examine while the engine is still at the machine shop is the starter mounting pad. Some blocks are machined with two starter bolt patterns (one for the 168-tooth flywheel the other for the 153-tooth version) others aren't. It's therefore advisable to ensure that the mounting holes in the block are compatible with the starter that's to be used.

The introduction of hydraulic roller lifters for the 1987 model year brought about other cylinder block changes. To accommodate original equipment hydraulic rollers—which are of a different design than aftermarket types—the tops of the lifter bores were raised and machined flat. The tapped bosses were also added in the lifter valley so the sheetmetal "spider" that holds the lifter link bars in place could be attached. Standard hydraulic or mechanical lifters can be installed in a "hydraulic roller" block, but original equipment roller lifters cannot be installed in a "non-hydraulic roller" block. "Hydraulic roller" blocks also have a tapped hole on either side of the camshaft hole for attaching the retaining plate that's installed to prevent the camshaft from "walking" forward.

Main Bearing Diameter

Another variation that can ruin an otherwise well-planned engine building party is main bearing diameter. Beginning with the 1968 model year, main journal diameter was increased from 2.30" to 2.45". On the other hand, all 4-1/8"-bore production blocks are machined for a 2.65" main journal diameter. Consequently, it's advisable to verify main journal, bearing and bearing saddle diameters to assure proper fit. It's also advisable to disregard model year when determining block characteristics. Considering that new cars are typically introduced in September or October of the previous

For serious horsepower efforts, production blocks are often inadequate. A Bow Tie or Rocket Block from GM Performance Parts is often required to handle the obscene amounts of horsepower that small blocks can produce.

calendar year, it's not at all unusual for a casting date to disagree with the model year of the vehicle in which it was originally installed. Prior engine swaps can also confuse the issue, so accurate measurements should always be made prior to the expenditure of money for parts and machine work.

Second Generation Blocks

Of course, the differences amongst "First Generation" small blocks are irrelevant when the focus is shifted to the "Second Generation" version which was introduced in the 1992 Corvette. For all intents and purposes, first and second generation small blocks are two completely different engines. Aside from camshaft and valvetrain, there are no interchangeable parts of any consequence. However, the machining and assembly techniques that make a First Generation small block roar will be equally successful when applied to a 1992 or later LT1.

If you plan to build a high performance LT1, be advised that Corvette blocks typically are of the four-bolt persuasion while Camaro/Firebird and Caprice blocks contain two-bolt main bearing caps.

A cylinder block is the foundation of any performance engine. No great revelation there, but a point that seems to be missed all too frequently is that you don't build a killer engine on a poor foundation. Although the block itself has little effect on horsepower (unless it's completely butchered) it does influence the ability of other parts to perform at maximum efficiency. It also plays a big role in determining durability.

BLOCK OPTIONS

If a new block is to be used, there are a number of choices. Part number 10066098 is a production cast iron 305 block which will accommodate bore diameters ranging from 3.740" to 3.770". The 4.000" to 4.030" bore

equivalent, is listed as part number 10105123.

Bow Tie Blocks

A Bow Tie alternative is GM Performance Parts' small bore Bow Tie block (which weighs 197 pounds compared to 181 pounds for the 4"-bore Bow Tie block) and is listed as part number 10051181. The maximum recommended bore diameter for this block is 4.030", but it takes a lot of cutting (about 16-pounds worth) to reach a 4" diameter. So unless you're building a small bore engine, it makes more sense to begin with a larger bore block. Part number 10051183 has cylinders rough bored to 3.980" diameter and can be safely bored to 4.150". According to GM, "This block is recommended for maximum effort competition engines. The deck surfaces are thicker than production blocks, and the head bolt holes are blind-tapped to improve gasket sealing. The main bearing bulkheads are .900" thick and the front and rear bulkheads are reinforced with strengthening ribs."

Chevrolet and GM Performance Parts also offer a number of race prepared Bow Tie cast iron blocks. Specifications are included in the accompanying chart. If the iron blocks don't suit your fancy, three aluminum Bow Tie blocks are also available. Weighing a mere 90 pounds, the aluminum blocks are approximately half the weight of a cast iron Bow Tie block.

Rocket Block

Yet another option from the vast GM parts bin is the Olds-developed Rocket block. Weighing in at a hefty 200 pounds, the cast iron Rocket blocks are offered for dry or wet sump

Cylinder block preparation should begin with align-boring (if required) and honing. All critical dimensions are taken off the main bearing saddles, so they must be true before other machining is done.

oiling systems in standard deck height (9.025") and in tall deck dress (9.300"). All Rocket blocks will accept a maximum bore diameter of 4.190", but blocks with standard deck height are supplied with either a 4.000" bore and tall deck blocks arrive with cylinders machined to a 4.125" diameter.

Other features of the Rocket blocks include camshaft positioning that's raised .390" compared to a standard small block (to clear crankshafts with strokes up to 4.125"), oil pan rails that are .800" further apart, big-block Chevy V-8 camshaft bearings, dual starter mounts, two-piece rear main seal and a main-priority oiling system. Rocket blocks are obviously overkill for a street engine, but offer a number of advantages for full-tilt boogie race engines.

BLOCK MACHINING

The quality of machine work is of vital importance. If you're building a high performance engine, be sure to take your parts to a machine shop that can provide the required level of quality. Some traditional shops are perfectly capable of achieving the finish quality and tolerances that are required, others simply are not. Don't believe all the Yellow Pages ads—what are they going to advertise, "We do shoddy work"? Get recommendations from people who have experience dealing with local shops. And don't trip over dollar bills to pick up pennies. Many of the shops that do quality work charge a little more than average. That's because it takes more time to do things right. What is the advantage of saving $25 on machine work and then grenading the engine because something wasn't machined accurately enough?

Sonic Check

But before any machine work is begun, a block should be sonic checked for adequate cylinder wall thickness. Any block that has less than .300" thickness on the thrust surfaces—before boring and honing—should be rejected unless the engine will see only occasional mild abuse. While sonic checking may seem unnecessary with a new Bow

Tie or Rocket block, it's always money well spent because of the possibility of core shift.

Crack Testing

Used blocks should be checked for cracks. You can use one or more of several crack-checking methods depending on the material being checked. Regardless of which method you use, the part being checked must be clean.

One of the better known crack-checking methods is Magnafluxing. The most common but unofficial methods of crack testing though is using the unassisted naked eye, making it the cheapest but least reliable method of crack checking. Other methods include using a dye penetrate and pressure testing. Let's first look at Magnafluxing.

Magnafluxing—This magnetic particle method of crack testing can only be used on ferrous-based materials, or iron and steel. To make the check, the suspected area is dusted with iron particles. Next, the area is magnetized with an electromagnet. If the poles of the magnet bridge a crack, the iron particles gather along it when the magnet is turned on, thus revealing the crack. If no crack is revealed, the magnet is turned 90° in the event the magnet is aligned with a crack. Any cracks are highlighted with white chalk so you'll be able to find it later.

Magnafluxing is also used to check iron or steel crankshafts, cast-iron cylinder heads, connecting rods and rod bolts.

Dye Penetrate—To use this crack-checking method, the suspect area is first sprayed with non-drying red dye penetrate. Next, the area is cleaned with solvent and allowed to dry,

Optimum piston ring seal can only be achieved if the cylinders are round. When head bolts are tightened, the bores distort several thousandths of an inch, so deck plates should be attached when honing so that the same loads are applied to the cylinder walls as exist when the heads are installed.

leaving only the dye in any cracks. For the last step, a white developer is sprayed over the same area. If a crack exists, it will show up as a bright red line as the dye in the crack bleeds through the white developer.

Another method also uses a dye, but rather than spraying the area with developer a black light is used to high light any cracks.

Align Honing

Once a suitable block is located, it should be align honed to assure that the main bearing saddles are of the proper diameter and in perfect alignment. Following align honing, it's wise to install the main bearings and check to verify that the holes in the upper halves are properly aligned with the oil supply holes in the block. Any misalignment can usually be corrected by simply elongating the saddle holes as required.

Many machinists either overlook or disregard the importance of align honing, but every critical block

dimension is taken off main bearing saddle alignment, so align boring and/or honing should be the first machining operation and it must be done accurately. When a block is align-honed, you absolutely must have the oil pump installed and the bearing caps tightened to the required torque, using the same type of fasteners (either studs or bolts) that will be installed when the engine is assembled. This is critical because when you tighten the main cap bolts or studs, or the oil pump bolt, it distorts the cap.

Deck Height

After align honing, the next step is to mathematically figure out deck height. Block decking not only ensures that a deck is flat, it also means it will have a consistent deck height for each cylinder. This ensures that the compression of each cylinder is the same providing all other work and parts are done correctly and within spec.

To deck a block, the machinist sets up the bare block in a milling machine or grinder to the main bearing bores, an important reason the block should have an accurate main bearing bore axis. The cutters or grinding stones then cuts the deck surface parallel to the main bearing bore axis, restoring the needed accuracy to your block. Remember, both cylinder banks should be decked the same amount.

When having your block decked, tell the machinist the type of head gasket you intend to use. If he's savvy—the only kind of machinist to deal with—he'll know what type of finish to use. Supply him with the gasket manufacturer's deck finish specifications as a backup.

Many engine builders use a BHJ True Deck plate to determine deck height and squareness and deck the block as required. Then they move on to the boring bar and use a deck plate, rather than the existing bores, to locate the boring bar. This operation is necessary because in a production block, the bores may be off center by .010" to .015".

Cylinder Boring & Honing

Cylinder wall finish is always a controversial topic, but a straight-forward procedure always works best. The biggest concern is cylinder wall movement so the use of torque plates during boring and honing is mandatory. Rather than using "trick of the week" honing procedures, the real trick is to stick with the basic stones that provide the desired finish, as determined by the type of rings being used. (See piston ring section for specific recommendations.)

Amongst high performance engine builders, there's a considerable

CRANKSHAFT RECOMMENDATIONS

Part No.	Material	Stroke	Rod	Rear Seal	Nitrided	ID
39411801053	forged steel	3.48"	2.10"	2-piece	No	1082
39411841053	forged steel	3.48"	2.10"	2-piece	Yes	1082
140960361053	forged steel	3.48"	2.10"	1-piece	No	N/A
14088527	cast iron	3.48"	2.10"	1-piece	No	SP

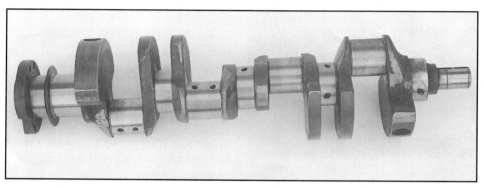

As horsepower climbs, the stresses imposed on the crankshaft rise dramatically. Forged crankshafts are often required to handle the loads. For most high performance engines, a properly prepared production crank is adequate. But for full-tilt boogie applications, use of a forging designed specifically for racing is advisable.

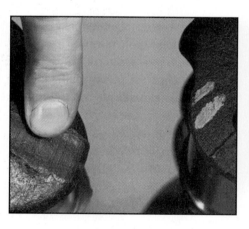

The easiest way to distinguish between cast and forged crankshafts is to look at the parting line. A broad surface like the one on the left indicates a forging. A thin line identifies a casting. If the parting line has been ground away, tap the crank with a hammer. A forged crank will ring like a bell, a casting will respond with a dull thud.

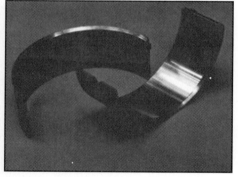

If a crankshaft's journals has been machined with large fillet radii, the bearing must be altered to match. Otherwise the edges of the bearings will wear rapidly.

difference of opinion as to what constitutes proper block preparation. As a minimum, a block should be align honed, decked to ensure that the surfaces are square and that piston-to-deck clearance is .000" to .005", and cylinders should be honed with deck plates attached. Oil drain back holes should be enlarged, all casting flash removed and all head bolt holes chamfered and retapped. For competition engines and street

engines that will be abused on a regular basis, it's advisable to add trash screens to prevent pieces of metal and "foreign material" from the cylinder heads from reaching the oil pan in the event of parts failure.

CRANKSHAFTS

The aspiring small-block builder has a number of options. For a high performance street engine, a standard cast crank is entirely adequate. Obviously, a forged crank is preferable, and if the budget allows, a good solid forging should be selected. But for a high performance street engine, if rpm is limited to the 6000 to 6500 rpm range, and horsepower doesn't exceed 400 to 425, a cast crank with no more than .010" undersized journals, that has been Magnaflux-checked to assure it isn't cracked, is sufficient. However, with any crankshaft, especially a cast type, use of a high performance vibration damper is advisable. See the External Components chapter for more information.

Recommendations

If you're cruising swap meets and wrecking yards in search of a good used crankshaft, keep in mind that you're setting yourself up to prove the old observation that "There's a sucker born every minute." Many cracks

Oil leakage through the rear main seal has been a persistent problem with small blocks. It can be minimized by rotating the seal slightly so that its ends aren't aligned with the cap/block mating surface.

Crankshaft Prep

As with most engine components, what you see isn't always what you think you see. As such, before any machine work is begun, a newly acquired crankshaft should be Magnaflux-inspected and checked for straightness (even if it's a brand new, out-of-the-box GM part). If everything looks good, have the mains cross-drilled and the journals ground and/or polished as required and chamfer the oil holes.

Also note that a generous (as opposed to stingy) fillet radius is desirable where the journal meets the flank. (A fillet radius eliminates the stock straight-line intersection which is a fertile ground for the growth of stress risers.) Bearings should be checked to be sure they're compatible with the fillet radius and fit with .002" to .0025" clearance. To ensure that they have a happy future, a top quality synthetic motor oil should fill the crankcase following engine break-in using a conventional mineral oil.

Which brings up the subject of oil pumps. For most small blocks, a standard oil pump is more than sufficient, provided bearing clearances are in the .002" to .0025" range. However, most engine builders install a high volume or high pressure pump as insurance against brain dead drivers. The additional load imposed by either of these pumps doesn't do any harm except for eating up a bit more horsepower and accelerating distributor gear wear. That's a trade-off for lubrication insurance that has to be decided on an individual basis. But irrespective of type or pressure, before installation, an oil pump should be disassembled and the gear-to-housing clearance checked; it should measure .0025" at the front and the

aren't visible to the naked eye, and repaired journals can also be disguised. Buying a used crankshaft that can't be returned if it's unsuitable is nothing more than a roll of the dice. It is possible to come up a winner, but chances are, you'll roll snake eyes.

Unless you can find a reputable source that will stand behind the components it sells, your best bet is to purchase a new crankshaft from a GM Performance Parts dealer. The part numbers of interest are listed in the chart nearby.

Also available are a number of raw forgings. Part number 10185100 is forged of S38 steel alloy and can be machined to provide a stroke ranging from 3.46" to 3.50". A 4340 steel forging is listed as part number 10051168 and can be finish-machined with a stroke of 3.20" to 4.00". Main bearing journals can be machined to 2.65" diameter to fit a 400 block or 2.45" diameter for 350 blocks. This forging also features large circular counterweights and lightened connecting rod journal arms. A third raw forging, part number 24502460 is

virtually identical to part number 10051168 except that it has added beef in the crank snout area so it can be machined to accept a big block vibration damper. All raw forgings are designed for use with pre-1986 two-piece rear main seals.

Although 305 and 350 engine both have 3.48" strokes, the crankshafts aren't necessarily interchangeable. Due to the difference in piston and connecting rod weights, crankshaft counterweighting is engine specific. While it is physically possible to install a 305 crankshaft in a 350 block and vice versa, such a swap makes it very difficult to achieve proper reciprocating assembly balance.

Unfortunately, GM Performance Parts doesn't offer high performance crankshafts for 305 or 400 cubic-inch small blocks. That being the case, stock castings or special aftermarket forgings are the only choice. Again, a properly machined production cast crank is acceptable for high performance street engines, so a custom forging isn't necessarily the only option.

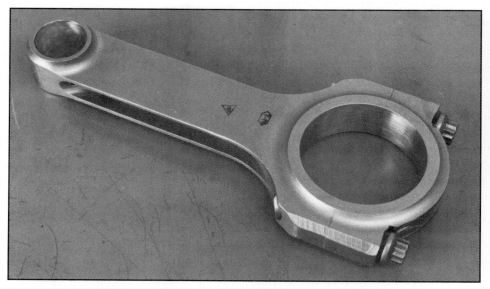

Some engine builders prefer an I-beam rod to the standard production H-beam configuration. Historically, I-beam rods have been preferred for maximum output applications, but with recent improvements in metallurgy and design, that's not always the case. Custom forged steel connecting rods are typically stronger than their production counterparts and are also available in a variety of lengths. Many high performance engines employ "long" rods with a 6.0" (as opposed to stock 5.7") center-to-center distance.

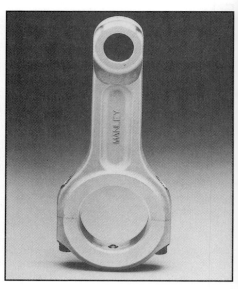

Aluminum rods are significantly lighter than their steel counterparts, which makes for a lighter, faster revving reciprocating assembly. Unfortunately aluminum work hardens, which places definite limits on life expectancy. Use of aluminum rods is pretty much confined to dedicated drag race engines and after a given number of quarter-mile runs, they should be routinely replaced—hopefully before they fail.

Rather than simply slapping a set of rods in an engine, legitimate high performance engine builders establish precise side clearances. In most instances, connecting rod side clearance should be between .018" and .026".

back. Before the pump is installed, it's *VITAL* that the pickup be welded or bolted to the pump body. See the chapter on Lubrication for additional oil pump information.

CONNECTING RODS

Any number of aftermarket rods are available, but stock Chevrolet rods are suitable—and usually a bunch cheaper. Standard production 350 large journal rods are not only forged, they're readily available and strong enough to survive in some racing environments. (But for years, the standard fare for high output small blocks has been part number 14096846, the infamous "pink" rod. (Pink refers to the rods identifying color code.) "Pink" rods feature 3/8" rod bolts and are machined for pressed wrist pins. These rods have achieved great popularity because they're heat-treated, shot-peened and Magnaflux-inspected to ensure they're crack-free.

Another offering from the GM parts bin is the Bow Tie rod which is specifically designed for maximum output small blocks. Bow Tie rods are available in 5.7" (part no. 14011090) and 6.0" (part no. 14011091) center-to-center lengths, are shot-peened and are supplied with 7/16" rod bolts that thread directly into the rod body. In addition to the standard models, Bow Tie forgings are available with profiled beams. (Part no. 14011082 for 5.7" length, 14011083 for 6.0"

Although most custom-forged pistons can be run as delivered, they're typically massaged to remove sharp edges. Note that the sharp edges around the valve reliefs have been rolled to make them smoother and less likely to create localized hot spots.

In applications where compression ratios of 12:1 or higher are desired, a piston with a healthy dome is a necessity. Numerous dome designs exist and in many cases they're precisely configured to match a particular combustion chamber. A slot in the middle of the dome is often added to promote flame front propagation.

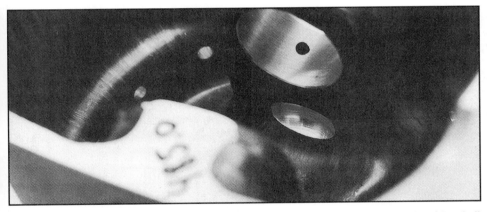

The preferred method of removing weight from a piston for balancing purposes is with a ball end mill in the side of the pin towers. Drilling or milling the underside of the crown, or drilling the bottom of the pin towers should not be done.

length.) The profiling operation reduces rod weight by approximately 50 grams and reduces rod-to-rod weight variation for easier balancing.

In recent years, there has been an outbreak of forged steel connecting rod manufacturers. Manley, Eagle, Childs and Albert, and Carrillo offer connecting rods in a variety of center-to-center lengths. Aluminum rods are another option, but their use is typically restricted to maximum effort drag race engines.

PISTONS

The best deal in town on small-block pistons can be found in the Keith Black and Speed-Pro catalogs. Both companies offer hypereutectic pistons which are ideal for high performance street (and some race) engines. These pistons are typically cheaper than their forged counterparts and are actually better suited for long-term operation in a high performance street engine. The hypereutectic material is extremely hard and has a very low expansion rate. Consequently, it can stand considerable abuse, and since it is installed with .001" to .002" piston-to-wall clearance, it can handle the abuse over a long period of time without the clatter that's associated with most forged pistons. Both flat-top and domed varieties are available, so just about any compression ratio can be achieved. A few caveats regarding pistons:

• If a piston has a dome designed for closed chamber heads, it can be used with open chamber heads, but not vice versa.
• Piston-to-wall clearance with forged pistons is typically .006" to .0075" whereas cast and hypereutectic pistons require .002" or less clearance. That makes for quieter operation and longer ring life.
• Before "massaging" a set of pistons, check to make sure they're of the proper diameter and have the correct compression height. If you're installing full floating-type wrist pins, make sure the holes are machined to accept retaining rings.

Piston Rings

Most performance and race engine builders have very strong opinions regarding brand and type of piston ring and the required cylinder wall finish. However, for long-term durability in any type of engine, a Total Seal ring set with a plasma moly top ring, gapless second and stainless steel low tension oil ring is tough to beat.

At Grimes Automotive Machine,

Without a proper finish on the cylinder walls, there are two chances of achieving adequate ring seal–slim and none. Regardless or the type of rings used, the cylinder walls should have a text book crosshatch pattern like this.

For optimum ring performance, a ring set that's .005" larger that the bore size should be used. Rings are then individually fit to each cylinder and filed until the desired end gap is achieved.

For optimum ring seal, nothing beats a Total Seal Gapless ring set. These sets contain a ductile iron plasma moly top ring, two-piece gapless second and either standard or low tension oil ring. This combination holds cylinder leakage to less than 2% for the life of the engine. Standard rings typically have a leakage rate of 5% to 8% after a surprisingly short amount of running time.

the standard cylinder preparation for this ring combination includes boring the block to within .005" of desired finished bore size then traveling the rest of the way with a hone. The typical procedure involves rough honing with 220-grit (500 series) stones, followed by a few passes with 280 grit stones (600 series). A final finish is then applied with 400-grit (800 series).

Although some engine builders use a super-slick cylinder wall finish, Grimes cautions against such procedures. He states, "When we do the final hone with the 400 stones, all we're doing is knocking the peaks off the ridges left by the coarser stones—

we don't remove any metal. We've found that this type of finish is best for quick ring seating and long term ring seal. Sure, you can go and put a mirror finish on the walls, but you better damn sure know what you're doing or the rings won't seat."

For optimum sealing, rings should be fit to the individual cylinders and end gaps filed to fit. In lieu of manufacturers' recommendations otherwise, the top ring should be given .020" to .022" end gap with forged pistons and .026" to .028" with hypereutectic pistons.

A 5/64", 5/64", 3/16" ring configuration is preferred for street and recreational marine engines. (Wider rings deliver better long-term durability.) Although a 1/16", 1/16", 3/16" ring combination will provide improved ring seal at high rpm, such considerations are unwarranted in a street or recreational marine engine because the engine doesn't spend enough time in the tachometer's "Twilight Zone" to justify the trade-

Although a standard flat file can be used on the ends of the rings, a proper ring filer is more accurate, makes it easier to keep the ends square and speeds the process.

It's not essential, but when file-fitting rings, use of a squaring tool ensures that the rings are properly positioned in the cylinders. Squaring tools are available for almost any cylinder size from Powerhouse Products in Memphis, TN.

off of reduced ring life. Another consideration is that with a 1/16", 1/16", 3/16" ring package, oil consumption tends to be higher than with wider rings.

Other ring options include .043" or Dykes-type top rings. Both of these ring types are intended strictly for racing and while they do offer exceptional ring seal, they tend to wear very quickly.

According to Joe Moriarty of Total Seal, Inc., *"The main reason to use a narrow ring is to reduce ring mass—the lighter the ring, the less it tends to hammer the ring groove. That's only a consideration at high rpm, so there's no need to use anything narrower than a 5/64" ring if an engine isn't going to be used exclusively for racing.*

"Piston rock is another factor that influences ring selection. With forged pistons, piston-to-cylinder wall clearance is greater than with cast or hypereutectic pistons, so the piston rocks more in the bore and that has a negative influence on ring seal—the wider the ring, the worse the effect. Cast or hypereutectic pistons, usually require clearances of .002" or less, so piston rock isn't a major factor and there's little advantage of running a narrow ring."

Moriarty also noted that .043" and Dykes rings are strictly for full-tilt race applications where gas pressures are high and the engine is regularly disassembled for maintenance. He states, "With a .043" top ring, you have much less mass which helps high rpm sealing, but you also have a reduced contact face. As a result, heat transfer to the cylinder wall is reduced and the rings wear faster. With a Dykes ring, sealing at low rpm and low gas loads isn't very good and may result in oil getting up into the combustion chamber. Since a Dykes ring only seals well with heavy gas loading, its only real application is for drag and similar types of racing where you're on the throttle all the time you're racing; Dykes rings are inappropriate for oval track and road racing because you're on and off the throttle."

The latest trend in oil rings is low tension. The oil rings are the most significant contributors to ring drag, so reducing tension significantly lowers internal friction. In a low tension oil ring, improved ring conformability (the ability of the ring to stay in contact with the cylinder wall) is achieved by manufacturing the oil rails from material with reduced radial thickness. Some companies are also experimenting with rails that are .015" thick rather than .024". in thickness.

As might be expected, the optimum ring package varies according to the type of life an engine is going to lead. What works best in a high revving Competition Eliminator or Winston Cup race engine won't even be close to the optimum ring set-up for a 350, 383 or 406 street engine. But having read this chapter, you're undoubtedly aware of the best ring combination for your short block. ■

INDUCTION SYSTEMS

3

CARBURETORS

Over the years, small-block Chevy engines have been factory-equipped with Rochester, Holley and Carter carburetors as well as Rochester mechanical and electronic fuel injection. By far, Holley four-barrels have been, and continue to be, the most popular carburetors for high performance and race applications. But with the variety of options offered by these systems, making the right selection usually involves a lot of catalog reading and head scratching. However, when all is said and done, selecting the right carburetor isn't overly difficult. It just requires a definition of priorities.

Holley Carburetors

Models 4150, 4160 & 2300—The 4150 and 4160 four-barrels and the 2300 two-barrel are closely related. The model 2300 two-barrel is nothing more than the primary two-barrel section of a 4150 four-barrel. The 4150 and 4160 models are virtually identical to each other with the exception of the hardware used to meter fuel in the secondary idle and main circuits. Rather than employing a block with removable jets (as used on the primary side), 4160 carburetors are fitted on the secondary side with a metering plate that contains non-replaceable fuel metering restrictions. The model 4150 has metering blocks

The Nineties may be the era of electronic fuel injection, but in most forms of racing, the Holley four-barrel still reigns supreme. This 850 cfm model 4150 has been modified for racing–the choke plate was removed and the air horn milled off for increased airflow potential. Far more radical modifications are made in classes where carb modifications are not limited. Holley modular-style four-barrels, are available in a variety of air flow ratings and with either vacuum or mechanically actuated secondaries.

with replaceable jets in both the primary and the secondary circuits. The four-barrel models also feature dual accelerator pumps and mechanical secondaries; single accelerator pump and vacuum secondaries; single "center squirter" accelerator pump with mechanical secondaries; adjustable idle screws on primary only; adjustable idle screws on primary and secondary; center inlet fuel bowls; standard idle mixture adjustment; and reverse idle mixture adjustment. The combination of items seems endless in this series which offers various airflow capacities

ranging from 390 to 855 cfm.

Models 4165 & 4175—These "Spread-Bore" carburetors, while very similar in appearance to the 4150/4160 models, differ considerably in construction, and share surprisingly few components with their relatives. This is in spite of the fact that fuel metering circuits are conceptually identical. Power valves, jets, fuel bowl vent accessories, secondary diaphragm springs, floats, needles-and-seats and some accelerator pump hardware are the only items that will successfully interchange between the 4150/4160

One of the reasons that model 4150/4160 and model 4165/4175 carburetors are called "modular" is that so many subassemblies can be removed. Four screws hold the accelerator pump cover to the float bowl. The diaphragm beneath the cover should be inspected whenever the float bowls are pulled off–more frequently if they leak.

Holley's model 4500 Dominator is a race carburetor and was originally available in 1050 and 1150 cfm capacities. That's a bit much for many small blocks, so the 750cfm model that was introduced a few years ago may be of interest. With "four corner" idle and no provision for a choke, the racing heritage is apparent. However, this carburetor can be used on street-driven engines.

Changing jets on a Holley is a relatively simple task, requiring removal of only four fuel bowl screws. Once the bowl is pulled off, the metering block, which holds the jets, can be separated from the carburetor's main body. However, if you really want to get with the program, get this recent addition to Holley's line of parts--Quick Change float bowl kits. Two plugs in the front of the bowl allow jets to be changed without removing the bowls. Each kit is supplied with a dual feed type bowl, fuel bowl, gaskets, plugs and a jet removal tool. Quick Change bowls are available in standard and chrome finish for Model 4150/4160 and 4500 carbs.

On single-feed Holleys, fuel reaches the secondary float bowl through a tube. Whenever the float bowls are removed, the O-ring seals on each end of the tube must be carefully extracted. Most times, they're reusable, but if you suddenly spring a leak, you know they weren't.

and the 4165/4175 series.

The reasons for the uniqueness of 4165/4175 components are both logical and straightforward. These carburetors were designed as direct bolt-on replacements for the Rochester QuadraJet and Carter Thermo-Quad, and as such must function in an emissions-sensitive environment. Therefore, carburetor components for the 4165/4175 family were designed to provide improved driveability while holding exhaust emissions within acceptable limits. They are offered in either 650 or 800 cfm versions; all have 1-5/32-in. diameter primary venturi, 1-3/8-in. primary throttle bores and 2-in. diameter secondary throttle bores. The 800 cfm model's extra airflow capacity is derived from 1-23/32-in. secondary venturis, as compared to the 1-3/8-in. venturis used on the smaller 650 cfm carb. Some 4165's use the reverse-idle system and two types of float bowls are also available. These are the only major differences between the Spread Bores.

Model 4500—These "Dominator" carburetors are conceptually identical to model 4150 four-barrels. Their primary distinguishing feature is their size; Dominators are physically much larger than other Holleys and have significantly greater airflow capacity than the largest 4150. They were designed strictly for racing, but at least one model is suitable for use on large displacement, high performance street engines. They have 2-in. diameter throttle bores and either 1-11/16-in. or 1-13/16-in. venturis. Dominators are available with a 750 cfm flow rating for the street; racing Dominators are available in either 1050 or 1150 cfm.

Power valves for Holley carbs are available from a variety of sources, but not all are suitable. The valve at left is a genuine Holley part, the one on the right, an aftermarket replacement. Note the difference in the opening, and it's not surprising that the replacement valve doesn't have the same fuel flow potential. It's unsuitable for performance use.

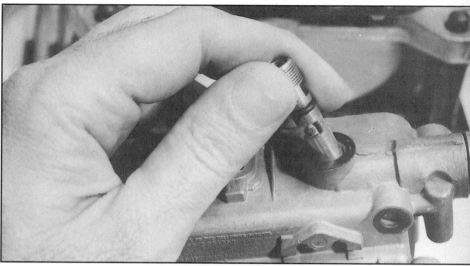

Holley inlet needle and seat assemblies are externally adjustable and removable. A 5/8-in. hex wrench is used to turn the adjusting nut and a wide bladed screwdriver is used to lock the assembly in place.

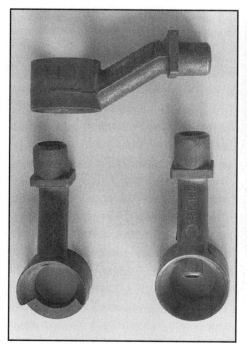

Holley has a number of different booster venturi designs and has used all of them over the years. Down-leg boosters offer less restriction than the straight-leg variety. The cut-out on the underside of one of these boosters was added to alter fuel distribution.

Some Holley carbs incorporate an accelerator pump transfer tube to link passages in the main body and metering body. This was done to minimize leakage from the accelerator pump circuit. O-rings seal the tube and you know the rest of the story.

Models 4010 & 4011—The latest additions to Holley's line-up of high performance four-barrels are the 4010 and 4011 series. Rather than having modular construction like other Holleys, these carburetors have a more simplified construction with only two major castings. These carburetors are also cast of aluminum rather than zinc and have a polished appearance. The 4010 carbs have either vacuum secondaries or mechanical secondaries with dual accelerator pumps. They have a square mounting flange and can be used to replace Holley 4150/4160 and Carter AFB/AVS carburetors. They are available in flow ratings of either 600 or 750 cfm. The 4011 models have a Spread Bore mounting flange and are intended as a direct replacement for the Rochester QuadraJet and Carter Thermo-Quad carburetors. The 4011 models come in either 650 or 800 cfm flow capacities.

Dialing in secondary diaphragm opening rate is considerably easier with this two-piece cover. Part no. 20-59 is for single carbs, 20-73 for dual four-barrel installations. Both covers in part no. 20-73 have a nipple so that two covers can be connected with a tube to balance the opening signal.

Holley carbs equipped with mechanical secondaries usually employ a link (arrow) from the primary throttle bracket for activation. Many times, this link must be bent (to shorten it) to ensure that the secondaries open fully.

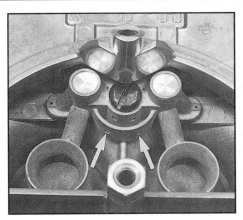

Holley model 4010 and 4011 are functionally quite similar to Holley 4150/4160 and 4165/4175 carburetors. However, construction is another matter completely. As an example. booster venturis are cast in a removable cluster which also incorporates the accelerator pump nozzle (arrows). On vacuum secondary carbs, no accelerator pump is used on the secondary side, so if you're looking for fuel to come squirting out of the pump discharge holes, you're in for a disappointment.

Whenever Holley float bowls are removed and reinstalled, or whenever the accelerator pump cam is moved, the pump override spring may need to be readjusted. There should be the slightest of preloads on the pump lever. Any clearance between override mechanism and the pump lever will delay the pump shot which may cause a hesitation.

An old trick for instant secondary opening on Holley four-barrels is to put a screw in the secondary throttle link slot. This effectively turns a vacuum-secondary carburetor into a mechanical secondary model. The only problem is that with no rear accelerator pump, the engine is sure to stumble when the secondaries pop open. Holley offers a selection of secondary diaphragm springs (kit number 20-13) for tuning secondary opening rate. Opening rate is affected by spring stiffness and overall height.

Carter Carburetors

Carter carburetors have also been a staple of high performance fuel systems, but they have never achieved the widespread popularity enjoyed by Holley. The primary reason is that Carter has always seemed to be out of step with the world of high performance engines. In fact, even finding a Carter four-barrel can be difficult. During the years that ACF Industries owned Carter, management indifference to the high performance market killed whatever momentum the carburetor had. That situation has changed in recent years with Carter's sale to Federal Mogul and Edelbrock's entry into the carburetor market. The Edelbrock carburetor is nothing more than a repackaged AFB and is available in 500, 600 and 750 cfm flow ratings.

Models WCFB & AFB—Only two Carter models ever saw much service atop a small-block Chevy. The WCFB models have electric chokes, others have manual chokes. Carter AFBs used to be very difficult to tune, however Carter now offers an assortment of jets, metering rods, metering rod piston springs, needle/seat assemblies and the like. Edelbrock also offers a selection of similar components.

ROCHESTER CARBURETORS

Rochester carburetors were manufactured by a division of General Motors, so it's not surprising that they have been installed on Chevrolet small blocks since the Fifties. Initially, Rochester 2GC two-barrels and 4GC four-barrels were used only on lower horsepower engines while Holley and Carter four-barrels were the carburetors of choice on high output engines. But by the late Sixties, the QuadraJet had moved in on the territory that had once belonged exclusively to Carter and Holley. And by the mid-Seventies, QuadraJets became the only original equipment four-barrel carburetors used on Chevrolet small blocks (and big blocks for that matter).

Although they were designed with emissions and fuel economy in mind, Rochester QuadraJets function quite well on high performance engines. In fact, when properly modified, they can be hard to beat. Their main drawback is price; they can be quite expensive.

SELECTING THE RIGHT CARB

When awareness of carburetor airflow capacity became commonplace, bigger was typically equated

Although dual Carter WCFBs were factory-installed on high performance 265 and 283 cid engines from 1956-1961, by 1962 the WCFB was too small to handle the airflow requirements of high horsepower engines, so Chevy began using Carter AFBs on some 327 cid engines. Dual AFBs were installed on the 409, but were never a factory option on a small block. Carter AFB and Edelbrock carbs utilize metering rods to control primary power enrichment. If you can find a "Strip Kit," it will have a good assortment of jets and metering rods so you can dial in air/fuel ratio to your engine's needs. At first glance, all metering rods may look pretty much identical, but small variations in diameter have a dramatic effect on fuel flow. Most AFB metering rods have a larger diameter step for cruise conditions and a smaller diameter tip for power enrichment.

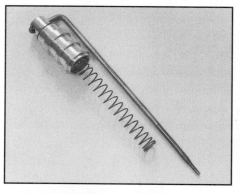

Power enrichment timing is controlled by a spring beneath the metering rod piston. Stiffer springs bring enrichment in sooner (at a higher manifold vacuum level).

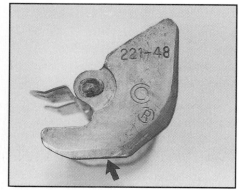

Removing weight on the edge with a grinder (arrow) from the secondary air valve of an AFB quickens opening rate. However, material removal must be done in small increments because if too much weight is taken off, the valve will open too quickly, causing a stumble.

(rated at 385 cfm), which was popular in the Fifties, is most noteworthy because it was the original equipment carburetor on 1956 and later 283 engines equipped with dual four-barrels. Although the AFB was used in dual four-barrel configuration on the legendary 409, small blocks were never factory equipped with more

than a single AFB.

Carter's 9000 series AFB carburetors (the only ones still in production) are available in four airflow ratings—500, 600, 625 and 750 cfm. All models have air valve secondaries which open in response to engine airflow requirements. Some

Rochester Quadrajets can be modified for performance applications but are more difficult to deal with than Holleys because of their construction. However, with any Q-Jet, the first order of the day is to make sure it doesn't leak. The lead plugs in bottom of the main body are notorious for allowing fuel to drip out. Epoxy can be used to seal the offending plugs.

Secondary opening rate on a Q-Jet is partially controlled by spring preload. When making changes to spring load, hold the adjustment screw with a screwdriver BEFORE loosening the Allen lock screw. Otherwise, the current setting will be lost (because the spring will cause the screw to unwind when the lock screw is backed off) leaving no reference point.

with better, and "too much" was just barely enough—even the largest available four-barrel was not capable of over-carbureting a highly modified small block. Two of the biggest early-model Holley 4150's provided a total airflow capacity of only 800 cfm (600 cfm four-barrels were not offered until 1958), and many factory dual four-barrel options utilized even smaller carburetors. It is interesting to note that dual four-barrels first appeared as original equipment on the 265 small block of 1956—just one year after the engine's introduction.

By comparison, the largest standard flange Holley four-barrel currently available flows 850 cfm and the larger square-flange "Dominators" flow up to 1150 cfm. Obviously, with the general availability of such grandiose carburetors, bigger no longer necessarily equals better. In fact, more often than not a smaller four-barrel is preferable to an extremely large one. While a 600 cfm unit with vacuum secondaries may not offer the glamour of an 850 double-pumper, the former will provide better driveability, greater fuel economy and crisper throttle response than the latter. It's also considerably less expensive.

Air Capacity—Choosing a performance carburetor therefore amounts to somewhat more than purchasing the largest model your budget allows. The first step is to determine the maximum airflow potentially demanded by the engine that is to receive the carburetor. On the surface, this appears to require no more than converting cubic inches (engine size) to cubic feet, multiplying by maximum rpm (to determine the engine cfm requirement), and selecting a carburetor that offers a corresponding airflow capacity. However, intended usage, engine efficiency, engine operating range and the total number of throttle bores must also be taken into consideration.

The basic mathematical formula for relating engine size and rpm to carburetor airflow capacity is:

$$cfm = \frac{\text{Engine cid x Maximum rpm}}{3456}$$

By way of example, consider a 350 cid powerplant with a maximum engine speed of 8000 rpm. By working it through the above equation, the cfm works out to 810 cfm. Therefore, a carburetor with an 800 cfm capacity would appear to be ideal.

Volumetric Efficiency—However, no adjustment has been made for volumetric efficiency (V.E.). Simply stated, volumetric efficiency is how many cubic inches of air and gas are consumed by an engine every two revolutions. Theoretically, a 350 cid engine with a 100% V.E. will consume 350 cubic inches of air and gas every two revolutions. However, except for well-prepared race engines, few small blocks reach 100% V.E. Volumetric efficiency is not constant throughout the rpm range, although it

Many later model QuadraJets have idle mixture screws sealed so that prying fingers and inquiring minds can't play. If idle quality has deteriorated, it may be necessary to grind the plugs away so the adjustment screws can be accessed.

When disassembling a Q-Jet, the external screws that hold the air horn to the main body are fairly obvious--except for the two hidden beneath the choke plate.

is usually highest at the engine speed where maximum torque is produced. According to Mike Urich, former vice president of engineering at Holley Carburetors and co-author of HPBooks' *Holley Carburetors and Manifolds:*

"An ordinary low-performance engine has a V.E. of about 75% at maximum speed; about 80% at maximum torque. A high-performance engine has a V.E. of about 80% at maximum speed; about 85% at maximum torque. An all-out race engine has a V.E. of about 90% at maximum speed; about 95% at maximum torque. A highly tuned intake and exhaust system with efficient cylinder-head porting and a camshaft ground to take full advantage of the engine's other equipment can provide such complete cylinder filling that a V.E. of 100%— or slightly higher—is obtained at the speed for which the system is tuned."

Urich goes on to recommend that you assume a V.E. of 85% for high performance street engines and a V.E. of 110% for all-out, highly tuned racing engines. As an example, consider the 350 racing engine running at 8000 rpm:

$$cfm = \frac{350 \text{ cid} \times 8000 \text{ rpm}}{3456} \times 1.1 \text{ V.E.}$$

$$cfm = 891$$

Theoretically, a carburetor with an 850 cfm capacity would be ideal. The 1.1, but the way, is 110% converted to a decimal. To calculate the street carb cfm, use the above equation only multiply by .85 (85% converted to a decimal) to arrive at a theoretical cfm.

These percentages of volumetric efficiency really mean that instead of consuming 350 cubic inches of air and gas every two revolutions, a 350 engine will use that percentage thereof. In other words, an engine with an 85% V.E. will only use 297 cubic inches of air and gas every two revolutions (350 x .85).

The laws of physics prevent these percentages from changing very dramatically. Intake manifold

efficiency, valve and port size, camshaft timing and exhaust manifold configuration are a few of the more readily identifiable factors affecting the volume of intake charge that will reach a cylinder prior to the power stroke. Since the low pressure created by a piston moving downward in a cylinder (during the intake stroke) is not sufficient to draw in 100% of the volume required to completely fill that cylinder (with the piston at the bottom of its travel), the effect of inertia is needed to keep the incoming air/gas mixture flowing after the piston has started moving upward (during the initial stage of the compression stroke). The inertia or "ram" effect increases with rpm, which is one of the reasons that internal combustion engines produce maximum horsepower in the upper rpm ranges

Vacuum vs. Mechanical Secondaries—The only other basic consideration with four-barrels is how the secondary throttle is activated. Vacuum control offers potentially smoother operation and in theory "sizes" the carburetor to the needs of the engine. If a vacuum actuating mechanism is properly tuned, maximum air velocity through the carburetor will be maintained at all operational levels. This is theoretically possible because secondary throttle opening responds to engine demands. Therefore, a 780 cfm carburetor may never flow more than 650 cfm, if that's all the engine requires.

Mechanical secondaries offer the advantage of allowing the driver to control precisely when the secondary throttles are opened. This is especially important in oval track and road

Edelbrock is now the source for QuadraJet carburetors, since GM has discontinued manufacturing them. In addition to new carburetors, Edelbrock also offers a variety of replacement parts which are useful for rebuilding and tuning.

racing where performance "coming out of the corners" is critical. In drag racing, positive secondary throttle control is also advantageous so use of vacuum secondary carburetors is uncommon except in Stock and Super Stock classes where rules dictate retention of the original equipment carb. Therefore, vacuum control is typically advised for street, RV, and recreational boat use, while mechanically operated secondaries are found in virtually all competition applications, the notable exception being off-road racing, because the inconsistent terrain doesn't allow the driver to maintain a smooth, constant application of power.

Recommendations

Regardless of horsepower figures produced on a dyno, engineering theory or mathematical formulas, the bottom line is the ability of a carburetor to function in a "real

world" environment. In many cases a carburetor is expected to compensate for inadequacies in the intake system. Some people mistakenly believe switching carburetors will correct certain problems (poor low speed response or lack of top-end power) that are actually caused by other factors.

For example, the combination of a big-port intake manifold, large-diameter headers and a super-lumpy camshaft will not allow any carburetor to meter fuel with optimum efficiency. Not only will fuel economy be poor, reduced vacuum at idle (created by long cam overlap and weak low-rpm exhaust scavenging) will delay activation of fuel flow through the main nozzles. This makes for poor low-speed throttle response, disappointing torque and possibly an off-idle stumble. Switching to a smaller carburetor is frequently viewed as a means of improving low-

speed operation. The reasoning is that velocities will be higher if venturi and throttle bore diameters are reduced. That's true at wide open throttle, but at part throttle, the effect is minimal. About the only advantage offered by a smaller carb is quicker activation of the main metering system. This may reduce the size of the performance "hole" but it will still be there.

Therefore, there is more to carburetor selection than mere size consideration. In spite of all the theories and reasoning behind proper carburetor selection, in the real world things usually boil down more to a matter of price and availability. With Carter and Edelbrock carburetors, only a few models are available, so it's pretty much a matter of selecting the carb that provides the desired airflow capacity. With a Holley the selection process is more involved, but not much. Part number 0-1850, which is rated at 600 cfm, and part number 0-3310, which is rated at 750 cfm, are "universal" carburetors that are produced in large volumes. Consequently, they're cheaper than other carburetors with similar airflow ratings. Other Holley carburetors with identical airflow capacities differ only in air/fuel calibration, linkage arrangement or choke mechanism. Since these carbs are tailored for engines of specific model years, they're easier to install and rarely require a change of jets. Emissions-type carbs will also clean up exhaust pollutants compared to a universal carb. The only real drawback is price: carburetors designed for specific applications are produced in relatively low volumes so they're more expensive than a universal carb of similar specifications.

Just about any street-type small

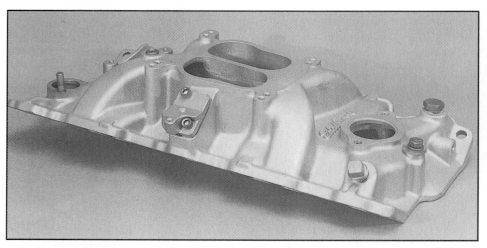

For street and even some race engines, a dual-plane manifold is the hot ticket. Edelbrock's Performer is a dual-plane manifold that offers strong low- and mid-range performance with relatively little compromise in top-end power. Two models are available—with and without provision for EGR—and both accept either spread-bore or square-flange carburetors. The RPM Performer (not shown) has a wider power band, but only accepts square-flange carburetors and may cause some hood clearance problems due to an extra .700 in. in height.

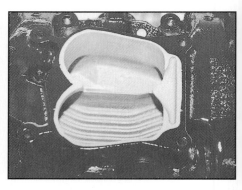

Cast-iron manifolds are universally scorned by performance enthusiasts, but some oval track organizations prohibit the use of anything else. Brzezinski Racing Products specializes in modification of cast-iron manifolds and reworks them extensively. This Q-Jet model is fully ported and has had a portion of the plenum divider removed for improved top-end horsepower.

block of 330 cubic inches or less will be well-carbureted by a 600 cfm four-barrel; small blocks of 350 cubic inches or greater displacement are equally well-served by a 750 cfm carburetor. Super high performance engines and race engines usually benefit from larger capacity carburetors with mechanical secondaries, such as those with cfm ratings of 750, 800, 850, 1050 and 1150 cfm. A variety of other carburetors are also available for specific applications.

However, before selecting a carburetor, check the emissions regulations that pertain to your vehicle so you don't run into problems if a governmental agency decides to check your vehicle's emissions levels.

INTAKE MANIFOLDS

The application for which an engine is designed dictates the specific rpm range in which power must be concentrated. Selection of intake manifold type should therefore be predicated upon a given design's ability to enhance performance at specific engine speeds.

All intake manifolds perform the same basic function, specifically that of providing a passageway between the carburetor and the intake ports of each cylinder. The configuration of the Chevy small block, like that of most V-8's, dictates that the passage connecting the manifold plenum to the cylinder head either travel a rather tortuous winding path, or take the shortest, most direct route. Both arrangements provide advantages and disadvantages which to some degree determine specific performance characteristics. In essence, each intake manifold configuration offers the potential for increased power within a particular rpm range while sacrificing performance somewhere else along the horsepower curve.

Dual-Plane Manifolds

Since passenger car engine designers are primarily concerned with low-speed driveability, they have always utilized the dual-plane design. Such manifolds are essentially two-in-one affairs, each plane or manifold half routing air and fuel from a separate plenum area to an individual group of four cylinders. With each half of the manifold isolated from the other, runners are grouped so that 180° of crankshaft rotation separates the intake cycles of cylinders fed by the same half of the manifold—hence the label "180° manifold." The 180° separation of cylinders, and relatively long runners which are required to snake around obstacles (like other runners), are the dual plane's greatest virtues. They are also the reasons that the design is conducive to the production of ample low-speed torque. At higher engine speeds, however, these assets become liabilities as the manifold runners are too restrictive to handle the volume of air required to produce maximum horsepower at 5500+ rpm. The high-rise design alleviates some restriction problems by allowing the runners to curve more gently, but it can't completely eradicate the inherent characteristics of the dual-plane configuration.

Single-Plane Manifolds

Conversely, a single-plane manifold is ideally suited to supplying great volumes of air to the cylinders. With eight large runners connected by the most direct route to a single plenum, this design offers comparatively little airflow restriction. The large open plenum offers an additional advantage in that it supplies a large reservoir of air/fuel mixture (the open plenum) from which the cylinders may draw, and this has the same effect as installing a larger carburetor. For high rpm operation, this arrangement is ideal, but the large plenum/short runner combination intensifies the problems of low air velocities at lower engine speeds; with insufficient velocity, cylinders don't fill with intake charge as well as they do with a dual-plane manifold, so low-speed torque is significantly reduced.

Another problem with the single-plane design is "mixture stealing" by adjacent firing cylinders. In the Chevy small-block V-8, at least two cylinders positioned next to each other fire in one-two succession. An example is number 7 cylinder firing immediately after number 5 cylinder. The first cylinder of the adjacent pair "steals" some of the intake charge that should go to the second, and at low engine speeds this can significantly reduce power output. At higher rpm levels, air velocities are such that each cylinder receives a full charge, but with the inherent low speed problem, a single-plane manifold can lead to objectionable off-idle performance, especially in heavy vehicles and those that are geared for good economy on the highway.

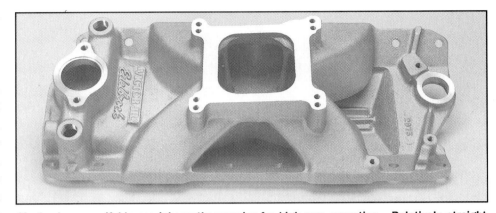

Single-plane manifolds are inherently superior for high rpm operation. Relatively straight runners and a large open plenum are typical features. Unfortunately, increased top-end power comes at the expense of low-speed torque. Because the plenum is wide open, runner walls can be extended, or ground back to change runner length. Longer runners shift the power curve down, shorter runners have the opposite effect.

Reducing Plenum Volume

One method of bolstering low-speed performance is to divide the plenum in half with an aluminum or steel plate. The resultant decrease in plenum volume reduces the air/fuel reservoir and intensifies the fuel metering signal that reaches the carburetor. The carb remains as the ultimate controller of airflow, but without a large open plenum between the carburetor and the runners, airflow velocities inside the manifold increase (which improves low speed operation) but maximum flow volume decreases (which limits top end power). In many instances, inserting a plenum divider will elevate manifold vacuum by one or two inches, and tremendously improve low-speed tractability. However, the fuel metering signal received by the carburetor will also be intensified resulting in a reduction in fuel economy unless the carburetor is rejetted.

Some engines may respond best to a dual-plane manifold with a portion of the plenum divider removed. Prior to the advent of single-plane manifolds, this was a common modification for improving top end horsepower. In the case of a dual-plane manifold, removing the plenum divider increases plenum volume, but there is an accompanying loss of carburetor signal. That can easily be overcome by rejetting. However, if competition class rules allow a single-plane manifold, that's the better choice.

If a dual-plane manifold is required, the term "cast iron" is probably in the same paragraph in the rule book. Surprisingly, most cast-iron four-barrel intake manifolds for small blocks aren't all that bad up to about 4500 rpm. In fact, some stock manifolds will produce more power than aftermarket high rise models in the off idle to 4500 rpm range. Increasing power above this level requires modifications of the type done by Brzezinski Racing Products of Pewaukee, WI, which has been known to perform magic on cast-iron manifolds.

As a general rule, reducing plenum volume has the same effect as reducing carburetor size; increasing plenum volume has the opposite effect. Adjusting plenum volume does

Weiand Team G single-plane manifolds were originally designed with the help of Bill "Grumpy" Jenkins. They've been updated over the years and are available for street and race engines. Model 7531 has a 2" raised plenum which eliminates the need for a carb spacer.

alter the rpm at which peak power occurs, but it isn't the only factor.

Intake Runners

Runner length also enters the picture and determines the rpm at which optimum efficiency is reached. Intake manifold runners are said to be tuned when their length and cross-sectional area are selected (based on the speed of sound) so that air movement is positively influenced. As with anything that moves, a column of air flowing into an engine has inertia. Movement of the air column is initiated when the intake valve opens and exposes the air in the intake manifold to a partial vacuum in the cylinder; pressure in the intake manifold is higher than in the cylinder, so the air naturally moves from an area of higher pressure to an area of lower pressure, thereby filling the cylinder. But when the intake valve closes, air movement does not stop immediately; the inertia of the air column keeps it moving and packs the runner with more air than it could otherwise accommodate. The inertia of the air column "rams" air into the runner's ports and has a slight pressurizing or supercharging effect. When the intake valve opens, the

SINGLE PLANE VS. DUAL PLANE

The engine used to compare a Holley 300-36 dual-plane manifold with a Holley 300-19 single-plane manifold had the following specifications: 355 cid small block, 11:1 compression ratio, Holley 650 cfm carburetor, ported 492 heads with 2.02/1.60-in. valves and a high performance hydraulic cam with 228 deg. of duration at .050-in. lift. The * in the chart indicates peak readings.

	Dual Plane		Single Plane	
rpm	CBT	CHp	CBT	CHp
2750	371	194	359	188
3000	381	218	365	209
3250	392	243	380	235
3500	405	270	395	263
3750	408*	292	398*	284
4000	405	308	398	303
4250	401	324	397	321
4500	398	341	389	333
4750	393	355	390	353
5000	390	372	393	374
5250	380	380	381	381
5500	374	391*	376	394
5750	357	390	366	400*
6000	340	389	346	396

Note that the dual-plane manifold produced higher torque and horsepower readings from 2750 to 4750 rpm. The single-plane manifold offers slightly more horsepower from 5000 to 6000 rpm, but the difference is significant only at 5750 where it offers a 10 horsepower advantage.

pressurized air in the manifold rams itself into the cylinder, filling it with an extra dense air/fuel charge, which translates into increased power. This effect isn't constant at all engine speeds, but it's significant within a defined rpm band. Longer runners lower the speed at which optimum ram effect occurs; shorter runners have the opposite effect. As a means of reference, the long, curving runners on a TPI manifold measure 17 in. in length.

One drawback of an intake runner that's tuned to produce peak torque below 4000 rpm is that total airflow capacity is compromised. The runners are too long, and of too small a diameter to permit sufficient airflow to support engine requirements at high rpm.

Runner sizing plays a significant role in establishing the rpm band in which an intake manifold is most effective and the premise of shrinking runner area to improve low speed

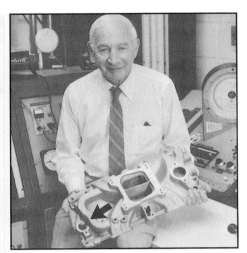

Zora Arkus Duntov, famed Corvette engineer, holds the "Z" series manifold he designed that is manufactured by Holley. This manifold concentrates power in the low and middle rpm ranges and offers excellent fuel economy. The "Z" series manifolds are single-plane, but incorporate a plenum divider to increase low-speed torque. The balance tube (arrow) connecting the runners for cylinders 7 and 8 serves to add volume to runner 7, which is usually robbed by cylinder 5, which fires immediately before it.

operating characteristics is also employed in single-plane manifolds designed for street operation. By altering runner cross-sectional area and plenum volume, a manifold designer can tailor a manifold to optimize performance at specific rpm levels. This accounts for the difference between street and race manifolds; they may appear quite similar externally, but there is a significant difference in internal dimensions, and the resultant effect on engine performance.

Single vs. Dual

Other considerations aside, a dual-plane manifold's relatively long runners make it less than the optimal design for high rpm use. By comparison, the shorter runners of a single-plane manifold are "tuned" to maximize the ram effect at higher engine speeds (above 5500 rpm).

Consequently, single-plane manifolds predominate on race engines and dual-plane manifolds get the job done on the street.

Alternate Designs

In the mid-Seventies, when fuel shortages changed the face of high-performance equipment, manifold designers came up with new configurations engineered to improve gas mileage and increase low speed and mid-range performance.

Z Series Manifold—Holley Carburetor's approach to pertinent intake manifolding was the "Z Series" manifold that was designed by Corvette engineer Zora Arkus-Duntov. A single-plane manifold with a divided plenum, the "Z" design also incorporates a balance tube that connects one plenum half with the other. In addition to providing additional air/fuel mixture to the adjacent firing cylinders that come out on the short end of things, the balance tube also transmits resonances created inside the manifold from one side to the other. This is said to increase charge density which improves low-speed engine response, and fuel economy. The "Z Series" intake

manifold for a small block (Holley part no. 300-28) works well on economy-oriented engines. Holley specifies an operating range of idle to 4800 rpm which is pretty accurate. On some engines, performance will take a nose dive at speeds above 5000-5250 rpm.

Edelbrock—Edelbrock took an entirely different approach to designing a manifold which optimizes low-speed performance and gas mileage and marketed it under the name SP2P. A minor variation on the dual-plane theme, the SP2P used extremely small runners to increase the velocity at which the air/fuel charge flowed from carburetor to cylinder. The theory behind this technique is that a faster moving mixture more readily keeps atomized fuel in suspension thereby reducing fuel consumption. However, the SP2P had a tendency to cause detonation under certain conditions and it wasn't compatible with some other types of performance equipment. Consequently, production was discontinued several years ago.

Tunnel Rams—While single- and dual-plane manifolds are most commonly associated with a lone

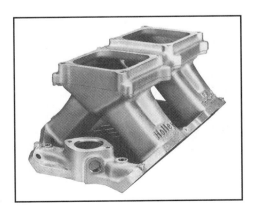

Holley's Pro Dominator dual four-barrel ram manifold has interchangeable tops and can be configured for either 4150 or Dominator carburetors.

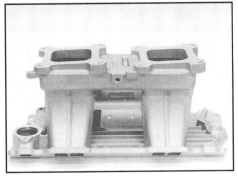

Edelbrock's Street Tunnel Ram is designed for lower rpm operation (3500-7500 rpm) than the race models. Runners are longer and have a smaller cross-sectional area for improved mid-range operation.

STOCK CAST IRON VS. ALUMINUM

Although a stock Chevrolet cast-iron intake manifold is heavy and ugly, it is ideally suited for low-speed and mid-range operation. The following dyno chart illustrates the advantage a stock manifold offers over an aftermarket version at lower engine speeds. In this case, the test engine was a 355 cid small block with 9.5:1 compression ratio, 1.94/1.50 in. valves and a mild performance camshaft with a duration of 216 deg. at .050-in. lift. The same stock QuadraJet was used in both series of tests. The * denotes peak readings.

	Cast Iron		Aluminum High Rise	
rpm	CBT	CHp	CBT	CHp
2000	331	126	320	122
2250	337	145	331	142
2500	332	158	335	159
2750	341	179	332	174
3000	358	205	344	197
3250	376	232	362	224
3500	390*	260	364	242
3750	385	275	371	265
4000	380	289	381*	290
4250	371	301	373	302
4500	365	313	365	313
4750	356	322	357	323
5000	345	329*	350	333
5250	324	324	333	333
5500	312	326	324	339*
5750	295	323	306	335

This comparison clearly shows that the stock manifold definitely has the handle on low-speed torque. While it produced only 9 lbs-ft. more than the high-rise manifold at peak reading, it's 12 to 14 lbs-ft. stronger from 3000 to 3750 rpm. But then the power curve starts to flatten out and begins to nose over at 5000 rpm. By comparison, the high-rise manifold's power curve continues to climb to a peak horsepower reading at 5500 rpm. In this case, the high-rise manifold produced only 10 additional peak horsepower. This is somewhat deceiving because of the influence of the stock cylinder heads and mild camshaft timing. A longer duration cam and mildly ported heads would have provided the needed airflow capacity to allow the high-rise manifold reach its full potential. With the right combination of parts, the high-rise manifold would have produced 15 to 20 additional horsepower. Once again, maximum performance boils down to assembling a properly coordinated combination of components.

two- or four-barrel carburetor, the tunnel-ram type design is linked to dual four-barrels. With long, gently curving runners topped off by a generous plenum area, a tunnel-ram manifold is strictly a high rpm, maximum horsepower affair. Various manufacturers—Edelbrock, Holley, Offenhauser and Weiand—each have their own ideas as to optimum runner size and shape, and plenum volume, but all ram type manifolds are primarily designed for full-tilt race engines such as those used in race boats and drag cars. Single four-barrel

tops are available for some models, but they generally prove unsatisfactory as fuel distribution is very erratic.

A tunnel-ram intake manifold can be run successfully on a street engine, but it usually requires some carburetor massaging. Edelbrock offers a street tunnel-ram manifold for small-block engines, but warns that it is, "intended for small-block Chevrolets operating below 7500 rpm where low-end torque is not a prime factor." This manifold has its runners sized to match stock and slightly modified

ports. Runner length and cross-sectional area is also tuned for a lower operating range than a race tunnel ram. Although Holley and Weiand do not have ram manifolds specifically designed for street engines, their race manifolds have been used with some success on street engines.

If you're planning to run a tunnel-ram manifold on a street engine, keep in mind that most carburetors are designed for single four-barrel applications, the exception being a few race carbs that are calibrated for twin four-barrel manifolds. As such, the idle and main metering circuits may have to be recalibrated to avoid an excessively rich mixture. Vacuum secondary carburetors should also have their secondary diaphragms tied together so that they open at the same rate. Holley offers a special diaphragm cover (part no. 20-28) which incorporates a hose fitting for this purpose.

General Recommendations

Laying down specific manifold selection guidelines is a difficult, if not impossible task, since the number of variables pertaining to engine/chassis combinations are virtually unlimited. However, there are some broad guidelines that will keep you out of trouble. Edelbrock, Holley, Chevrolet and Weiand offer dual-plane high-rise manifolds that are ideally suited to stock and modified engines. These models produce strong low- and mid-range power and allow an engine to pull strongly up to about 6000 rpm. They represent the best all-around choice for any high performance street engine. More exotic race-type manifolds can be used successfully on the street but since they are designed to deliver maximum power at higher rpm (above 5000) they tend to compromise driveability and torque below 4000 rpm. Another drawback of a race-type single-plane manifold is lack of heat at the base of the plenum. This is a particular problem with certain models that have an air gap between the bottom of the plenum and the manifold base because it takes so long for the manifold to reach normal operating temperature. This isn't an insurmountable problem, but one you should be aware of when selecting an intake manifold.

Remember, you will have to live with the manifold you choose. An engine that talks back every time you attempt to accelerate away from a stop light is about as much fun as driving in stop-and-go-traffic. If you're not prepared to make all the changes and some of the sacrifices necessitated by a race-type manifold, stick with something tamer. Your car will be easier to drive, and a lot more fun. It will also run faster.

Most street engines run out of camshaft, cylinder head or carburetor before they ever get to the rpm at which a single-plane manifold makes maximum power. There are exceptions, but every time I've run a single plane versus dual plane dyno comparison test, the dual plane outperforms the single plane up to about 5000 rpm. If you shift at 5500 rpm, that doesn't give you much of an rpm range to take advantage of the increased top-end power.

ELECTRONIC FUEL INJECTION

Electronic fuel injection easily does things that a carburetor and intake manifold could never do, no matter how much they are modified. EFI represents the best method of achieving maximum performance while keeping exhaust emissions as low as possible and fuel economy as high as possible. While the myriad of electrical, computerized components of EFI may seem intimidating, this really isn't so. While certainly more sophisticated than a Holley four-barrel, it still performs the same basic function—mixing fuel and air. These systems are intimidating at first because they're so different. But after working with one for a short time, you'll find that most of the same rules apply.

Throttle Body Injection

Throttle body injection (TBI) systems position the injectors within the throttle body, rather than in each individual port. A TBI unit is similar to a carburetor in that it can be bolted directly to the type of intake manifold commonly associated with two- and four-barrel carburetors. However, unlike a carburetor which requires airflow to draw fuel through it, a TBI unit injects fuel under pressure. Chevrolet's Crossfire Injection, used

The TPI system that was introduced in 1985 provides excellent street performance and has become extremely popular. It is routinely installed on older cars and trucks. However, improvements can be made.

Although the nozzles found in an electronic fuel injection system are precision components, they are mass produced and subject to variations in spray pattern and total flow. Accumulation of deposits can also alter pattern and flow. For optimum performance, nozzles should be chemically cleaned so that spray patterns are uniform. Each nozzle should also be flow tested so that cylinder-to-cylinder fuel distribution is equalized.

on 1982-1984 Corvettes, and the injection found on many late-model plain vanilla passenger car and truck small-block V-8s, are TBI systems.

Crossfire Injection—This throttle body system is a band-aid that Chevrolet used to make the transition from carburetors to fuel injection. There's nothing wrong with throttle body injection, but in the Crossfire system, the manifold has very small runner outlets which makes the system inappropriate for use on a high performance engine—it just won't

flow enough air and can't be modified without extensive welding and reshaping of the runner outlets.

Tuned Port Injection

The outstanding performance of factory small blocks produced during the late 1980s and early 1990s is largely a result of Chevrolet's Tuned Port Injection (TPI) system. The first TPI systems (installed on 1985-1989 model year engines) employed a mass air flow sensor to monitor the volume of air entering the manifold. A heated wire serves as the actual sensing device and air flowing past the wire cools it, altering its electrical resistance. Higher airflow has a greater cooling effect. The ECM monitors the resistance and adjusts fuel flow accordingly.

In 1990, Chevrolet switched to speed/density systems which rely on programmed information, rather than measured air flow to determine fuel flow. Although speed/density systems offer increased performance potential because they eliminate the Mass Air sensor, which is somewhat restrictive, they are more difficult to work with when making engine modifications. Since there's no Mass Air Flow sensor to tell the EMC what's going on, custom PROM calibrations become much more critical since they're in total control.

With both types of systems, a variety of other sensors feed input to the computer so adjustments can be made for changes in manifold air temperature, throttle position and engine coolant temperature. When the system goes into "closed loop" operation, an Exhaust Gas Oxygen (EGO) sensor is used to monitor the oxygen content of the exhaust. Based on input from the EGO sensor, the

ECM makes the adjustments required to keep the air/fuel mixture at the chemically correct ratio (14.7:1).

Primary Components

The primary electronic components of a TPI system are not as complicated as they may seem.

ECM—Electronic Control Module. This is the brains of the outfit. Essentially, the ECM receives all sensor input and performs all the calculations required to establish fuel flow rates. The ECM also controls ignition timing. In the early 90s, the capacity of the ECM was expanded to included control of automatic transmissions and the initials were changed to PCM—Powertrain Control Module.

PROM—Programmable Read Only Memory. This simply means that once programmed, a computer can read it, but can't alter it. The PROM or chip holds all the data that the ECM needs to match a given set of sensor inputs to fuel and ignition control outputs. The data inside a PROM is arranged in a multi-dimensional array that looks like a topographical map. The reason that computer-controlled

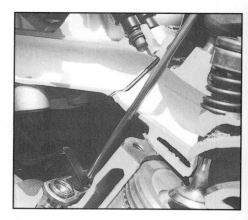

Cutaway view of a TPI manifold shows the path that air must flow to reach the cylinder head. Combined with the external runner tube length, the manifold section adds up to a total of 17" of overall runner length.

Tuned Port systems employ a three-piece intake manifold—the base mates to a pair of curved tubular runners which in turn connect to an upper plenum. Although high performance bases and large tube runners are available, stock plenums are the order of the day. However, extensive internal modifications are applied for high performance applications. One of the easiest ways to hop up a TPI system is with a Fast Pak from TPI Specialties. Included are an adjustable fuel pressure regulator, throttle body air foil, plug wires, low-restriction air filter element and throttle body cover plate.

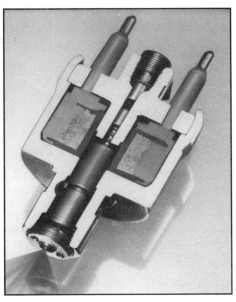

The fuel injector nozzle exposed. Fuel enters under high pressure at the top, flows through the injector body and exits at the spray tip. The ball valve is normally closed and opens while current is supplied to the coil assembly. The length of time that the coil is energized (known as pulse width) controls the amount of fuel discharged. As pulse width widens, the mixture becomes richer. Total maximum flow rate is governed by injector sizing which varies from engine to engine.

engines don't always respond well to modifications is that the ECM can't match the sensor input to the data in the map, so it can't come up with the proper output data. The computer continues to "hunt" for a recognizable combination input data, and does the best job it can in coming up with proper output data—which makes for erratic engine operation. However, aftermarket PROMs can be programmed to include conditions not recognized by a standard PROM. All it takes is the right programming to make computerized controls capable of handling just about any engine requirement. Starting with the 1994 model year, removable PROMs were no longer included in the PCMs found in Camaros, Firebirds and Corvettes. Instead, *electronically erasable programmable read only memory*

(EEPROM), also called "flash" memory, is used. With these systems, new calibrations can be downloaded into the EEPROM without removing it from the PCM.

MAF Sensor—Mass Air Flow. These sensors were incorporated in 1985-89 TPI and 1994 and later LT1 systems. This sensor monitors the amount of air flowing through by sensing the voltage of heated wire it contains. At wide-open throttle, maximum air flow will exert a strong cooling effect and voltage through the wire will be close to the five-volt maximum in order to maintain temperature; at idle, with not much air movement, only about .4 volts are required to heat the wire.

EGO or O_2 Sensor—Exhaust Gas Oxygen. This sensor measures the amount of oxygen in the exhaust and

alters fuel flow so that the air/fuel ratio is maintained at stoichiometric, which is the chemically ideal ratio of 14.7:1. One of the problems with standard EGO sensors is that they must be located relatively close to the heads so they reach operating temperature. Heated EGO sensors are the solution and are used on many original equipment and custom installations. A heated EGO sensor is mandatory when an engine is equipped with headers because the sensor is too far downstream and the exhaust is too cool for proper operation.

MAT Sensor—Manifold Air Temperature. As its name implies, this sensor keeps track of the air temperature within the manifold. This

For more horsepower in the upper rpm ranges, a MiniRam manifold is available from TPI Specialties. This manifold is very similar to the one found on LT1 engines and delivers a sizable increase in mid-range and top end horsepower.

information is sent to the ECM so that calibrations can be finely tuned.

TPS—Throttle Position Sensor. It doesn't take a rocket scientist to figure out that the TPS tells the ECM the position of the throttle. What isn't so apparent is that this sensor also sends data concerning the rate of throttle opening. This rate is used to calculate the degree of air/fuel enrichment required for acceleration (in a carburetor this function is handled by the accelerator pump). TPS position is physically adjustable, and a volt meter is normally used to determine the proper position. When placed in the stock position, the TPS will have an output of .54 volts with the throttle closed. Rotating the TPS counterclockwise increases the voltage which results in a richer air/fuel ratio and usually crisper throttle response. But too much of a good thing is still too much and if the sensor is moved too far, the "Check Engine" light will come on during idle. With TPI systems, this condition can usually be avoided by keeping TPS voltage at .54 to .55 volts with the throttle closed.

LT1 engines incorporate a non-adjustable TPS. Rather than relying strictly on voltage to determine throttle position, the LT1 system equates the lowest voltage encountered with 0% throttle opening (throttle closed). The computer then bases throttle position (persentage of opening) on that voltage. If the PCM subsequently sees a lower voltage, it revises its calibrations with the new voltage equated to 0%.

Coolant Temperature—The name for this sensor is self-explanatory, but the output of this sensor has a pronounced effect on performance. Both air/fuel ratio and ignition timing are altered depending upon coolant temperature. Lower temperatures result in richer mixtures and more aggressive spark timing. High temperatures have the opposite effect.

Knock Sensor—This is a device that protects the engine from destruction. The sensor itself is like a small microphone. When the ECM "hears" detonation, it temporarily retards timing.

IAC—Idle Air Control. This device incorporates a small electric motor that controls an air bypass valve (a separate air channel not controlled by the throttle plates). If the idle speed established by throttle position is too high or too low, the PCM moves the IAC to open or close the bypass valve as required to achieve the desired idle speed.

MAP Sensor—Manifold Absolute Pressure. This is another way of stating manifold vacuum. The MAP sensor is essentially an electronic vacuum gauge that tells the ECM the amount of load under which an engine is operating. The ECM alters air/fuel ratio to accommodate varying load conditions, just as a power valve or metering rods perform this function in a carburetor. Speed/Density systems rely heavily on MAP sensor input to calculate the fuel curve.

Limp Home Mode—Of course, with all these sensors, something can very well take a wrong turn so TPI systems incorporate what's known as a "Limp Home" mode. In the event of a major system or sensor malfunction, the ECM automatically slides into "Limp Home" mode where upon it holds timing to about 22 deg. and establishes a relatively rich air/fuel mixture. The whole idea of "Limp Home" mode is to protect the engine from damage while it is being driven a short distance. Some custom wiring harnesses (designed to allow installation of TPI systems in vehicles not originally so equipped) force activation of "Limp Home" mode. This isn't desirable, nor is it necessary. Proper harnesses are available from a variety of sources.

MODIFICATIONS

Even though the use of electronics sets TPI apart from a garden variety carburetor and intake manifold, that doesn't alter the fact that it takes a substantial amount of airflow to develop a substantial amount of power. In the case of a Tuned Port intake manifold, that means porting the manifold base and plenum, and installing oversized runners.

A number of companies, including TPI Specialties, Accel and Arizona Speed and Marine, specialize in performance modifications to TPI hardware. Additionally, TPI Specialties, Accel and Edelbrock have developed replacement intake manifolds with higher airflow capacities than a fully modified Tuned Port system. The Accel manifolds were designed by John Lingenfelter.

One of the keys to inducing higher air flow capacity in a Tuned Port or LT1 engine is a larger throttle body. The standard one has two 48mm openings whereas high performance models contain 52mm or 58mm openings. The 52mm models are modified stock throttle bodies, the 58mm versions are complete new castings.

As originally designed, Chevrolet's TPI manifold components are intended to produce strong mid-range torque, but the system is too restrictive for high rpm operation. Even on a fully modified engine, the most extensively altered TPI system will reach peak horsepower at 5000-5250 rpm. At 17-in. in length, the runners (which are responsible for such strong mid-range torque) are just too restrictive. Since horsepower is partially a function of rpm, a four-barrel carburetor and high performance intake manifold will always pump out more top-end horsepower—and less mid-range torque—than a TPI system.

Myron Cottrell of TPI Specialties addressed this problem by creating a "Mini Ram" intake manifold. With runners measuring only 3-in. in length, the Mini Ram doesn't attempt to provide a tuning effect. Instead, it offers minimal restriction and increased airflow. The trade-off is a bit of mid-range torque for a bunch of top-end power.

This trade-off was embraced by Chevrolet engineering in development of the LT1 engine which employs a Mini-Ram-style manifold rather than the TPI system found on the 1985-

1991 L-98 engines. According to John Juriga, V-8 Engine Laboratory Development Manager of the GM Powertrain division:

"Any time you tune an intake system, you increase power in the middle of the curve, but you lose at the top and bottom. The power curve looks like a peaked roof. With the LT1 intake manifold, we've lowered the peak, but raised the sides—more like a flat roof—so power doesn't drop off so quickly. As a result, the LT1 puts out 50 more horsepower than the L-98."

However, for many street-driven engines, a modified Tuned Port manifold/runner combination is entirely suitable. Depending upon the type of driving you do, it may actually be preferable because it concentrates power in the rpm range where an engine spends most of its time. Modified TPI systems produce outstanding results, but it takes quite a bit of experimentation to optimize power. Myron Cottrell of TPI Specialties has spent countless hours on the dyno testing various plenum, runner and base modifications and has been able to achieve outstanding power output with modified engines equipped with TPI systems.

The PROM—One of the keys to maximizing power is having the right PROM. Many times, a modification to a TPI-equipped engine has the potential to make a significant power increase. But that potential won't be realized until the proper air/fuel calibration is achieved. Remember, unlike a mechanical distributor, the ECM contains calibration data for virtually every operating condition and every engine speed. If a change to

the intake tract alters airflow significantly, the ECM may misread actual operating conditions and adjust air/fuel ratio for conditions that don't exist. These problems tend to be minimized when a mass air sensor is included in the system, but they still exist.

For stock and lightly modified engines, Cottrell's formula for improved power output includes an air foil to smooth the flow of air entering the throttle body, a low restriction air filter and an adjustable fuel pressure regulator. These parts deliver a measurable power increase and can be used with the stock PROM as the adjustable pressure regulator allows the fuel curve to be altered to some degree. Higher pressure results in a richer mixture (and vice versa) which usually results in increased horsepower, up to a point. If pressure is raised too high, power will fall off because the mixture becomes too rich. However, if a new PROM is installed, horsepower will take another step up because fuel atomization is improved as pressure is increased.

That sounds like a case of "more is better unless it's too much, in which case even more is what you need." Actually, there's a good deal of logic to it all. With electronic fuel injection, fuel flow is primarily governed by three factors—injector flow rate, system fuel pressure and pulse width. Pulse width refers to the length of the electronic pulse that tells the injector nozzle to stay open. Increasing pulse width keeps the nozzle open longer so fuel flow is greater. Injector flow rate refers to the amount of fuel a nozzle is capable of flowing (usually expressed in pounds per hour). A richer air/fuel mixture may be achieved by lengthening pulse width, switching to

Increasing the airflow potential of a standard TPI system requires a manifold with larger runners such as TPI Specialties' "Big Mouth" model. Here, the grimacing Pete Gray is installing one on Jim Monteith's 1990 Corvette. Along with a number of other modifications, the car went on to run 12.30s at over 112 miles per hour. Gray also installed large tube runners to compliment the "Big Mouth."

larger capacity nozzles, increasing fuel pressure or some combination of all three. However, if the mixture is too rich, power will drop, just as it does in a carbureted engine.

When pressure is in the range of 46 to 55 psi, and an increase causes a drop in power, the air/fuel ratio is simply too rich. Installing a new PROM corrects the situation by shortening the pulse width so the ratio is brought back to the optimum setting. Certainly, the proper calibration leads to more horsepower, but in this case you get a bonus because of the improved fuel atomization that accompanies

increased pressure. It takes quite a bit of experimenting to determine the most desirable fuel pressure/pulse width combinations, but specialists in TPI modifications have figured out most of the answers.

Replacement Injectors—For a time, the hot tip was to install injectors from a Buick Grand National (27 lbs./hr.) in modified 383 and 406 engines. However, Cottrell has found that in most cases, this is exactly the wrong change to make. Provided total flow capacity is adequate, smaller injectors (in combination with higher fuel pressure) produce more horsepower and better fuel economy—if fuel pressure and pulse width are correctly set—because of improved atomization. The one caveat is that it takes fuel to make horsepower so maximum injector flow rate must be consistent with engine demands at maximum power. At part throttle, the computer reads the EGO sensor input and adjusts injector pulse width so that the proper air/fuel ratio is achieved. When fuel pressure is increased, the computer automatically shortens pulse width to compensate. However, at wide-open throttle, the system switches from closed loop to open loop and ignores EGO sensor input. When this occurs, it relies totally on the calibrations stored in the PROM.

Testing has shown that 305 injectors (19 lbs./hr.) can deliver adequate fuel for engines up to about 355 horsepower. Standard 350 injectors (22 lbs./hr.) can handle the demands of 450-horsepower engines. In some cases, when 305 nozzles are installed in a 350, raising fuel pressure to 50 psi is the only change required and the stock PROM can be maintained. Irrespective of nozzle capacity or fuel

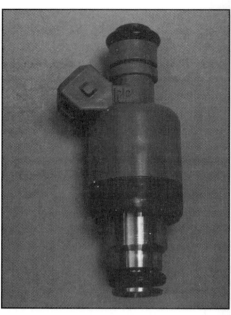

Port type injectors operate under the same principles as their throttle body counterparts, but they're considerably smaller. Both types of injectors are available in a variety of flow ratings. Stock 305 Tuned Port injectors are flow rated at 19 pounds per hour; 350 TPI injectors are rated at 22 pounds per hour and LT1 injectors are rated at 25 pounds per hour.

pressure, horsepower may come up short if flow varies too much from one nozzle to another. Sizable flow variations are not uncommon, so if you're after every possible bit of horsepower, blueprinted nozzles, with equalized flow rates, are required.

Fuel Flow Numbers

If you're used to dealing with carburetors, you'll find that total fuel flow numbers seem to be a bit off. Eight 305 injectors have a maximum flow capacity of 152 pounds of fuel per hour (19 lbs./hr. times eight injectors). With a carburetor, that's only enough fuel for about 310 horsepower. But fuel injection is so much more efficient that it takes considerably less fuel to produce the same amount of power. This is reflected in the Brake Specific Fuel

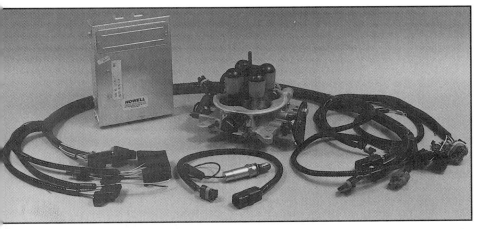

The HP/TBI system from Howell Engine Developments utilizes a Holley ProJection throttle body which is controlled by a GM Electronic Control Module (ECM) through a custom harness. This system allows owners of older small block Chevys to sample the convenience, fuel economy and power of a state-of-the-art throttle body electronic fuel injection system. Full GM diagnostic capabilities are retained so calibrations and troubleshooting are simplified.

Consumption (BSFC) numbers which relate fuel consumed to horsepower produced (BSFC = Fuel Flow/Horsepower). TPI-equipped engines typically produce BSFC readings of .40 to .43 at peak power while a carbureted engine will usually have readings in the range of .46 to .50.

Custom PROMs

Although high performance PROMs are available from several companies, they are typically designed for stock or lightly modified engines. As such, they won't optimize the power output of engines equipped with high performance cams, modified cylinder heads, headers and the usual assortment of intake system alterations. Until recently, a custom PROM for such engines had to be ordered from an "off-road" specialist. However, in 1994, Steve Cole of The Turbo Shop (Compton, CA 310/215-0147) introduced "MasterTune", a program that enables custom PROMs to be created with an IBM-compatible PC.

Using MasterTune, it's possible to develop calibrations for virtually any TPI-equipped small block, regardless of the extent of engine modifications. However, unless you can see how the engine is responding to changes in calibrations, you're flying blind. So in order to use MasterTune's capabilities fully, you'll need another piece of software known as Diacom. This program monitors all the sensors and controllers that communicate with the ECM or PCM, displays the data and also has storage capability. Typically, after a new chip is programmed and installed, a car is driven with Diacom set to store data which can then be reviewed to determine the effect of the changes.

Regarding the capabilities of a standard GM Mass Air or Speed Density ECM, personal experience has shown that with a properly programmed PROM, it can easily control a 525-horsepower 406 small block. The only problem with this particular engine is that it was being run with a TPI-style Mass Air Flow sensor which can only measure up to 255 grams per second of air. The engine reached that flow rate at 4800 rpm, so fuel enrichment had to be "fudged" above that level. The point is that the stock GM ECM has the capability to control virtually any streetable small block.

Replacement TPI Systems

Although TPI systems and aftermarket versions thereof are very attractive in both appearance and performance, they're also fairly expensive. Connecting one to a vehicle that was originally equipped with a carburetor requires purchase of a computer, wiring harness and the required sensors. All of these are available from a variety of sources, but they have to be considered when figuring total cost of a TPI installation.

Companies specializing in Tuned Port Injection usually have complete systems available for sale. Another alternative is to find a system in a wrecking yard and either modify it yourself or send it off for the full treatment. But before such a system can be installed in a vehicle that didn't originally have a TPI or LT1 engine, a custom wiring harness must be used. Howell Engine Developments in Marine City, MI (810/765-5100) is a good source for these.

Howell also markets a complete high performance throttle body fuel injection system. Known as the HP/TBI, it features a GM ECM a Holley two-barrel or four-barrel injector body and one of Howell's custom harnesses. Since the system relies on GM sensors and electronics, it's dead reliable, and replacement sensors and controllers are readily available. It also maintains all GM diagnostics which eases service and repair, if needed.

HOLLEY PROJECTION SYSTEM

Holley's ProJection systems are designed to bolt right onto any four-barrel intake manifold with a standard Holley carb flange. Available in both two-barrel and four-barrel versions, Pro-Jection is a self-contained electronic throttle body system. While it doesn't offer the fuel efficiency or torque potential of a Tuned Port Injection system, it costs a good deal less and installation is considerably simpler. The ProJection system is also vastly superior to a carburetor.

The ProJection systems originally employed a rather simplistic analog controller which seemed to require constant adjustment. The subsequent digital ProJection system is vastly superior. Consisting of a a four-barrel throttle body, wiring harness, electronic control unit (ECU) computer, high-pressure fuel pump and all required sensors and hardware, the system can also be used to control ignition timing.

Installation isn't terribly difficult and compared to a carburetor, Holley's digital ProJection systems offer significantly better throttle response, smoother operation, increased efficiency and a broader power range. After it's installed, the ProJection system is very easy to tune. Instead of having to remove fuel bowls and change jets, air/fuel calibrations are altered by simply typing a few keys on a lap top computer and downloading the data to the ECU.

As with any electronic fuel injection system, the ProJection requires a return line to the fuel tank because pressure is controlled by bypassing unused fuel back to the fuel tank. To assure that pressure doesn't get out of hand, the return line must be adequately sized; return line inside diameter should be a minimum of 5/16 in.

Another supplier of aftermarket electronic fuel injection is Holley. The original ProJection systems were analog and offered limited tuning capabilities. Although adjustments are provided for idle, power enrichment, accelerator pump, choke and mid-range calibrations, analog ProJection systems rely strictly on throttle position, change in throttle position and rpm as a means of establishing fuel flow. Consequently, air/fuel ratios are not as precisely controlled as with digital systems that utilize a number of other inputs.

Holley's latest ProJection systems are of the digital persuasion and include an ECU (electronic control unit) that can be programmed with a laptop computer. Digital ProJection systems are conceptually similar to original equipment speed/density systems and include Manifold Absolute Pressure, Manifold Air Temperature, Throttle Position and O2 sensors. Holley's systems will also control spark timing and will provide automatic knock retard is an Electronic Spark Control module is wired into the system.

Irrespective of the induction system you select, keep exhaust emissions in mind. With the November 15, 1990 amendments to the Federal Clean Air Act, it has become illegal to install "... any device whose principal effect is to bypass, defeat or render inoperative an emissions-control device or element design installed on a motor vehicle." The fine for each violation is $2,500. Depending upon the model year of your vehicle, you may or may not be impacted by the Clean Air Act, so be sure to check things out, and make sure your intended modifications are in tune with Federal regulations.

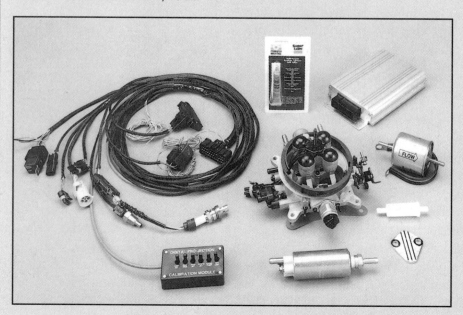

TPI MODIFICATION KIT

If you've never worked on a TPI system, the thought of disassembling the intake manifold and making component changes may be enough to bring on Excedrine headache number L98. But once you get over the initial fears of taking your wrenches into uncharted territory, you'll find that the TPI hardware is no more difficult to deal with than a carburetor-based induction system. The following modifications can all be accomplished in a few hours, making a TPI hop-up an ideal project for a Saturday afternoon. The modifications pictured here involve installation of a TPI Specialties Fast Pak and a few ancillary modifications. According to TPI Specialties, the kit will provide an average increase of between 25 and 30 horsepower with proper tuning. To order your kit, contact TPI Specialties, 4255 County Road 10 East, Chaska, MN 55318. (612) 448-6021.

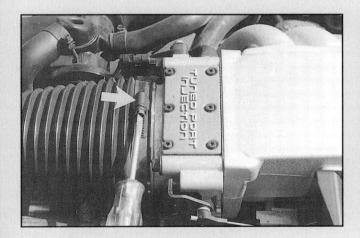

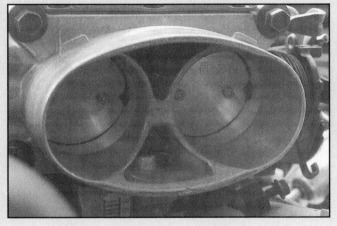

1. Begin by removing the clamp that holds the ducting in place on the throttle body. The ducting and its attachment method differ according to year and model.

2. It's not necessary to remove the throttle body from the plenum to install the air foil. Leave it in place so you don't have to wrestle with it while installing the air foil. But the four-throttle body attaching screws will have to be pulled out later so the plenum can be broken loose, a requirement for installation of the adjustable fuel pressure regulator.

3. To install the air foil, remove the six Torx head screws that hold the cover plate in place.

4. The air foil nut (arrow) slips right into a small hole between the throttle bores.

5. Hold the nut in place and put the air foil in position. Then thread the retaining screw into place and tighten it. Replace the cover plate.

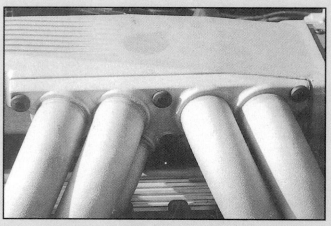

6. Four Torx head bolts hold each runner section to the plenum. After removing the throttle body, remove the runner attaching screws from each side. It may be necessary to loosen the bolts that hold the runner sections to the manifold and lightly rap the plenum with a rubber hammer to brake it loose from the gaskets. But before you do that...

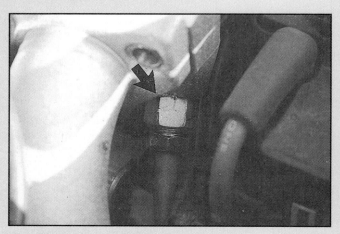

7. ...disconnect the fitting that attaches the power brake vacuum line to the plenum and...

8. ...remove the three bolts that hold the cable bracket to the plenum body. The cables can remain attached because only the plenum must be lifted out—the throttle body can remain in place.

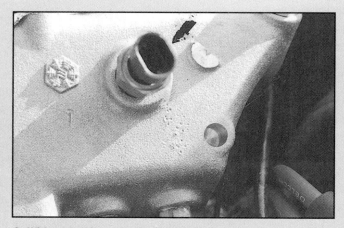

9. With everything else disconnected, the plenum may be lifted, but can only be moved a few inches. The wire that plugs into this fitting must be pulled out so the plenum can be swung to the side.

10. With the plenum flipped over as shown, you have all the access you need to the fuel pressure regulator. Don't forget to reconnect all electrical and vacuum lines during reassembly.

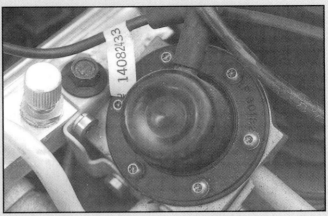

11. The stock pressure regulator is held in place by six security Torx screws (note small tang in the center of each screw head—that's the security feature). Special wrenches are available from a variety of sources and are included in TPI Specialties adjustable regulator and Fast Pak kits.

12. Before removing the stock pressure regulator, remove the gas cap (to eliminate pressure in the tank) and bleed off system pressure at valve/gauge connection. This valve functions like a tire valve. As you can see, the fuel pressure adjustment screw can be easily accessed after the system is reassembled. If you're smart, you'll check system fuel pressure before making any changes so that you can re-establish the baseline after the adjustable unit is installed.

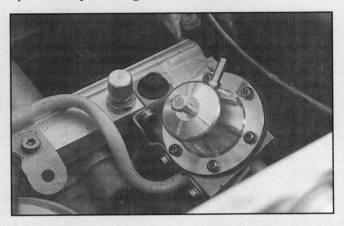

13. Once the adjustable pressure regulator is bolted in place, the vacuum hose can be attached and the plenum reinstalled. Use new plenum/runner gaskets which are supplied with the adjustable regulator.

14. If your TPI system is equipped with a Mass Air Flow sensor, it has screens on each side. Flow capacity can be improved by removing these screens.

The easiest way to remove the screens is to roll a knife blade around the seam between the screen retainer and the MAF sensor body. Once you cut through all the way around, the retainer will pop off.

CYLINDER HEADS

4

Cylinder heads are understandably vital in any recipe for horsepower, so whether an engine is being built for street performance, drag racing, oval track, road racing, marine or off-road applications, the heads must be properly matched to the pistons, camshaft and intended engine usage if maximum power is to be extracted. Countless numbers of small blocks have had all visions of glory destroyed by misdirected "experts" who either selected the wrong cylinder heads, or took a wrong turn while modifying them. Such mistakes aren't difficult to make because the selection of small-block heads seems nearly endless.

CAST-IRON PRODUCTION HEADS

In spite of the vast array of cylinder heads produced by Chevrolet and a host of aftermarket manufacturers, there are usually only a few models that are truly applicable for an engine of a particular personality. Just as passenger car heads rarely provide the ultimate power levels on a race engine, race heads usually provide less than impressive results when installed on a true street engine. It all has to do with combustion chamber volume, port size and casting integrity.

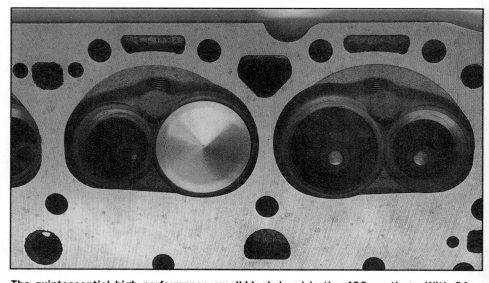

The quintessential high performance small-block head is the 492 casting. With 64cc combustion chambers, 2.02 in. intake and 1.60 in. exhaust valves and generously proportioned ports, it has been used in a variety of street and race applications. Like most traditional combustion chambers, the ones in this 492 head are nominally rated at 64cc's. In real life, they typically measure 66-68cc's. For high performance use, this is generally the most popular type of chamber because of the compression ratio it allows. With a true 64cc chamber, it's possible for a 350 cid engine to squeeze a 10.5:1 compression ratio with flat-top pistons.

Identification

Chevrolet small-block cylinder heads are most commonly identified by their casting numbers, which may be found in a variety of locations, depending upon the particular head. However, the complete casting number is usually located beneath the valve cover, directly above a pair of intake ports. Additionally, the last three digits of the casting number can usually be found beneath one of the ports when a head is viewed from the combustion chamber side. These are the three digits that are used when referring to cylinder heads. As an example, in machine shops, bench racing parlors and other houses of high performance, casting number 3991492 is called simply a "492" casting. In the real world, the first four digits are virtually meaningless, as is the actual part number (3987376) which is used only when ordering new heads from a Chevrolet dealer's parts department. However, once a cylinder head is out of its original box, a part number is of no use because the only identifying marks on the head itself are the casting numbers.

Many Chevrolet cast-iron

Complete cylinder head casting numbers are usually located on the head's upper surface, which is visible when the valve cover is removed. The last three digits, in this case "492" are the ones used most commonly for identification.

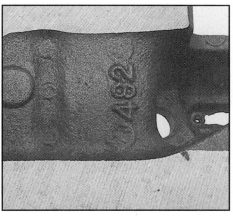

A casting number, usually limited to the last three digits, can also be found beneath an intake port.

Most original equipment standard production small-block heads have an identifying mark cast into the end. The same mark can usually be found on many different castings. However, irrespective of the size valves originally installed, the infamous double hump shown here invariably indicates large ports and a 64cc combustion chamber.

production heads also have an identifying mark cast into their ends. The most sought-after castings are the ones with a "double hump," which indicates a performance head with large ports. Some performance heads also have a triangular identification mark.

Cast-Iron Production Heads

From the time the small block was introduced, Chevrolet has offered a variety of cylinder heads. Most of the pre-emissions era high performance heads have 64cc combustion chambers. Note that this is a nominal engineering dimension; in real life, most "64cc chambers" actually measure 67 or 68cc's. Head milling is usually required to achieve a combustion chamber that actually measures 64cc's.

896—Old timers talk fondly of the "Power Pack" heads that were released back in the late Fifties. While these heads may have been the hot ticket for the modified 283s at that time, they are far from being the best

choice for a state-of-the-art performance engine. Power Pack heads (number 896 casting) are characterized by 1.72/1.50" intake/exhaust valves, 137cc intake runner volume and 59cc combustion chambers.

492 (double hump)—By comparison, a 492 casting (routinely referred to as a "fuel injection," LT1 or Z/28 head) commonly features 2.02/1.60" valves (some 492 heads were supplied with a 1.94/1.50" valve combination, but these heads can be easily machined to accept the larger valves), 64cc combustion chambers and 160cc intake runner volume. The 492 casting is the only high performance head with 64cc chambers still available from Chevrolet. As part number 3987376, this head features screw-in rocker arm studs and pushrod guide plates. But as part number 3958603, (discontinued in 1991) a 492 casting had pressed-in studs and was machined for 1.94/1.50" intake/exhaust valves.

In the early Seventies, 492 castings were available with angled spark plug holes, but this version, part no. 336746, was offered for only a short

time, and only through the Chevrolet parts department; angle-plug 492 castings were never factory-installed on a production engine. Angled spark plug holes are advantageous primarily in engines with pistons having extremely high domes. The angled drilling of the plug holes repositions the firing end of the plug higher in the combustion chamber so the flame front isn't blocked by the dome. If a piston doesn't have a large dome, this repositioning isn't quite as advantageous, but the angled orientation places the plug tip closer to the center of the chamber for more efficient combustion. (Note that Chevrolet ultimately adopted angled plugs heads for production engines; both the L98 and LT1 aluminum heads found on late-model Corvettes, Camaros and Firebirds have angled spark plugs.) The latest version of the 492 casting has increased diameter spring pockets which accommodate valve springs having a 1.440" diameter; early versions accommodate only 1.250" diameter springs.

This 441 casting houses 76cc chamber chambers which became the rule in the early 70s. Although this larger chamber doesn't allow for particularly high compression ratios (the maximum in a 350 cid engine is about 9:1 with flat-top pistons and 11:1 with high domed pistons), it offers excellent power potential because it doesn't shroud the valves.

One of the reasons that double-hump castings are so appropriate for high performance use is their generously sized exhaust ports. Although not the hot lick for professional caliber race engines, these ports, with just a little clean-up, are ideal for street and mild race engines.

462 & 186 (double hump)—These castings have specifications similar to the 492 head. The 186 was the first large valve/64cc chamber head with accessory bolt holes.

461 & 461X (double hump)— These heads also feature 64cc combustion chambers and a 2.02/1.60" valve combination, but have slightly larger intake ports; 461

PLAYING THE ANGLES

Beginning with the 1987 model year, production cast iron small block heads incorporated a revised angle on the two center manifold bolt holes. On earlier heads, these bolt holes are at a 90-degree angle to the manifold face; on '87 and later heads, they're at a 73-degree angle. The revised angle of these bolt holes is obviously a consideration when installing an intake manifold. Late model intake manifolds originally mated to '87 and later cast iron heads are machined to accommodate the 73-degree angle; intake manifolds designed for earlier cast iron or any aluminum heads are not. Obviously, manifold/cylinder head compatability must be verified before engine assembly is completed. Some aftermarket manifolds are machined with oval hole center bolt holes and the appropriate spot facings so they can be used with either type of head. When a manifold/head mismatch occurs, it can be corrected by machining and spot facing the center bolt holes as required.

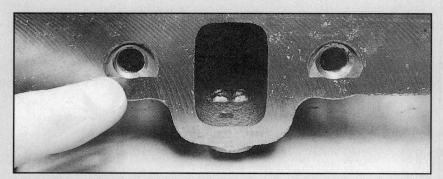

Cylinder heads with 73-degree center bolt holes can be identified by the relief around the holes.

castings typically have 165cc intake ports while 461X castings have 170cc intake ports. These heads achieved notoriety during the heyday of Super Stock drag racing when porting was not allowed. They offer no particular advantage if port modification is planned. Another point to be considered if shopping for used heads is that 461 castings do not contain accessory mounting bosses and bolt holes, so they can't be used in many late-model vehicles unless special brackets are installed. The 461 is the original "double hump" casting.

441—A late-model "smog" head

installed on 350 cid engines, the 441 casting has 76cc combustion chambers and 1.94/1.50" valves. Although the intake ports are only 155cc's, these heads deliver amazingly good performance, especially when modified and machined for 2.02- or 2.05" intake valves.

441X—This version of the 441 casting was used on 350 and 400 cid small blocks. It's virtually identical to the 441 casting except that it has 80cc combustion chambers and 1.60" exhaust valves when factory-installed on 400 cid engines. 441X heads

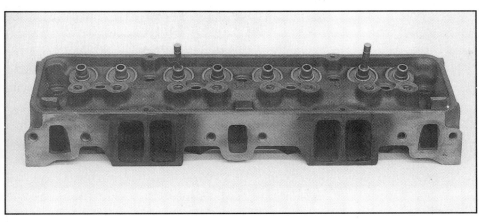

Small-block intake ports can be deceiving because from one casting to another, cross-sectional area can vary even though outlet size is about the same.

installed on 350's have 1.50" exhaust valves.

041 (triangle)—This head was originally supplied with either 1.94" or 2.02" intake valves. It is virtually identical to the 186 casting, but has accessory bolt holes.

624 (double triangle)—Originally used on 1971-72 LT1, 1971-74 Z/28 and 1973-79 L-82 engines (with 9:1 compression ratio), this head has 76cc combustion chambers and is still available as a service replacement for high-performance, low-compression engines. As part number 464045, it's supplied with 3/8" screw-in studs and is machined for 2.02/1.60" valves. This casting isn't a lightweight type, but weight reduction was incorporated in its design. Although it is suitable for mild performance applications, it should not be used if power output is above 350-360 horsepower.

997 & 493—These are late-model "smog" heads with 76cc combustion chambers and 1.94/1.50" valves. Functionally almost identical to the 441 head except intake ports measure 160cc's.

If you've gotten the idea that the 492 casting is the best production cast-iron head for a street engine, you're right.

But other castings offer virtually identical performance characteristics. When looking for used heads, you just may find a good pair of 462 and 186 castings, before you stumble onto a pair of 492's. There's virtually no performance difference between these castings, but there is one caveat; for high performance or race applications, a pair of heads will have to be machined to accept screw-in rocker studs and 1.440" diameter valve springs. The cost of machining may turn a bargain into a bad deal. In the long run, you may be better off purchasing a new pair of 492 or aftermarket heads.

Vortec V-8—The 305 and 350 Vortec V-8s introduced for 1996 pickup trucks feature one of the best cast-iron cylinder heads ever produced by GM. Combined with the unique Vortec intake manifold, these heads are responsible for a 250 SAE net horsepower rating for the 350. Although Vortec heads are equipped with 1.94" intake and 1.50" exhaust valves, they offer exceptional potential for high performance applications. However, they feature unique intake manifold bolt positioning, so conventional small-

block manifolds won't fit without modification.

CHEVROLET RACING HEADS

292 Turbo Head

In 1973, Chevrolet realized that there was a tremendous demand for cylinder heads that brought horsepower potential to higher levels than could be achieved with production heads. The 292 turbo head was the first casting designed specifically for racing. The turbo moniker arose from a turbocharged Indy engine project that never materialized. Although these heads weren't used on the Indy engine, the name somehow was transferred to the 292 castings which have been called "turbo heads" ever since.

Although the 292 intake ports have a 180cc volume and provide better airflow potential than any production heads, the ports as cast can be lacking. Like virtually all Chevrolet "off-road" heads, 292 castings were poured with the anticipation that they would be extensively modified before ever being installed on an engine. Consequently, as-cast port shape isn't a high priority during manufacturing. The primary advantage of castings designed for "off-road use only" is that they have plenty of material in the places needed for port modification and also have angled spark plug holes.

Bow Tie Heads

Throughout the Seventies, Chevrolet, like all other auto manufacturers, concentrated on downsizing and cleaning up in an effort to improve fuel economy and reduce exhaust emissions. At the

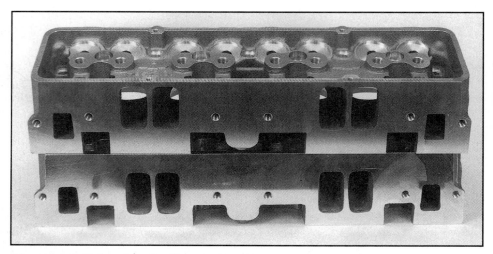

Other recent offerings from the Chevrolet RaceShop are conventionally designed heads with an 18° valve angle. Both low and high port models are available.

same time, racing was becoming more competitive, so specialty parts designed strictly for racing were also developed. By 1979, the 292 casting was coming up short in performance potential so a replacement was released—the 034 "Bow Tie" casting. "Bow Tie" refers to the Chevrolet emblem which is cast into race-oriented cylinder heads, cylinder blocks, connecting rods and intake manifolds. Over the years, the "Bow Tie" emblem has become synonymous with Chevrolet's high performance parts program.

034—The 034 head, with its 190cc intake port, established a new benchmark in the evolution of Chevrolet racing cylinder heads. As a completely machined casting the Bow Tie cast-iron head was originally listed as part number 14011058. Subsequently, changes were made in external machining—the front face was machined flat and the parting line between the exhaust ports was machined rather than left as cast. Another change was a recontouring of the combustion chamber so that its volume was actually 64cc's.

The revised 034 head was given a new part number—10134392. Although the earlier 14011058 head was listed as having 64cc combustion chambers, in real life, the chambers typically measure 67-68cc's as cast. The Bow Tie iron head was also available in semi-finished form, with no spark plug holes and no pushrod holes; listed as part number 10051108, it was discontinued in 1990.

Phase 6—In addition to the cast-iron Bow Tie head, Chevrolet also offers an aluminum version (introduced in 1980) as casting number 14011049. Like its iron counterpart, the aluminum Bow Tie head features angled spark plug holes, but the current "Phase 6" version has a 55cc rather than a 64cc combustion chamber and "D"-shaped exhaust ports. "Phase 6" aluminum Bow Tie heads also have an additional .050" between intake and exhaust valves making it possible to install 2.100" intake and 1.625" exhaust valves. This casting is available with no seats or guides as part number 14011049; it is also available as part number

10051167 with cast-iron valve guides and seats that accommodate standard length 2.02/1.60" valves. Part number 10051179 pertains to the same casting but includes bronze valve guides and seats that accommodate 2.10" diameter intake and 1.625" exhaust valves that are .100" longer than stock.

101—Another variation on the aluminum Bow Tie theme is the raised runner 101 head released in 1986. This head features intake ports that are .200" higher than in standard production and race heads. With this repositioning of the ports, use of a special intake manifold (Chevrolet part no. 10051103 or an aftermarket equivalent) with appropriately positioned runners is required.

Intake ports in the 101 (raised runner) cylinder head provide for a larger short turn radius (where the floor of the port curves down towards the valve) which in turn reduces turbulence and increases airflow capacity. The "D"-shaped exhaust ports in the 101 casting have also been altered to incorporate a larger short-turn radius. This head was

The difference between the low and high port 18-deg. Chevrolet heads is obvious when you look at the distance from the top of the port to the valve cover rail. This is a low port version.

supplied without pushrod holes so that the intake ports can be extensively widened. Once all the port work is finished, the machine shop must drill eight pushrod holes in each head. The 101 casting, (10051101) which requires valves that are .100" longer than stock, was discontinued in 1991.

352 & 363

Chevrolet has two other inline valve aluminum race heads in its parts catalog. Both heads feature an 18° valve angle as opposed to the 23° angle found in production and other Bow Tie heads. Valve centerlines are also relocated and the valves are on the cylinder bore centerline to minimize shrouding and accommodate the largest possible valve diameters. Casting number 10134352 (which is also the part number) is referred to as the low-port design because the intake ports are .65" above the deck surface. Casting and part number 10134363 is a high-port design with the intake ports located 1.22" above the deck.

Both heads have 45cc combustion chambers (which are typically finished at 50cc's) and 80cc exhaust ports. However, the 352 head has 200cc intake ports and will accommodate a 2.150/1.625" valve combination while the 363 head incorporates 223cc intake ports and will handle a 2.20/1.625" valve arrangement. The 352 head requires valves with a nominal length of 5.250" (.300" longer than stock) while the 363 head requires valves that are 5.350" long.

A variation of the 363 head carries part number 10134364. Specifications of the two heads are the same except that as part number 10134364, the largest intake valve size is 2.15".

Splayed Valve—Chevrolet also has a unique splayed-valve head that was modeled after the splayed-valve 90° V-6 head that was instrumental in Chevrolet's winning the 1990 SCCA Trans-Am manufacturer's and driver's championships. The V-6 head traces its lineage to the symmetrical port big block head. Listed as part number 10185040, the splayed-valve head was introduced in 1991. Some of its vital statistics look like they were lifted from a big-block specification sheet—263cc intake runner volume, 2.20" intake valves and intake ports that are 2 in. high. The splayed-valve head also features 1.60" exhaust valves, a 45cc heart-shaped combustion chamber and compound valve angles. The intake valves are angled 16° from the deck and canted 4°; exhaust valves are pitched at an 11° angle and also tilted 4° to the side.

Splayed-valve heads require the use of part number 10185041 rocker mounting bars, 10185042 intake manifold gaskets, 10185043 valve cover gaskets and 10185045 valve covers. A shaft-mounted rocker system, 5.70"-long valves and special

Aluminum Bow Tie heads with 18° valve angles feature a uniquely shaped combustion chamber which is filled in behind the valves for improved combustion efficiency.

length pushrods are also required as is a special camshaft because of the change in intake and exhaust valve sequence. Since splayed-valve heads are legal only in unrestricted classes, Chevrolet's initial intake manifold offering consisted only of a base plate, part number 10185044. Individual fuel injector stacks can be attached directly, or a manifold can be fabricated to accommodate other types of induction systems.

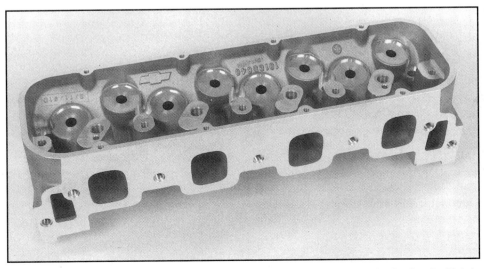

The latest offering from Chevrolet's high performance group is the splayed-valve head which is quite obviously a radical departure from traditional small-block cylinder head design. This head will accommodate 2.20" intake valves and features 263cc intake ports.

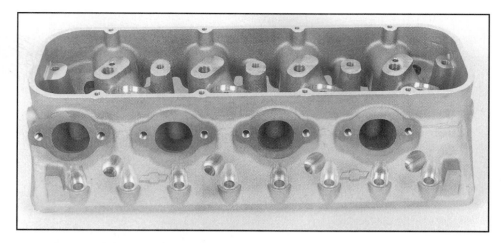

Uniformly spaced exhaust ports and angled spark plug holes are also included in the splayed valve head. The 1.6" diameter exhaust valves are angled 11° from the deck and canted 4 °.

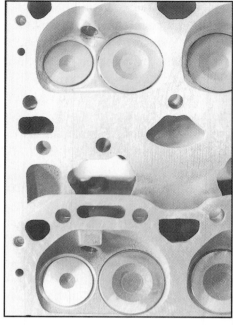

Combustion chambers of Corvette aluminum heads are routinely polished and reshaped for high performance use (top). Standard valve sizes are 1.94" intake, 1.50" exhaust. Lower head has unmodified chambers.

CORVETTE ALUMINUM HEADS

While the Bow Tie castings are intended strictly for maximum output race engines, the Corvette aluminum heads released in the middle of the 1986 model year are suitable for high performance street engines. These heads have 58cc combustion chambers, 1.94" intake, 1.50-in. exhaust valves and angled spark plugs. Although they're reasonably priced (considering that they're aluminum), and offer excellent performance potential, Corvette heads do have some notable limitations; maximum valve size obtainable from the original valve seats is 2.00" and 1.60" for intake and exhaust respectively.

For the 1988 model year, Corvette aluminum head castings were revised to increase exhaust port flow. The port roof was raised .100" and the floor was flattened to create a "D" shape. Exhaust valves were also treated to a 65° back cut to improve flow capacity. These changes brought about a 15% increase in exhaust port flow. However, the raised exhaust

exits can cause a mismatch when earlier model exhaust manifolds or headers are installed. According to Chevrolet engineering, any such mismatch should have an insignificant effect on performance because exhaust gas flow is concentrated in the center of the port. However, with certain headers, there may not be enough contact area at the top of the port to form an effective seal.

In stock form, the Corvette aluminum head (casting No. 10088113, part no. 10185087) has

good airflow characteristics which are sufficient to support the needs of an engine producing a maximum of about 330 horsepower. Properly ported, however, these heads are suitable for 400+ horsepower engines.

No Heat Riser—Another

Although not a legitimate race head, Corvette aluminum heads work well in high performance street applications after they've been ported. Later versions of this casting offer improved port shape and spark plug positioning. Guideplates used on Corvette aluminum heads are not hardened because self-aligning rocker arms (part no. 10089648) are used.

consideration is that these heads were designed for use on fuel-injected engines. As such, they have no heat-riser passages to bring heat to the bottom of the intake manifold (many aftermarket heads do not have heat-riser passages either).

This is by no means an insurmountable problem, but on a carbureted engine it will cause poor driveability immediately after start-up in cold weather. Even in warm weather, lack of heat at the bottom of an intake manifold can cause a carbureted engine to stumble and backfire. In order for a carburetor to function properly, the air flowing through it has to be moving at a sufficient velocity to cause a pressure drop so that fuel vaporizes. Once through the carburetor, the environment has to be warm enough to prevent chilling the vaporized fuel to the point that it reliquifies. With no heat at the bottom of the intake manifold, some of the fuel that is in vapor form will condense and fall out of suspension. Liquid fuel doesn't burn very well, so the engine sputters, pops, bangs and occasionally backfires until it reaches operating temperature. Oversized intake ports compound the problem, because they reduce airflow velocities which have a negative impact on vaporization.

Corvette aluminum heads may not be the ultimate choice for a killer small block, but when properly ported, they'll deliver air flow capacities that are as good or better than most aftermarket street heads. The weight savings of aluminum is also attractive (a bare Corvette aluminum head weighs 19 pounds; a typical cast-iron head weighs 44 pounds), but for engines that will be fueled by a carburetor, it might make

more sense to purchase aftermarket heads that have heat riser passages.

As sold through Chevrolet dealers and Goodwrench Performance parts, Corvette aluminum heads are available as complete assemblies (part no. 10134336) including valves, springs, retainers, screw-in 3/8" rocker studs and guide plates. The valve springs on these heads (part no. 10134358) are heavy-duty chrome silicon types which have a seat pressure of 110 pounds at an installed height of 1.70 in. By comparison, in production trim as installed on a Corvette engine, the aluminum heads are fitted with standard springs that have a seat pressure of only 80 pounds at the same installed height.

LT1 Heads

LT1 aluminum heads incorporate ports that are similar to those in L98 castings, but the intake ports offer higher flow capacity in unmodified form. When fully ported, LT1 heads will flow sufficient quantities of air to support 425 to 450 horsepower. Due to the reverse-flow cooling system utilized in LT1 engines, these heads aren't suitable for use on conventional "First Generation" small blocks.

AFTERMARKET CYLINDER HEADS

Prior to the Seventies, Chevrolet Motor Division was the only reliable source of cylinder head castings for the small block. But since that time, companies like Brodix, Dart, Air Flow Research, Edelbrock and All-Pro have jumped in with a variety of cast iron and aluminum heads that in most cases are a step up from the factory parts. Even Pontiac and Buick have developed their own head

There are significant differences between LT1 (bottom) and L98 (top) cylinder heads. Note that intake ports have a different shape and the LT1 casting has no water passage exposed to the intake manifold. That means the intake manifold can be removed without draining the radiator.

castings which can be used on a small-block Chevy. They are available through the GM Parts Performance Catalog.

Brodix

Brodix offers a wide variety of aluminum cylinder heads. The Brodix Street Head is intended for general high performance use and offers excellent value. This head features 69cc combustion chambers, screw-in studs and guide plates, and a three-angle valve job. It is supplied completely assembled with stainless steel 2.020" intake and 1.60" exhaust valves, valve springs suitable for a

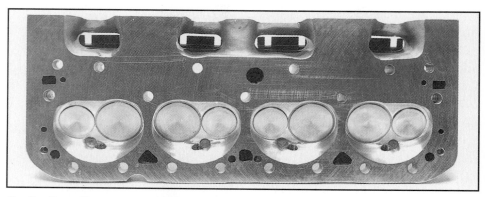

Brodix -8 castings are popular for both street and race applications. These heads offer excellent long-term durability because they have ample material in all the right places. The only difference between street and race versions is that the street heads usually have a heat-riser passage.

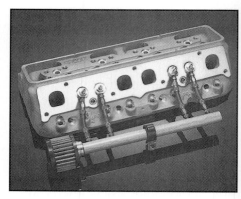

One option found on heads intended for injected alcohol-burning sprint car engines is side nozzle injection. This arrangement brings the fuel discharge point very close to the intake valve which is advantageous in these applications. Pictured is a spread port -11 Brodix head. Note space between the two center exhaust ports.

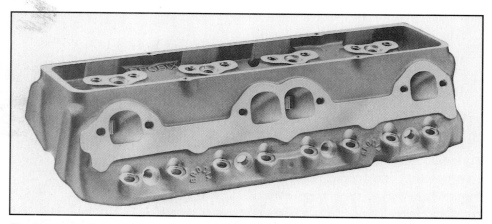

The Brodix Track I cylinder head is a relatively low-priced aluminum head intended for short track engine. The head features 215cc intake runners, 70cc chambers and angled spark plug holes.

hydraulic lifter camshaft, steel retainers, valve locks and seals. Unlike most race heads, the Brodix street head includes heat-riser passages and is 50-state legal.

Brodix also offers its -8 race head with heat risers. This casting dates back several years and although it was originally intended for race engines, it is entirely suitable for a high performance street engine if it isn't ported extensively.

Other cylinder heads available from Brodix are -10, Track I, -11, -12 and -18 head castings which are successive designs released to accommodate the ever-changing

demands of professional oval track and drag racing. These heads have achieved tremendous popularity because they provide an engine builder with port configuration options not available with factory high performance cylinder heads. Brodix -8, -10, -11 and -12 heads are available with either standard or raised intake ports. The Raised Intake (RI) series offer the potential for increased intake port airflow because of the less severe corner that the mixture has to turn on its way to the combustion chamber.

The -8, -10, Track I and -11 heads are variations on the original small-

block cylinder head theme and differ only in port volume; they all have 23-degree valve angles. Brodix developed different port designs in response to specific demands and the number assigned to each design pertains to the relative time it was released. A larger "dash" number (-8, -9) indicates a later release date, but does not always imply a larger intake port. Most Brodix heads are available with either standard or spread exhaust ports. Spreading the two center ports allows large diameter headers to be installed without the need for dual flange header plates, but more importantly, it allows a waterjacket to be added between the exhaust valves for the two center cylinders. This allows the center of the head to be cooled properly, which improves durability.

The Brodix -12 head features a 15° valve angle and intake port volume can range from about 225cc to 280cc. A -18 casting, with an 18-degree valve angle is also available as is a canted valve head which features intake valves angled at 14° and inclined (or canted) 4° and exhaust valves angled at 10° and inclined 2°.

Dart

Another company that offers a wide selection of small-block cylinder heads is Dart Machinery. Dart conventional design "220" aluminum heads (23° valve angle) feature 64cc combustion chambers, 220cc intake ports and can be ordered with standard or spread exhaust ports. Raised exhaust ports and standard Chevrolet accessory mounting holes are also featured as are maximum valve sizes of 2.20" for intake valves and 1.680" for exhaust valves. Dart also offers raised runner heads with 64cc combustion chambers and 215cc intake ports. These heads are available with either standard or spread exhaust ports and 23° or 17° valve angles. Another Dart casting features 50cc combustion chambers, 15° valve angle and spread exhaust ports.

Dart's Buick Head—Dart also manufactures the Buick head for small block "corporate" engines. This head incorporates the port and combustion chamber design used on the Buick Stage 2 V-6 race engine and requires the use of special rocker arm assemblies. Dart "Buick" heads feature intake valves positioned at a 10-degree angle (compared to 23 degrees for a standard small block head) symmetrical ports and 235cc intake ports. A variety of valve spacings are available.

Note that a completely different camshaft is also required because of the different valve arrangement. On a conventional head, the valves are arranged in an exhaust/intake, intake/exhaust pattern. With the Dart Buick head, intake and exhaust valves alternate, so the cam lobes must be

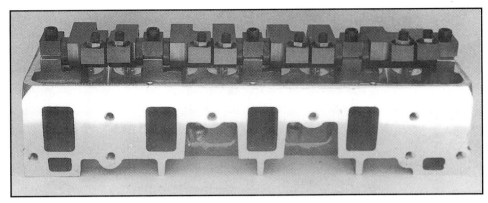

The Buick version of the small-block Chevy head is patterned after the Buick Stage II V-6 head. It offers 235cc intake runners, 42cc combustion chambers and 2.100" intake 1.625" exhaust valves. With its unique port layout, the Buick Stage II head shares no components with standard Chevy heads and requires special intake manifold, headers and camshaft.

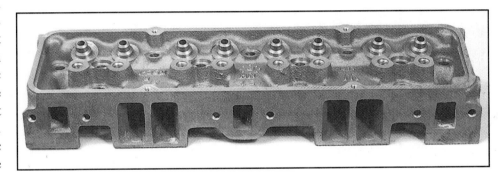

Dart II cast-iron heads have become extremely popular because of their low price and high quality. The Sportsman head is the hot ticket for high performance street and mild race engines. These heads have better airflow characteristics than any Chevrolet production head and respond nicely when ported.

arranged accordingly.

World Products—While all the heads sold under the Dart name are strictly hard-core race pieces, World Products heads (formerly known as Dart II) are suitable for street, street/strip, oval track, drag race, marine and off-road applications. (World and Dart are related.) World Product's original orientation was towards the standard replacement market.

As good used Chevrolet castings have become more difficult to locate, the demand for a replacement has risen. World Products introduced the S/R head (Stock Replacement) as just that. However, it does have excellent air flow capacity, has enough meat to

allow for extensive porting and is an excellent choice for stock and lightly modified engines.

For more highly modified engines, World Products offers Torquer, Torquer II and Sportsman II castings (all cast iron). For most street applications, the Torquer cast-iron heads with 1.94/1.50" exhaust valves or optional 2.02/1.60" valves and 171cc intake ports are more than adequate (the biggest intake port in a standard production Chevrolet head is 170cc's). Torquer 305 and Torquer II 305 castings are designed for 305-cu. in. and other 3.875" bore engines. Large displacement and high horsepower street engines (especially 372, 383 or 406 cid models) may look

Dart II cast iron heads have plenty of material in all the right places. The S/R castings are used by stock engine rebuilders because good used stock castings have become so difficult to locate. Sportsman castings have larger ports.

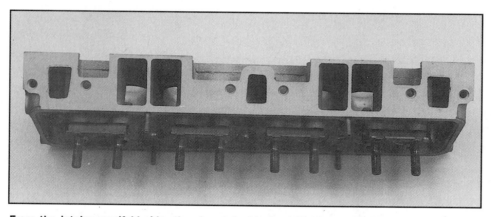

From the intake manifold side, there's no doubt about the intent of the Dart II Sportsman castings. Note the height and width of the intake ports.

more approvingly at Sportsman II heads, which are 50-state legal (as are all other World small-block heads).

Sportsman II—Sportsman II heads were revised in 1996 to incorporate raised valve cover rails and to accept either conventional or center-bolt valve covers. Either 64cc or 72cc combustion chambers may be specified and spark plug orientation may be straight or angled. Intake port volume has been increased to 200cc's and the exhaust face contains seven bolt holes so that either of the two standard exhaust manifold types may

be connected. All World Products heads are available as bare castings or complete assemblies. For dimensions, see the specification chart on page 58.

Air Flow Research

Air Flow Research (AFR) offers a selection of aluminum heads for the small block including three distinct race heads and two street heads, all featuring "cast billet" construction and a 3/4" thick deck surface (increased deck thickness improves long-term head gasket sealing). For race

applications, the three models have intake port volumes of 210cc's, 220 cc's and 227 cc's. All three heads are supplied with 68cc combustion chambers that can be modified to as little as 53cc's or as large as 76cc's. Heads with 220 and 227cc intake ports have spread exhaust ports while the 210cc intake port is matched up with a standard exhaust port.

AFR street heads feature 66cc "D"-shaped exhaust ports and are available with either straight or angled spark plug holes. The 190 casting is designed to accept standard intake manifolds while the 195 is intended for "tall port" manifolds like the Victor Jr. and Holley Strip Dominator. Beginning in 1991, all AFR street heads (which are 50-state legal) had a high swirl intake fin located near the valve guide to enhance turbulence for improved fuel economy and reduced exhaust emissions. In AFR's race head line up, the 210 and 220 accept standard rocker arms but the 227 has revised valve centerlines which make offset rocker arms (or shaft-mounted rockers) necessary. AFR heads are

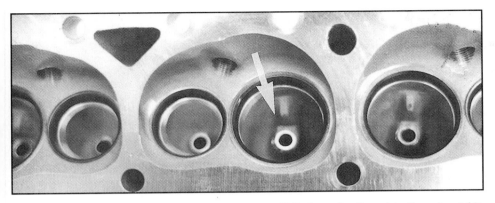

Some Airflow Research (AFR) heads incorporate a swirl fin (arrow) adjacent to the valve guide in the intake port. This fin is designed to enhance mixture homogenization for more efficient combustion.

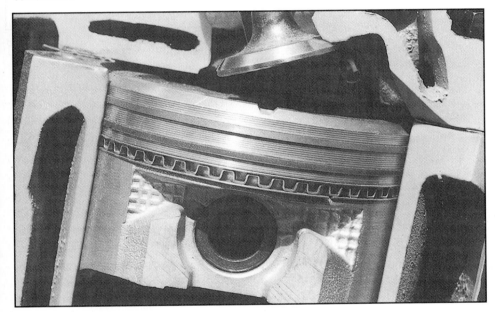

If the term "wedge head" confused you before, it shouldn't any more. Small-block Chevy heads have a textbook wedge-shaped combustion chamber, hence the name. Note the space between the top of the piston and the head surface (at the left side). At top dead center, this is known as deck clearance; for optimum performance, it should be as close to zero as possible.

Edelbrock

Edelbrock's Performer and Performer RPM aluminum cylinder heads are designed for street-type high performance applications while the Victor Jr. is the company's race head. The 50-state legal Performer head is available in "early" and "late" versions. The former has a available as bare castings or complete assemblies.

conventional valve cover bolt pattern, accepts equally conventional intake manifolds and contains 170cc intake ports and 70cc combustion chambers. The latter incorporates 165cc intake ports, 60cc combustion chambers, center bolt valve covers, and the revised intake manifold bolt pattern found on 1987 to 1995 cast iron heads. This casting is also available to fit 1987 to 1991 Corvette aluminum heads.

Other Edelbrock castings include the Performer LT1, designed for 1992 and later LT1 engines, and Performer RPM, for 1986 and earlier engines that are not emissions controlled. All Edelbrock heads are available as bare castings or complete assemblies. See the accompanying chart for specifications.

Holley

After countless years of manufacturing carburetors and intake manifolds, Holley entered the cylinder head business in 1996. Designed as part of its SysteMAX II engine package (which includes camshaft, lifters, intake manifold, timing chain set, heads and head bolts) SystemMAX aluminum heads are supplied as complete assemblies. They feature 185cc intake ports, 68cc exhaust ports, 68cc combustion chambers, 2.02" intake, 1.60" exhaust valves, screw-in studs with guideplates and dual valve springs. When used with the other components of the SysteMAX package, these heads will enable a 350 cid engine with 9.8:1 compression ratio to crank out approximately 425 horsepower.

Trick Flow Specialties

Trick Flow initially concentrated on heads for Ford small blocks. But with the popularity of the small-block Chevy, it wasn't long before the product line was expanded. TFS Twisted Wedge cylinder heads feature rotated or "twisted" valve angles which unshroud the intake valve for improved air flow characteristics. Twisted Wedge heads are supplied as complete assemblies with 2.02" intake, 1.60" exhaust valves, screw-in studs and guideplates. ■

DART & DART II CYLINDER HEADS

Casting	Max. Valve Size (intake/exhaust)	Combustion Chamber Vol.*	Intake Port Vol.
S/R Torquer	2.02/1.60	67/60/75cc	171cc
S/R Torquer	2.02/1.60	76/60/75cc	171cc
Sportsman	2.100/1.625	64/47/75cc	200cc
220	2.100/1.625	64/55/75cc	220cc
Raised 220	2.125/1.625	64/55/75cc	215cc
15-deg.	2.125/1.625	50/47/60cc	215cc
Buick Stage	II2.100/1.625	42/19/50cc	235cc

*as supplied/minimum/maximum

BRODIX CYLINDER HEADS

Casting	Max. Valve Size (intake/exhaust)	Combustion Chamber Vol.*	Intake Port Vol.
Street	2.020/1.600	69/52/76cc	168cc
8	2.100/1.600	69/52/76cc	194cc
10	2.100/1.600	69/52/76cc	210cc
Track I	2.080/1.600	69/52/76cc	215cc
11**	2.125/1.625	68/52/76cc	221cc
12SP S	2.150/1.600	64/40/65cc	230cc
12SP FF	2.150/1.600	64/40/65cc	250cc
12SP B	2.150/1.600	64/40/65cc	260cc

*as supplied/minumum/maximum
**With optional .040/.060-in. valve centerline, larger valves can be installed.

CHEVROLET CYLINDER HEAD CASTINGS

Casting No.	Material	Combustion Chamber Vol.	Intake Port VoL.	Valve Size (Max Stock)
034	CI, BT	64	184	2.02/1.60
040	AL, BT	45	240	N/A
041	CI, P	64	160	2.02/1.60
049	AL, BT	55	180	2.10/1.625
101	AL, BT	55	196	N/A
113	AL, Corv	58	163	1.94/1.50
186	CI, P	64	160	2.02/1.60
292	CI, BT	64	180	N/A
352	AL, BT	45	223	N/A
363	AL, BT	45	210	N/A
441	CI, P	76	155	1.94/1.50
441X	CI, P	80	155	1.94/1.60
461	CI, P	64	165	2.02/1.60
461X	CI, P	64	170	2.02/1.60
462	CI, P	64	160	2.02/1.60
492	CI, P	64	157	2.02/1.60
624	CI, P	76	160	2.02/1.60
867	AL, PM	62	196	2.10/1.625
896	CI, P	59	137	1.72/1.50
997/493	CI, P	76	160	1.94/1.50

CI- Cast Iron, AL- Aluminum, P- Production, BT- Bow Tie, Corv- Corvette, PM- Pontiac Motorsport

AIR FLOW RESEARCH CYLINDER HEADS

Casting	Intake Valve	Exhaust Valve	Combustion Chamber Vol.*	Intake Port Vol.
190	2.020/2.100	1.600/1.625	74/58/76cc	190cc
195	2.050/2.100	1.600/1.625	74/58/76cc	195cc
210	2.055/2.100	1.600/1.625	68/53/76cc	210cc
220	2.080/2.125	1.625/1.625	68/53/75cc	220cc
227	2.100/2.125	1.625/1.625	68/53/75cc	227cc

Indicates valve sizes as supplied and maximum valve size.
*as supplied/minimum/maximum.

CYLINDER HEAD MODIFICATIONS

5

Now that you've read more than you ever wanted to know about the types of small-block heads available, you can turn your attention to the proper modification and preparation of the heads for maximum performance.

PORTING

Modification of intake and exhaust ports has been done since the dawn of high performance engines. While much has been written on porting techniques and their effect on airflow capabilities, misinformation still abounds. This is largely because most people fall victim to BIBS—"Bigger Is Better Syndrome." Huge, gaping ports may be the answer for full-on race engines that operate in the 7500 rpm range. However, for street engines and race engines that operate in lower and middle rpm ranges, porting should be done with a little more discretion.

Mild Porting

Rather than indiscriminately grinding material, porting of heads for a street or mild race engine should consist of smoothing and blending. Particular attention should be given the valve bowl area because it's the most critical part of the port.

As supplied, most cylinder heads

Cylinder head modifications are the key to horsepower and with the right modifications, wonderful things happen. The 350 small block in this Camaro is equipped with modified Corvette aluminum heads and blasts through the quarter mile in 12.31 seconds in emissions legal trim.

(except for some aftermarket types) have rough edges where factory machining ends and as-cast surfaces begin. These junctions are primarily adjacent to the bowl area just beneath the valves. Typically, the factory uses a 70° cutter to machine the port throat and provide a transition from the cast surface to the valve seat. There is almost always a sharp edge down in the port left by the cutter. Some sharp edges may also be evident adjacent to the valve seat. Porting of street heads concentrates in this bowl or pocket area. Blending for a smooth transition from machined to the raw cast surface is the first priority. Some porters also slightly enlarge the bowl area, primarily by blending the bowl into

the port wall and narrowing the portion of the valve guide that protrudes into the port.

In instances where class rules prohibit porting, additional flow capacity can be achieved by either machining deeper (than the factory did) with a 70° cutter, or by machining the throat with a 75° cutter. Larger angle cutters, such as 80°, should be avoided because they can actually hurt flow. Tech inspectors rarely, if ever, measure the angle or depth of the cut below the valve seat. Rather, they look for evidence that a die grinder has paid a visit to the ports.

Chemical Milling—Chemical milling is another technique used to remove material from port walls that are supposed to be unmodified. As the acid eats away the metal, the original as-cast surface contour is maintained, so without measuring port volume, it's virtually impossible to detect the modifications. Glass beading a set of heads further obscures evidence of modification, however, some sanctioning bodies prohibit glass beading or similar procedures.

Short-Turn Radius—Another section of the port that is deserving of special attention is the short-turn radius—the section area that transitions from the valve seat to the port floor. Opinions vary as to what constitutes the ideal short-turn radius, but in an intake port, what's desirable is at least a .090" straight, vertical drop between the bottom cut below the valve seat and the curve that leads to the port floor. Many times this profile is difficult to achieve unless oversized valves are installed. In fact, it's not at all unusual for 2.055" intake valves to be installed in place of standard 2.02" valves for no other reason than to improve the contour of the short-turn radius. Installing 2.02" valves in heads originally machined for 1.94" valves has the same effect. Contrary to popular belief, the exhaust ports also need to have their short-turn radii carefully massaged, so don't overlook them.

Gasket Matching—Additionally, it is beneficial to gasket-match the openings of both intake and exhaust ports. Fel-Pro offers a wide variety of gaskets for both the intake and exhaust ports that can be used as a template so you can open the intake ports and manifold runner openings to the same dimensions. For more specifics, contact your local Fel-Pro dealer.

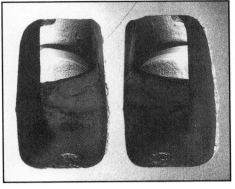

Bigger isn't always better. When modifying cast-iron heads for maximum horsepower, some porters add material to the intake port floor. This allows for an improved short-turn radius and improved airflow. A unique cast-iron welding capability is required to make these modifications Similar work can be done more easily on aluminum heads using heliarc welding.

Port Size—Having the intake port opening slightly larger than the manifold runner opening won't hurt and may help control reversion if a long duration camshaft is used. However, having a port mouth that is smaller than the runner will impose a serious performance handicap as the incoming air/fuel mixture will be disrupted as it strikes the sharp ledge created by the undersized port opening.

Whether modified for street or race, intake ports are typically matched to the intake manifold runners. An intake manifold gasket serves conveniently as a template. If the entire port isn't modified, the revised opening is usually blended about an inch into the port.

On the exhaust side, the opposite is true. If the port mouth is larger than the header tube, the exhaust gasses will strike a sharp ledge as they exit. On the other hand, if the header tube is larger than the exhaust port opening, no serious ill effects will result and the resulting ledge may serve to control reversion.

Race Heads
Porting of race heads is

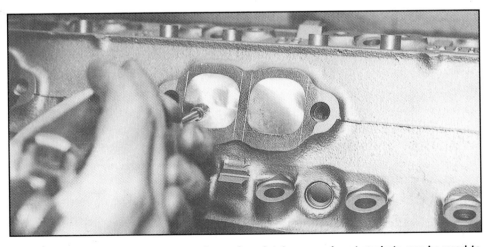

Exhaust ports require the same type of rework as intakes so exhaust gaskets can be used to establish the outlet contour that will best match the headers to be installed. Many times it isn't practical to rework the port to the precise contour of the header opening. This doesn't cause a performance penalty as long as the port opening is smaller than the header tube that mates to it.

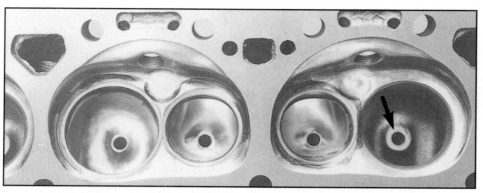

When a head is fully ported, the boss around the valve guide is usually narrowed. Both the intake and exhaust guides in the port on the left have been modified. Only the exhaust valve guide has been reworked in the chamber at the right. A stock intake guide is shown on the far right.

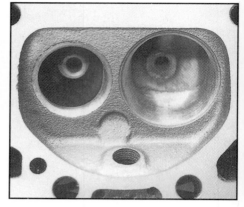

Pocket porting" involves smoothing and blending the area below the valve seat (arrow). Particular attention is given the short-turn radius.

considerably more involved than the procedure for street heads. However, the proper way to port race heads isn't something that can be learned by reading a book—no matter how good the writer. Cylinder head specialists spend countless hours testing on the flow bench and engine dyno and have developed highly specialized port configurations, many of which they keep secret. If you're convinced that you want to do your own competition-style porting, proceed cautiously. It's a lot easier to remove metal than to put it back. The problem with getting carried away with a grinder is that ports that are too large for an engine's requirements do not support good port velocities. Slow-moving intake charges don't fill the cylinder very well and aren't conducive to the development of maximum horsepower. An exhaust port that's too large doesn't hurt quite as much because the exhaust gasses move at high velocities as a result of the heat and pressure that accompany them. However, oversized exhaust ports are difficult to achieve because in a small-block head, they rarely match the flow capacity of intake ports. If you can't create a port configuration that's optimized for a particular application, you're better off with a port that's too small than one that's too large.

If you're a novice at porting heads and absolutely feel you want to tackle this job yourself, start by reworking the bowl area and gasket-matching the port mouths. Narrow the OD of the valve guide as much as possible and then concentrate on straightening the port walls. In both intake and exhaust ports, the walls should be as straight as possible from the bowl to the mouth. The biggest obstructions to a straight-line path are humps around the pushrod and head bolt holes. The size of these humps can be reduced, but they can't be completely removed. Care must also be taken to avoid grinding through into the water jackets.

CNC Porting

Within the past few years, CNC porting has been used more frequently in place of conventional hand-porting.

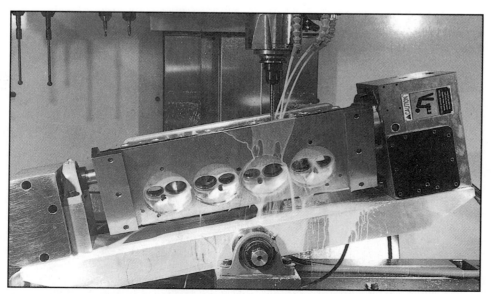

The latest development in cylinder head modification is computerized numerical control (CNC) machining. The beauty of CNC-modification is that once the program is developed, every port is machined identically. Once reserved exclusively for maximum effort race heads, CNC porting is now available for virtually any type of small block cylinder head.

Due to the orientation of the cutter to the surface it's machining, CNC-machining is characterized by a unique ridged surface. Many engine builders feel this is an advantage as it minimizes "wet out," a condition where fuel falls out of suspenion. While acnc-modified port may marginally less than one that's been hand ported and polished, it will typically make more horsepower.

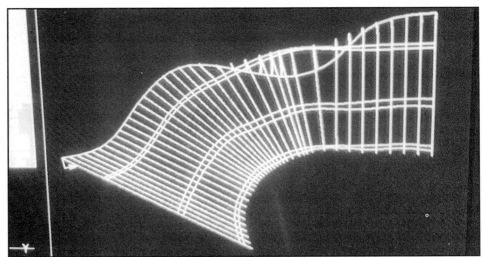

Without computer-aided design, (CAD) CNC porting wouldn't have progressed so rapidly. Port designs translated into computer-generated images are translated into tool positions that are used to perform the actual modifications.

techniques. The beauty of CNC (Computerized Numerical Control) modification is that every port in every head is virtually identical. The inconsistencies of hand porting are completely eliminated.

However, a CNC ported head is only as good as the person doing the original port modification and the programmer who translates that port into a program that can reproduce it. There's no magic to CNC porting, other than the incredible consistency of the port and combustion chamber modifications.

When CNC porting was first introduced, it was a relatively expensive proposition and therefore limited to professional race teams. However as technology progressed, costs dropped and use of CNC-ported heads has become more widespread. According to Pete Incaudo of CNC

Cylinder Heads, Pinellas Park, FL, "We introduced CNC-ported LT1 and L98 heads for street applications and they've been very successful. For about the same cost as a pair of hand-ported heads, you can have modifications made with Winston Cup technology. That's leading edge stuff. And it gets pretty good results. With standard street-type

modifications, a late-model Camaro or Corvette with our CNC ported aluminum Corvette heads will easily run 12.50s in the quarter-mile and still be emissions-legal."

Combustion Chamber

Just as porting and a good valve job are essential for top performance, so is a properly shaped and sized

Airflow testing involves measuring airflow through a port at various valve openings. Special fixtures are often used to improve repeatability. Another common practice is to add a radius at the port inlet to minimize turbulence.

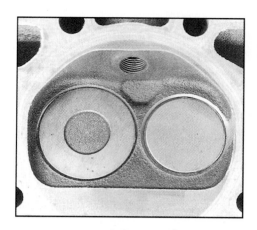

Beginning in 1971, large chamber (73-76cc) heads became the norm as exhaust emissions requirements became more stringent. In spite of the bad rap given to "Smog" heads, many of them offer excellent performance potential. The large chamber unshrouds the valves which improves airflow characteristics.

combustion chamber. To assure that compression ratio is consistent from one cylinder to another, combustion chamber volume must be checked and equalized. Since adding material to a chamber is neither easy nor desirable, the most common approach taken to equalizing volume is to find the largest chamber in a head, and then grind all the other chambers to match. If the final desired volume is less than that of the largest chamber, the head can be milled after all individual chamber work is completed. As an example, if the smallest chamber in a head measures 64cc's, and the largest is 68cc's, the chamber wall around the intake valve can be ground back which will unshroud the valve. That operation and some blending and polishing should easily add 4cc's of volume. Once this has been done, the head can be milled as required to bring all chambers to 64cc's.

Sinking Valves—Some people advocate sinking the valves to enlarge chamber volume. This should never be done. Although it may bring you

the chamber volume you want, it will disturb airflow. Sinking the valves was once a common technique applied to race engines built for classes with rules prohibiting grinding or polishing in the combustion chamber. Those types of rules are pretty much a thing of the past, and where they still exist, most racers have developed "new interpretations" (sometimes called cheating) that allow chamber volume to be increased without sinking the valves.

CC'ing—CC'ing the chambers is a measuring operation that requires nothing more than a clear plastic plate to seal the chamber, a burette to hold the fluid used for the measurements and some means of holding the cylinder head level from end-to-end and at a slight angle side-to-side. Once the head is properly anchored, place the plastic plate (which must have a small hole in it to admit fluid) over the chamber. The plate should be positioned so that the hole is at the highest point over the chamber. Your measurement won't be accurate if any of the fluid leaks out, so keep an eye on the seal between the plate and the head, and around the valves and spark plug. Use grease to effect a liquid-tight seal between the plate and the head. If the valve job hasn't been completed, you may also have to smear grease around the valve seat to seal the valves. Obviously, you'll also need to install a spark plug to prevent leakage through the plug hole.

Once everything is in place, position the burette over the hole in the plastic plate and open the petcock so the fluid flows slowly into the combustion chamber. Be careful not to overfill the chamber and make sure no air bubbles are trapped beneath the plastic plate. Once you measure and

record the volume of one chamber, repeat the process on the next one and continue until all four have been completed. Then set up the other head and measure all of its chambers.

CYLINDER HEAD MACHINING

Three-Angle Valve Job

A good multi-angle valve job (three angles are most commonly used) includes a bottom cut ranging from 50° to 70° depending upon the casting. A 70° cutter is typically used on stock-type heads to smooth the area below the valve. In a stock port, the 70° cut meets the 45° cut of the valve seat. But when a 3-angle valve job is done, a 60° cut is added to smooth the transition from the valve seat and narrow the valve seat. The

If you want to cc your own heads, you'll need a burette like this model from Powerhouse Products. To properly check combustion chamber volume, a clear plastic plate is sealed to the head surface with grease. Then fluid from a burette is allowed to flow in and fill up the available space. Of course, the valves and spark plug must be in position and leak-free

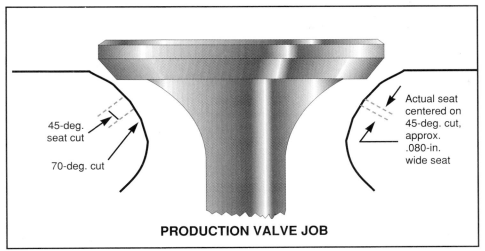

PRODUCTION VALVE JOB

45-deg. seat cut

70-deg. cut

Actual seat centered on 45-deg. cut, approx. .080-in. wide seat

A production-type valve job has a single cut on the valve and on the seat. The resulting sharp edges aren't the hot lick for maximum airflow, which is the reason that high performance engines are typically treated to a multi-angle valve job.

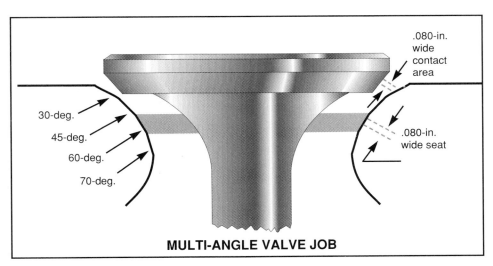

MULTI-ANGLE VALVE JOB

30-deg.
45-deg.
60-deg.
70-deg.

.080-in. wide contact area

.080-in. wide seat

The infamous three-angle valve job exposed. The valve itself has a 45° face which contacts the actual valve seat which is also cut at 45°. The contact area on the valve should be centered on the 45° face. Below the 45° seat face is a 60° cut and then a 70° cut. On the top side, a 30° cut blends the seat into the combustion chamber. Depending on how you look at it, a three-angle valve job may actually involve four different angles (30°, 45°, 60° and 70°).

This is a text book example of a three-angle valve job. Even on stock, unmodified ports, a valve job like this can add 10 horsepower.

seat itself is cut with a 45° cutter and a 30° cutter machines the transition from the top of the valve seat to the combustion chamber surface. The accuracy of the valve job exerts a significant influence over performance because it affects the quality of the seal between the valve face and seat, and airflow. Compared to an inexpensive stock valve job, a high performance 3-angle valve job

can be worth a solid 10-15 horsepower. If you consider the 30° cut on the combustion chamber side of the valve, a 3-angle valve job is actually a 4-angle valve job.

Although some engine builders vary intake valve seat width according to application, Chad Hedgecock, the cylinder head specialist at Eagle Racing Engines, relies on a .060" wide intake valve seat for both street

and race engines. However, he prefers exhaust seats .080" wide for street applications but holds them to .060" for racing. Hedgecock's reasoning for this is that the narrower seat provides a slight flow improvement and the heads on a race engine are removed for service frequently enough that the seats will be recut before they get beat up too badly. With a street engine, the slightly wider seat is required for longevity.

While these dimensions have been used successfully in thousands of high performance and race engines, they are by no means written in stone. Hedgecock feels it's important to note that some cylinder head specialists may have other ideas or have developed other combinations that they prefer. If you're paying someone to do a valve job, don't try to tell him or her how to do it. If you feel you have to, find another shop.

Garry Grimes of Grimes Automotive Machine, also notes that in many cases the trade-off with a valve job is between flow and heat dissipation. He states:

"A wider seat provides more area for the valve to transfer heat into the

head. That's why you can't use the same valve seat dimensions on heads built for the street or oval track that you can on drag race heads. Every engine builder has his own technique, but there are still certain things that are either right or wrong for a particular application. You can get by with narrow seats that are out near the edge of the seat surface in a drag engine because it's going to come apart before any damage is done. But on street, oval track or bracket engines, where you're trying to get long-term durability, you have to give up a little flow to get reasonable valve life. And regardless of the application, the valves should be lapped. We can cut the prettiest-looking seats, with every angle just what it's supposed to be, and there's still no assurance that you'll get the best possible seal. When you lap the valves, you know for sure."

Valve Seats

Another aspect of the valve job to be leery of is the positioning of the valve head with respect to the combustion chamber roof. This is especially true with used heads. Each time a valve job is done, some material is removed from the valve seat. If a head has been the victim of numerous valve jobs, or was used for on-the-job training, the seating surface may have been ground so much that the valves are sunk. As previously noted, sinking the valves should be avoided because it hurts airflow and consequently power output. Sinking the valves shortens the distance between the seat and the short-turn radius which is exactly opposite of the desired condition.

Raising the Seats—If a pair of heads has a lot of redeeming features,

but has seats that have been sunk like the Titanic, either new valve seats should be installed or larger diameter valves substituted for the original ones. One of the reasons that small valve (1.94/1.50") 492 and similar castings respond so well when 2.02/1.60" valves are installed, is because the valve seats are raised, which increases the distance from the seat to the short-turn radius. Remember, larger valves improve airflow two ways—with increased diameter and better seat positioning.

Replacing Seats—Ever since leaded fuel all but vanished from the pumps, valve seat life has been a big question. Numerous tests have shown that without lead to provide a cushion between the valves and their seats, rapid seat erosion results. Consequently, all factory-installed small-block heads manufactured after 1971 have induction-hardened exhaust seats. While they're certainly advantageous, they're not always necessary. Valve seat erosion is typically only a problem when an engine is run continuously under a heavy load. While valve seat wear is unquestionably greater with unleaded fuels, it won't be severe enough to cause problems under normal operating conditions. If you're uncomfortable with unleaded fuel, add a lead or lead substitute additive—it's a lot cheaper than having hardened seats installed. You'll also find that it's usually cheaper to buy a new head than to have hardened seats installed.

Installation of hardened seats (made of stellite material) is justified if a pair of heads is particularly valuable or impossible to replace (such as an out-of-production casting). In such an instance, only the exhaust seats need

Guideplates and screw-in studs are standard fare on aftermarket cylinder heads such as these Brodix castings, but are not found on many stock heads. Stepped guideplates and 7/16-" studs comprise the preferred combination.

to be replaced. However, this isn't a job for a shade-tree mechanic; extremely accurate equipment run by an experienced machinist is required for proper installation.

Screw-In Rocker Studs

On many Chevrolet head castings, the rocker studs are pressed into place. That's fine for engines in luxocruisers, but pressed-in studs

Before screw-in studs and guideplates can be installed on heads not originally so equipped, the stud bosses must be milled down and the stud bosses tapped.

have no place in a high performance engine. Rather than pulling a tap out of your tool box, you should take the heads to a competent machine shop. It's almost impossible to keep a hand tap perfectly vertical while wrestling with a head on your work bench. If the tap isn't perfectly aligned, the studs will screw in on an angle which will place a side load on the rocker pivots or bearings and on the valve and valve guide. None of those conditions are particularly conducive to a long and happy engine life.

In addition to tapping the stud holes, you'll also have to mill the top of the bosses so that the hex on the stud clears the bottom of the rocker. Unless you've got the necessary equipment, this is strictly a job for a machine shop.

Spring Seats

If you're planning to use a camshaft that will rattle the fenders and the nerves of mothers, fathers and pillars of society, it will be necessary to machine the spring seats to accept larger diameter valve springs. Stock production heads are machined to accept valve springs measuring 1.250" in outside diameter. The stoutest spring with this dimension will yield only about 120 lbs. of seat pressure and less than 300 lbs. of open pressure. That won't be sufficient to control the lifters on aggressive camshafts. The 1.250" diameter spring seats also preclude use of dual valve springs which typically have a 1.460" or larger outside diameter. Consequently, for high performance and race applications, it's advisable to have the spring seats machined to accept larger-than-stock diameter valve springs.

Also note that some valve springs won't precisely match categorical outside diameter dimensions. As an example, manufacturer specifications for 1.460" OD springs can range from 1.437" to 1.465". Valve springs for small-block Chevy heads fall into one of three general OD size ranges— 1.250, 1.460 and 1.550"—and the same dimensional variations apply to all diameters. Larger-than-stock diameters are needed to achieve the higher pressures required by high performance hydraulic, mechanical and roller camshafts. For specific valve spring pressure and installation information, see Chapter 7.

Valve Seal Machining

Machining for special valve seals is another routine operation when a head is prepared for use on a high performance engine. Most high performance valve seals clamp on the outside diameter of the valve guide. In a stock-type cylinder head, valve sealing is accomplished through one of, or a combination of, the following: an O-ring that fits over the valve stem, an oil splash shield that fits between the retainer and spring and an umbrella seal that simply slides over the outside of the valve guide. High performance seals clamp on both the OD of the valve guide and the valve stem. These seals are considerably thicker than stock umbrella seals and consequently won't clear the inner spring of a dual valve-spring assembly. It is therefore necessary to machine the OD of the valve guide to .530" or .500" to accept most high performance seals. Appropriate machining tools and arbors are available from major high performance camshaft manufacturers. Some companies offer combination tools which machine the valve guide

OD and spring seat in one operation. Most high performance cylinder head specialists prefer rubber seals with teflon inserts and specifically do not recommend all-teflon valve seals. Irrespective of the type of seal used, retainer-to-seal clearance (or retainer-to-guide clearance if stock type seals are used) should be at least .100" at maximum valve lift. This amount of clearance is impossible to achieve with some stock late-model heads when a high performance cam is installed. In such instances, the heads must be removed from the engine and machined as required.

Valve Guides

Of course, it doesn't make much sense to install high performance valve seals and ignore the valve guides. Stock valve guides in cast-iron heads are an integral part of the head casting. In aluminum heads, the guides are essentially thick-wall silicon bronze tubes that are pressed

Installation of replacement cast-iron valve guides begins by drilling out the original guide. Next the drilled hole is reamed so the replacement guide can be installed with the proper press fit. An impact wrench is used to drive the replacement guide into place. As a final step, the replacement guide's inside diameter should be honed, not reamed, to size. Honing is the preferred method of machining the ID because it does not fracture the material—unlike reaming.

Solid bronze valve guides are found in aluminum cylinder heads and some cast-iron heads destined for high performance applications. Bronze is also advantageous in marine applications because it won't rust.

into place.

Clearances—Clearance between the valve guide and valve stem is critical to both oil control and durability. Several valve guide preparation options are available. New heads shouldn't require extensive valve guide work, but guide-to-stem clearance should always be checked. Cast-iron heads being groomed for a high performance or race engine are frequently treated to a set of bronze guide liners. Cast-iron liners are also used on occasion. Both types are installed by drilling the stock guide oversized and then pressing the liner of choice into place. Once in position, the liners should be honed, not reamed, for a more consistent finish. Reaming tends to fracture and distort the material and does not provide a consistent finish. With honing, clearances and concentricity are much more accurately controlled.

Knurling—Stock cast-iron valve guides can also be knurled if valve guide ID is too large, but this is a

stock rebuild rather than a high performance technique. It should be avoided because knurling fractures the guide material which isn't exactly the hot tip for longevity. Knurling essentially cuts a thread on the ID of the guide. Although the deep part of the "thread" is larger than the original ID, the material displaced by the cut "humps" up into a ridge which has a smaller ID. After knurling, the guide must be honed to a finished dimension.

Replacement Liners

Rather than knurling worn guides, replacement liners should be installed. For performance applications, bronze rather than iron liners are preferred—especially with stainless steel valves. Bronze is more compatible with stainless steel than cast iron. For marine engines or powerplants that run only occasionally, bronze liners also eliminate the possibility of rust and corrosion seizing the valve in the guide.

Bronze Liners—Several methods of bronze liner installation are

available. Solid liners are pressed into place, then either knurled or broached to lock them against the original cast-iron guide. With knurling, the knurled "thread" offers a small reservoir of oil to keep the stem lubricated. On the other hand, knurling bronze fractures the material just as it does with iron, which is a detriment to longevity and makes the ID less consistent. However, acceptable results can be achieved if the liners are honed to size after knurling.

Many engine builders prefer to use a ball broach to lock solid bronze guide liners into place. A guide insert that is locked tightly in place offers superior heat dissipation. A ball broach locks the liner against the guide without fracturing the surface material and cuts the guide to the required ID at the same time. For the best possible finish and consistency, an undersized broach can be used and the liners honed to final size.

Bronze liners are more expensive than iron but offer the option of running much tighter clearances and almost eliminate the possibility of the

The latest advance in cylinder head machining is the valve/guide/seat machine which uses a cutter, rather than stone, to machine a valve seat. The cutter can have virtually any shape desired so it's possible to do a three-angle valve job in a single pass. These machines also offer excellent repetition so machining time is reduced.

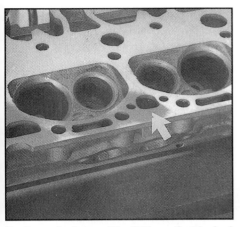

To the naked eye, this 882 casting looked perfectly flat. However, after making a light skim cut, it's obvious that some low spots existed (arrows). Most heads must be milled only a few thousandths of an inch to eliminate the effects of warpage.

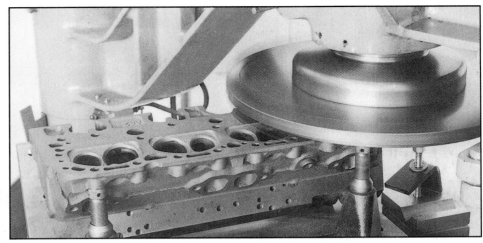

Used or "seasoned" cylinder heads should always be milled before being reused. An absolutely flat surface is essential for optimal head gasket seal.

valve stem sticking in the guide. Typically, intake stem-to-guide clearances with bronze guides (and 11/32" valve stems) can be as tight as .0008" for drag race applications. Generally though, stem-to-guide clearance is .001" for intake and .0015" for exhaust valves. Engines pulling a high amount of manifold vacuum may frequently require tighter than stock clearances to avoid pulling oil through the guide.

Cast-Iron Liners—Cast-iron liners are occasionally recommended for street engines because they're claimed to offer longer life. Iron liners require less effort to install because they generally require no ID machining once they're pressed into place. After an iron liner is cut to length, it need only be relieved at top and bottom (where it's been cut) to ensure that these areas aren't undersized as a result of the cutting operation. However, the quality of cast-iron guides varies tremendously, and if you get the cheap kind, they're only liable to last for 20-30,000 miles. For all high performance engines, it's

money well spent to go with premium guides.

Winona Guides—Rather than solid bronze liners, some engine builders prefer Winona-type threaded inserts. With this method, the guide is threaded with a coarse tap or roller and a strand of thin bronze wire is threaded and wedged into place. The ID of the guide is then honed to the desired diameter. In addition to providing a bronze surface for the valve stem, Winona-style inserts allow a small reservoir of oil to be maintained between the bronze threads, providing a bit of lubrication insurance and a path for heat transfer.

Guide Height—Although the size and condition of the valve guide ID is of vital importance, it isn't the only part of the guide that demands attention. You also have to consider valve guide height, especially if you've installed a high performance cam. Specifically, if the valve guide is too tall, it may cause the keeper or retainer to crash against the seal if maximum valve lift exceeds .470" This has been a problem with many late-model 305 and 350 engines;

consequently, many cam grinders limit valve lift to .460" on camshafts designed for stock-type "emissions" engines. See Chapter 7 for specific details on clearances

Head Milling

Like any other piece of equipment, cylinder heads are subject to warping as a result of repeated heating and cooling cycles. The thick deck surfaces of older original equipment castings and many aftermarket heads minimize or eliminate warpage, except under extreme operating conditions. However, it is advisable to check the flatness of any used cylinder head.

Warped head surfaces are milled a minimal amount to return them to their original perfectly flat condition. Milling is also occasionally done as a means of improving head gasket sealing; the comparatively rough surface left by the cutter grips the head gasket better than a smooth surface.

Head milling also serves as a means of reducing combustion chamber volume. Many aftermarket heads have

The intake manifold mating surface may also require a light cut to achieve absolute flatness. This step is often overlooked with poor manifold gasket seal being the result.

CYLINDER HEAD/INTAKE MANIFOLD MATERIAL REMOVAL GUIDE

IF HEAD IS MILLED:	MILL MANIFOLD SIDES/END RAILS:
.005	.006/.009
.010	.012/.018
.015	.018/.027
.020	.024/.035
.025	.032/.044
.030	.038/.053
.035	.044/.062

Figures in thousandths of an inch. Use as a reference, not absolute dimensions. Other variables such as block deck machining, previous cylinder head or intake manifold machining and heads and manifolds not manufactured to original specs must be considered.

Manifold Milling—Milling the deck surface alters geometry at the head/intake manifold interface, necessitating removal of material from the manifold mating surface. As a general guideline, whenever a head is milled, the same amount of material should be cut from the intake manifold side to re-establish original gasket space and port alignment. Thus if .010" are cut from the deck, .010" should also be cut from the intake port face. It is usually necessary to alter the bottom of the intake manifold as well. When a head is milled, the intake manifold mating surface moves closer to the block. That reduces the clearance between the bottom of the intake manifold and top of the block along the front and rear rails. In fact, if a head is milled excessively, the front and rear rails may keep the manifold so high that the intake gaskets won't be thick enough to seal.

Gasket thickness compatibility problems can be avoided by cutting approximately 50% more from the bottom of the manifold than has been cut from the head. Thus if a head is milled .010", the bottom of the intake manifold should be cut .015". In many cases, it's best to trial-fit the intake manifold before making any cuts. If a block has been decked, its manifold rails may have also been machined and machining the manifold rails may lead to severe gaps. Heads that have been angle milled additionally require machining of the intake face at a complimentary angle to make sure the two surfaces are parallel.

The easiest way to seal the manifold/block end rail interface is to follow the procedure used by most race engine builders who do not use manifold end rail gaskets—they opt for silicone sealer (RTV which stands

extra thick deck surfaces because the manufacturers have anticipated extensive milling (to reduce combustion chamber volume) prior to installation. As an example, Brodix -8 heads are supplied with 68cc chambers which can be reduced to 56cc's if required. Each .001" cut from the surface reduces combustion chamber volume a given amount which is determined by chamber

shape. Obviously, only so much material can be removed before the mill will be cutting into the valve seats.

Angle Milling—One means of getting around this is angle milling. By tilting the head so that more material is removed from the spark plug side of the head, the chamber volume can be reduced significantly more than from standard milling.

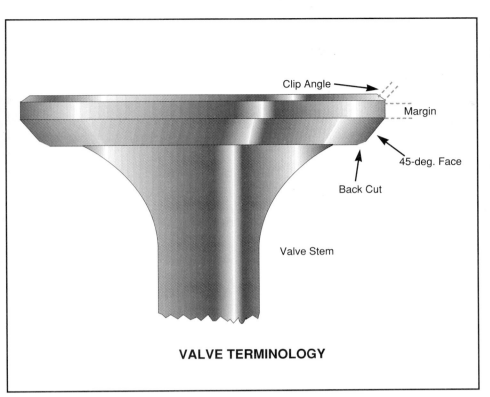

Clip Angle

Margin

45-deg. Face

Back Cut

Valve Stem

VALVE TERMINOLOGY

Most engine builders advise grinding valves before they're installed. Due to generous production line tolerances, many brand new valves are imperfect in both finish and concentricity. Both valves and seats should be ground to precise dimensions for high performance use.

Valves vary considerably depending upon supplier and application. Some valves are supplied with a back cut and a clip angle or top cut may not be included. Generally, a margin of .050" to .080" is desirable. Except in unusual circumstances, if a valve has a margin of less than .030", it should be discarded.

for Room Temperature Vulcanizing) instead. Standard end rail gaskets may keep the intake manifold from seating firmly against the heads, especially if block-to-manifold end rail clearance isn't sufficient. Silicone is much more conformable and will seal any reasonably sized gap without interfering with manifold/head seal.

VALVES

Think you know small blocks, do you? Then you should have no trouble with this question. What size valve stems are found in all stock small-block heads? If you said, "11/32, everyone knows that," you win—the booby prize. It's a little known fact that valves with 3/8" stems are found in some small-block truck engines.

Aftermarket Valves

Although Chevrolet offers several swirl-polished valves, aftermarket suppliers such as Sealed Power/Speed-Pro, TRW, Ferrea and Manley offer equivalent or superior valves that can usually be purchased at lower cost. Aftermarket valves are used by virtually all high performance and racing cylinder head specialists because of their lower price and wider selection.

Racing Engine Valves (REV) of Fort Lauderdale, FL, Ferrea Racing Components of Fort Lauderdale, FL and Manley Performance Products of Lakewood, NJ offer a very wide selection of high performance and racing valves for small blocks. It would take several pages to list all the small-block valves available from

both companies, so be sure to leaf through their respective catalogs before making a selection. In addition to standard sizes, Manley and Ferrea also offer valves that are longer-than-stock and both companies market valves with undercut stems for increased flow and valves with 5/16" stems.

Note that nearly all factory replacement type valves have a .001" taper from one end of the valve stem to the other. The taper doesn't mean the valves are poorly machined; the stem diameters are smaller near the head to accommodate heat induced expansion which would otherwise cause galling.

As noted, the standard small block valve has an 11/32" (.3415") diameter stem which couples up with a 4.950" nominal overall length. Reducing stem diameter to 5/16" (.3085") may not seem like much of a change, but it's enough to knock off a few grams of weight and also bring about a measurable increase in airflow—

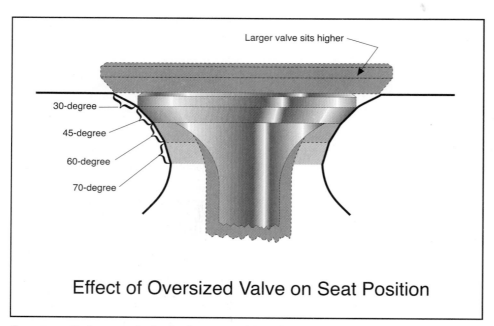

Effect of Oversized Valve on Seat Position

One reason that an oversized valve increases airflow (in addition to its larger diameter) is that it "unsinks" the seating position–with the valve sitting higher (in the combustion chamber) the distance from the seat to the short-turn radius is increased, and that improves flow.

The difference between a swirl-polished (left) and stock valve (right) is evident here. The polished valve has less of a lip and smoother head/stem transition area which contributes to increased airflow.

especially at lower valve lifts. Several companies, including Speed-Pro and Manley, offer valves with 5/16" stems; but before they can be installed in a set of heads, the valve guides have to be modified so the stems don't rattle around. That obviously adds quite a bit of expense to cylinder head preparation and that's difficult to justify in many cases. However, there is a way to take advantage of increased airflow potential without breaking the bank.

Undercut Valves—A number of years ago, Manley introduced a series of high performance stainless steel valves with the stem undercut adjacent to the valve head. That portion of the stem that fits into the valve guide has an 11/32" diameter, but the portion of the stem that extends into the port measures only 5/16". If your valves need to be replaced, or if you're assembling a new set of heads and have to purchase valves, installing Manley Pro Flo or

Race Flow (both are undercut, but each series is made from different material) will bring you some extra horsepower at no extra cost—Race-Flo and Race Master one-piece stainless steel valves are priced the same.

Titanium Valves—Titanium is the material of choice for valves used in "damn the expense, let the sponsor pay for it" classes of drag, oval track and road racing. Owing to their light weight and high strength, titanium valves allow for more radical cam profiles and higher power potential. However, at seven to eight times the cost of a top quality stainless steel valve, the expense can't be justified in anything less than a professional class of competition.

HEAD GASKETS

It wasn't too many years ago that head gaskets were viewed as safety valves; they would burn or blow out

before abnormally high pressures could cause any internal damage. But like every other component found in a small-block Chevy, head gaskets have enjoyed the benefits of technology. Current gaskets are so good, that the pistons or valves may well be damaged before the head gaskets let go.

Composition Gaskets

One of the reasons that head gasket sealing has improved so dramatically over the years is the improvement made in composition gaskets. The stock steel-shim head gasket, with raised beads around the cylinders and water holes, is adequate for a stock engine, but it is marginal in many performance applications. Chevrolet lists three steel shim head gaskets: part number 10105117 has a compressed thickness of .014"; part number 3830711 has a compressed thickness of .022"; and part no. 6269477 is a stainless steel gasket with a compressed thickness of .014" These gaskets are designed for use on 4" bore blocks with cast-iron heads.

A composition gasket which is suitable for racing is also available through Chevrolet and GM

Performance Parts dealers. Listed as part number 14011041, this gasket, like all high performance/racing composition gaskets has a solid wire O-ring, encapsulated in a stainless steel armor, around each cylinder. This gasket has a compressed thickness of approximately .040" and can be used on blocks with 4.125" diameter bores if steam holes are drilled. Another composition gasket is listed as part number 14088948 and is intended for engines with Corvette aluminum cylinder heads. Its stainless steel fire rings are said to stop galvanic action between the aluminum heads and cast-iron block, but it's primary appeal is for lowering compression ratios that have gotten out of hand (or have been miscalculated). This gasket has a compressed thickness of .051"

When selecting head gaskets, match them to the bore size of your engine. All blocks with cylinders smaller than 4.060" are usually handled by the same gasket. As an example, Fel-Pro, which offers a wide variety of race-quality composition head gaskets, offers part number 1003 for 350 cid and smaller engines. This gasket has a 4.166" bore and a compressed thickness of .038" Although part number 1003 will obviously fit a block with a 4.125" bore, it should not be used in this application; the sealing armor will be too close to the cylinder wall and will have a tendency to overheat and burn through.

By comparison, Fel-Pro's part number 1004, which is designed for 4.125" cylinders has a 4.190" gasket bore. Also available is part number 1034 which has a 4.200" gasket bore and is suitable for use with aluminum heads. According to Jerry Rosenquist, Performance Products Engineer at Fel-Pro:

"Part number 1034 has a new combustion seal design and it's the strongest Fel-Pro has ever offered. It has a pre-flattened steel wire O-ring around each cylinder opening so it will not brinnell (leave indentations) aluminum heads. We also offer part number 1010 for 4" bore blocks with aluminum heads. It has a copper, rather than steel, wire ring and a compressed thickness of .037"." Fel-Pro Gasket specifications are listed on p. 198.

Gasket Thickness

Head gasket thickness is often overlooked, but it is an important part of any engine build. Keep in mind that a minimum of .035" piston-to-head clearance should be maintained if an engine is equipped with steel connecting rods. This dimension should be increased if aluminum rods are used. Since a "zero deck" condition (that is, no deck clearance—the top of the piston deck flush with the top of the block when the piston is at Top Dead Center) is desired for maximum power and reduced octane sensitivity, a gasket of appropriate thickness must be installed. Some amount of deck clearance must obviously be built into engines equipped with steel shim head gaskets. On the other hand, maximum power can't be achieved if a deck clearance of.020-.030" or more is combined with a thick composition head gasket.

LT1 Gaskets—LT1 engines require entirely different head gaskets than conventional small blocks. The GM replacement gaskets for Corvette and Camaro engines, which have aluminum heads, is part number

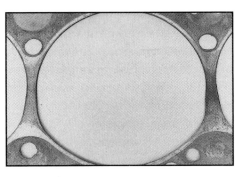

Head gaskets can be an invaluable source of information about internal engine conditions. Note that the area between the cylinders on the right is darker and wider than the one on the left. That's because it was situated between two center cylinders where the exhaust valves are side-by-side. The heat generated by this valve placement leads to higher gasket temperatures and more gasket relaxing. This is the most likely place for leakage to begin.

10168457. But the iron-headed engines found in the Impala SS and Caprice utilize a slightly different gasket which is listed as part number 12553160. The advantage of this gasket is that it has a compressed thickness of .030", which is about .020" thinner than the stock gasket. Using the "160" gasket is a quick, easy and economical way to simulate the effect of a "zero deck." The thinner gasket not only raises compression ratio slightly, it reduces the volume of air and fuel left in the quench area and that translates to lower emissions, more power and reduced octane sensitivity.

Clamp Load

While temperature certainly plays a role in gasket life, the most influential factor is the clamp load exerted by the head bolts or studs. According to the engineers at Fel-Pro, the key to sufficient clamp load is to have adequately stretched bolts or studs.

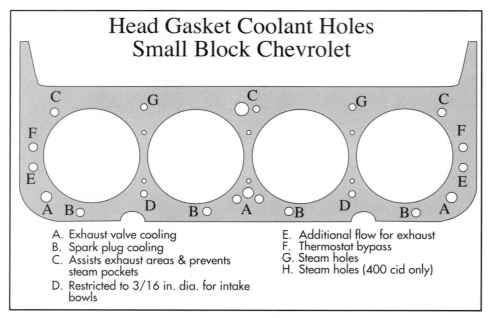

Head Gasket Coolant Holes
Small Block Chevrolet

A. Exhaust valve cooling
B. Spark plug cooling
C. Assists exhaust areas & prevents steam pockets
D. Restricted to 3/16 in. dia. for intake bowls
E. Additional flow for exhaust
F. Thermostat bypass
G. Steam holes
H. Steam holes (400 cid only)

Note that steam holes are included for 400 blocks, which have siamesed cylinders (no waterjacket between cylinders). When using cylinder heads not originally designed for a 400 block, steam holes must be drilled in the head's deck surface for low-speed operation. A head gasket may be used as a location template. This modification is necessary only for engines which will be operated continuously at less than 3500 rpm. At higher speeds, coolant flow is sufficient to eliminate steam pockets. With adequate cooling system pressure and a high efficiency water pump, steam hole in the head may not be necessary.

This can't be achieved if thread friction is too high because when the desired torque reading is reached, the bolts or studs won't be adequately stretched. Also note that clamp load can decrease significantly if an engine is overheated or subjected to detonation.

Some form of lubricant, usually racing oil, anti-seize or a non-hardening sealer, is required to assure the proper amount of stretch. Sealer must be used on all the bolts that enter the waterjackets. Another worthwhile addition is a hardened washer (under the head of each bolt or nut) to prevent galling and reduce friction.

O-Ringing

As cylinder pressures increase, so does the load on the head gaskets. Although current composition gaskets have been used successfully in virtually every type of racing engine imaginable, the pressures encountered in some supercharged, turbocharged or nitrous assisted powerplants may require that the block be machined to accept O-rings around each cylinder.

The most commonly used system employs stainless steel O-rings and a solid copper gasket. While this does an excellent job of sealing the cylinders, coolant leakage is an all too common problem. About the only way to prevent coolant leakage with copper head gaskets is to apply a small bead of silicone around each coolant hole in the block and head.

An alternative solution is to O-ring the block and use a composition gasket such as a Fel-Pro 1034 installed upside down (standard composition gaskets can't be used on blocks with a separate O-ring groove around each cylinder). O-ring grooves should be cut so that the .041" stainless steel wire sticks up .010" above the block deck surface.

TORQUING HEAD BOLTS

When tightening the head bolts, follow the proper sequence and pull smoothly on the torque wrench. The idea is to "sneak up" on each setting because a sudden or jerky motion will give false torque wrench readings. What follows are some tips for torquing head bolts from Jerry Rosenquist at Fel-Pro:

• Necked-down short bolts and studs are a good idea. Bolts with a full shank stretch only .002" to .005" If the gasket and/or casting relax .002", over 50% of the clamp load is lost. The necked-down bolts can increase stretch 100% over full shank bolts. "Short" bolts refers to the eight 1-3/4" long bolts used in the outer row of holes on each head. Seven 3-13/16" and two 3"-long bolts are also used to hold each cylinder head in place.

• With new bolts or studs, the clamp load won't be at its best; it takes two or three tightenings for the threads to burnish in.

• Bolts can be reused several times as long as they don't feel spongy when they're tightened. Discard washers when they become cupped or scored.

• It's difficult or impossible to get a proper seal if the head castings are too thin in the deck area. Weak castings bend, causing the bolts to lose clamp load. ■

CAMSHAFTS

6

As it relates to internal combustion engines, a camshaft is a shaft containing one non-concentric or "egg-shaped" lobe for each valve. A gear to drive the distributor and one special lobe to operate the engine's fuel pump are also usually included. The motion generated by each cam lobe as it rotates will open and close its mating intake or exhaust valve by imparting a raising and lowering action to the valvetrain. In an overhead valve engine, like the small-block Chevy, the valvetrain typically consists of lifters (also called followers or tappets), pushrods, rocker arms, valve springs, valve retainers, valve locks and the valves themselves.

By opening and closing the valves, the camshaft controls the timing of the flow of intake mixture and the exhausting of burnt gasses into and out of the cylinders. In terms of a functional definition, the previous paragraph is adequate. But to fully define a camshaft, it's necessary to be familiar with all the components of a cam lobe. However, it goes beyond mere definitions; camshaft technology has progressed to the point that a thorough knowledge of lobe terminology is helpful in selecting the correct camshaft for optimum performance.

Although Stock Eliminator engines are only allowed limited modifications, a high performance camshaft can make a whopping difference in horsepower. Even 4000 pound "tanks" like this Impala record impressive quarter mile times when cammed properly.

CAMSHAFT TERMINOLOGY

As with any rotating shaft, a camshaft must be supported by a number of bearings spaced over its length. The portion of the camshaft that contacts each bearing is called a journal and is obviously round. Camshafts for small-block Chevy and other V-8 engines have five journals. Although each cam lobe is egg-shaped, a portion of it, called the base circle, is concentric with the journal. In effect, the base circle, also called the heel, is that portion of the lobe where no lift is generated. Directly opposite the base circle is the nose or toe of the lobe. The sections leading up to and away from the nose are called the opening and closing flanks, or ramps, respectively.

Lift

Maximum lift, which is the height to which a cam follower or lifter is ultimately raised off the base circle, results when the lobe is rotated so that the tip of the nose is directly beneath the lifter. Ideally, the transition from no lift to maximum lift would be instantaneous, but the laws of physics make such motion impossible to achieve. Therefore, the areas of the lobe between the nose and base circle must be engineered to raise the lifter quickly, but at a very smooth, specified rate. The precision with which the transition is made is often overlooked, but it plays a major role

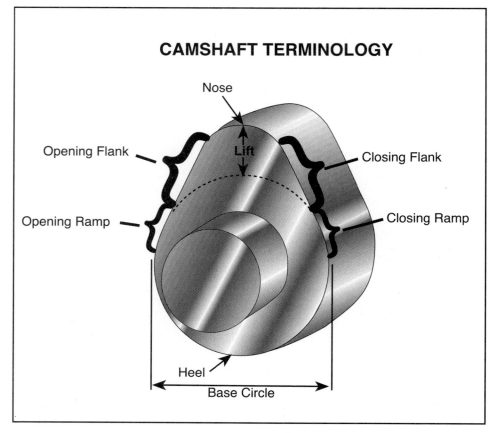

CAMSHAFT TERMINOLOGY

Nose

Opening Flank

Lift

Closing Flank

Opening Ramp

Closing Ramp

Heel

Base Circle

To the naked eye, any cam designed for standard (non-roller) hydraulic or mechanical tappets looks pretty much the same. The black finish on the lobes is parkerizing. Most hydraulic and mechanical tappet cams are machined from cast iron billets.

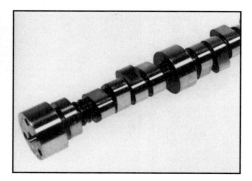

Roller tappet cams are characterized by shiny lobes which have a relatively broad nose. Roller cams are machined from 8620 steel billet cores.

in determining camshaft performance—which is one of the reasons that two cams with "identical" specifications can offer significantly different operational characteristics.

Ramps

Coming off the base circle, the first segment of the lobe that contacts the lifter is the opening clearance ramp. While many people associate ramps with mechanical lifter cams, they are also essential to hydraulic lifters. Ramps were originally put on cam lobes for one purpose only—to make the valves quiet at the operating lash specified. Typically, early engines had .010-in. lash and the ramps were put on to take that .010-in. slack out gradually so that when the valve started to move off the seat and come back on to it, it did not make any appreciable noise. In fact, they were called "quieting ramps" and they were patented back in the Twenties.

Theoretically, a hydraulic cam runs at zero lash all the time. So why do you need a ramp? You have to look at a hydraulic lifter and see how it functions. The only reason that a hydraulic lifter works is because as you lift the valve, spring pressure increases and causes the hydraulic tappet to get shorter. It actually collapses a small amount by pushing the plunger deeper into the lifter body. Therefore you must have opening and closing ramps to allow for this loss of length during the opening and closing cycle. Very few high performance cam manufacturers have thought about that carefully and many are not putting the correct closing ramp on their cams.

Typically, the ramp area of the lobe brings the lifter off the base circle by raising it at relatively low velocity, so that shock loads are kept to a minimum. Once the tappet is riding on the flank, it is lifted at continuously increasing velocity until it has traveled approximately half the distance to the nose. At that point, lift velocity begins to decrease in preparation for reaching the maximum lift point where velocity is zero. As the lifter rides over the nose, it reaches the closing side of the lobe where it is lowered back down towards the base circle. While descending on the closing flank,

Late-model small blocks with original equipment hydraulic roller cams employ a unique means of keeping the lifters in place. Each pair of lifters is held in position by a guide bar that is held in place by a sheet metal "spider." (Photo by Jim Monteith)

A normal camshaft wear pattern. Due to the crowned shape of the lifter bottom, most of the contact area is offset to one side. This offset causes the lifter to spin as the cam rotates, resulting in the pattern shown.

Automotive Engineers (SAE), duration of hydraulic lifter cams should be rated by establishing the timing point baseline at .004-in. cam lift, assuming a 1.5:1 rocker arm ratio. However, it is common practice for cam grinders to juggle numbers for any number of reasons, so while some cams have advertised durations computed at .004-in. cam lift, others are referenced to a different cam lift figure, like .006".

Duration-at-Fifty—Because of the various rating data points, it is often difficult to compare two different cams. However, the industry standard for evaluating camshaft performance potential is the duration at .050-in. cam lift. Duration at .050" lift, also called *net duration*, is simply the number of degrees during which a lifter is raised .050" or more off the base circle. This figure was chosen because it usually requires this amount of lift to open the valve sufficiently to initiate a significant amount of airflow. It's also true that at .050" lift, the tappet is well off the

velocity increases until it becomes necessary to slow things down in preparation for transition to the low velocity of the closing ramp. This is the part of the lobe that sets the valve back on its seat so it must be properly designed both for quiet operation and long valve life.

On either side of the maximum lift point, which occurs in the center of the lobe, the tappet is moved at relatively high velocities. But at the opening and closing ramps, lifter velocity is slowed so that the transition onto and off of the base circle is smooth and gentle. So even with no clearance to take up, hydraulic lifter cams require opening and closing ramps to effect a smooth transition from the base circle to the flank and back again.

Duration

While lift at the cam and at the valve (valve lift equals cam lift multiplied by rocker arm ratio) are

straightforward, duration is not. To be meaningful, duration must be referenced to a given amount of lift. Obviously, the lower the lift point at which duration is rated, the greater that duration will be.

According to the Society of

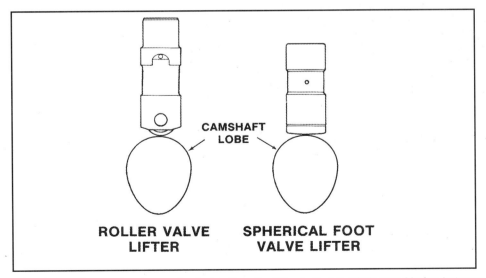

One of the primary advantages of a hydraulic roller lifter is that it eliminates friction between the cam lobe and lifter. This pays off with increased horsepower and fuel economy. More aggressive valve opening and closing rates can be achieved with roller lifters, but most stock hydraulic roller cams are non-aggressive in the name of durability and reduced valve train noise.

Original equipment hydraulic roller cams made their first appearance in engine produced for the 1987 model year. Since the roller lifters don't preload the cam toward the rear of the block, a retainer had to be added to the front. The cams used in these engines have a step machined on the front to accommodate the retainer which bolts to the front of the block.

ramps so duration at this reference point pertains to the lobe itself and is not influenced by ramp design. Many lobes with widely varying advertised durations look almost identical when profiled at .050" lift.

But duration at .050" lift doesn't tell the whole story. Advertised duration provides a key as to the idle quality that will be delivered by a particular camshaft. However, before cam comparisons can be made, you must know the lift at which the advertised duration is computed. To get an accurate comparison, the advertised durations must be computed at the same lift. Some hydraulic cam durations may be computed at a lift other than the SAE .004" lift standard. This can make cam comparisons downright confusing. However, when duration at .050-in. lift, lobe separation and intensity are used in the assessment of a cam's performance potential, you can be fairly sure of making the right selection. For more details on comparing camshafts with advertised

COMPUTING HYDRAULIC DURATION

There are a number of reasons that a hydraulic lifter cam may have its duration computed at something other than the SAE recommended figure of .004" cam lift. In some instances, a cam designer who has used a particular timing point for many years may be reluctant to change. Other cam designers may prefer another rating point—like .006" lift—as a means of ensuring that the lobe is well out of the ramp area. Another valid reason is that new technology can alter performance relative to duration at .004" lift. Using a different timing point baseline in the computation of advertised duration may therefore be instrumental in reducing the tendency to over-cam an engine.

What it all boils down to is that you have to know the lift at which advertised duration is computed if you're going to make comparisons between different cams. Otherwise, you're comparing apples and oranges. As an example of the surprise you're likely to get if you don't check out duration numbers thoroughly, consider the following horsepower and torque numbers taken from a dyno test I ran, shown in the chart. The "test mule" engine was a 350 small block with 11:1 compression ratio, street ported cylinder heads, 2.02" intake and 1.60" exhaust valves, and a 650 cfm Holley carburetor.

| CAMSHAFT 1 | | | CAMSHAFT 2 | |
rpm	CHp	CBT	CHp	CBT
2750	188	359	169	324
3000	209	365	198	346
3250	235	380	225	364
3500	263	395	251	376
3750	284	398*	272*	381
4000	303	398	286	376
4250	321	397	305	377
4500	333	389	323	378
4750	353	390	343	379
5000	374	393	361	379
5250	381	381	372	372
5500	376	394	381	364
5750	400*	366	387*	353
6000	396	346	379	332

*Peak readings

Camshaft number 1, has an advertised duration of 284°; camshaft number 2 has an advertised duration of 280° However, while the 284° cam was rated at .004" of lift, the 280° cam had its duration computed at .006" of cam lift; at the .004-in. lift figure, this cam had a duration of 289°—nine more than advertised. So the cam with the shorter advertised duration actually has more duration than its rival when both cams are rated at the same lift point.

While both cams lift the valves .480" off their seats, the one with 284° of advertised duration has a duration at .050" lift of 228°; the cam with an advertised duration of 280° has a duration at .050" of 230° All other things being equal, the cam with the slightly longer duration would be expected to make more horsepower—but it didn't. Due to differences in lobe design, lobe separation—112° versus 110°—the shorter 284° cam actually produced more torque and more horsepower.

With all the variations in timing point baselines, making cam duration comparisons can be more confusing than trying to figure who's really doing what to whom in a television soap opera. As the dyno test demonstrates, even duration at .050" lift doesn't always tell the whole story.

However, when duration at .050-in. lift, lobe separation and something called intensity are used in the assessment of a cam's performance potential, you can be pretty well assured of making the right selection.

durations computed at lifts other than the industry standard, see the sidebar nearby.

Valve Lash—Whatever is said about hydraulic lifter cams also holds true for mechanical lifter versions—except valve lash must be considered and that alters the lift at which advertised duration is computed. According to SAE specifications, the timing point baseline for a mechanical lifter cam is .006" plus the specified valve lash. Therefore, if the manufacturer specifies a lash of .030", advertised duration is computed at a valve lift of .036" which computes to a cam lift of .024-in. assuming a 1.5:1 rocker arm ratio. This computation method does little besides make a confusing situation even more confusing. Valve lash figures chosen by original equipment manufacturers are largely arbitrary numbers that are easy for the mechanic to use when the engine is in the shop. It's almost always a number that applies when the engine is cold. But lash changes when things get hot so there's no point in relating timing points to lash. Most high performance cam manufacturers compute the advertised duration of mechanical lifter camshafts at .020-in. cam lift.

Lobe Separation

Another term that is useful in describing a camshaft's performance characteristics is lobe separation (also called lobe centerline). Lobe separation is the displacement angle between the center (maximum lift point) of the intake lobe and the center of the exhaust lobe. Typically, lobe separation runs between 102 and 114 camshaft (not crankshaft) degrees and is established through design and manufacturing—it cannot be changed. Most small-block street engines produce maximum usable power with a lobe separation of 110-112 degrees.

Intake Centerline—Now for the confusion factor. Intake centerline, which is often referred to simply as "centerline," pertains to the position at which the cam is installed in the engine with respect to the crankshaft.

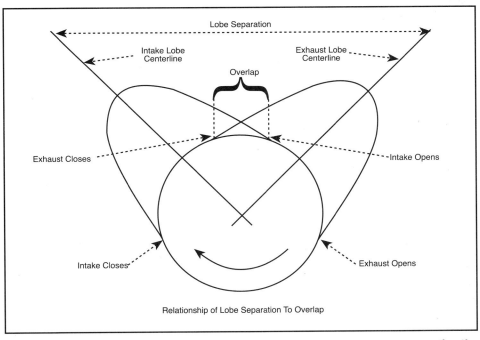

Relationship of Lobe Separation To Overlap

Lobe separation, also called lobe center angle, refers to the number of degrees separating the centerline of the intake lobe from the centerline of the exhaust lobe. As lobe separation is increased (spread further apart), overlap is decreased and vice versa.

This figure relates to the angle (in crankshaft degrees) at which maximum intake lift occurs relative to Top Dead Center. An intake centerline of 108° means that the intake valve reaches maximum lift at 108° after Top Dead Center. As Murphy's Law would have it, intake centerline will frequently be between 102 and 110°, so it and lobe separation are often confused simply because the numbers are in the same ballpark.

But there is a reason to all this rhyme. Lobe centerline is not adjustable by the engine builder; it is ground into the camshaft. Seeking to eliminate some of the terminology confusion, some people refer to intake centerline as the intake maximum lift point (expressed in crankshaft degrees after Top Dead Center). Its counterpart is exhaust maximum lift (expressed in crankshaft degrees before Top Dead Center) and both

figures are frequently noted on camshaft specification cards.

Varying Degrees—For many years, virtually every high performance camshaft, whether intended for street use, drag racing, circle track racing or any other form of automotive competition, was ground with 108° of lobe separation. Then, someone figured out that if the lobe separation was changed to 106°, an engine made more mid-range torque (at a slightly

EFFECTS OF LOBE SEPARATION ON POWER

According to theory, assuming that two cams have otherwise identical specifications, spreading lobe separation (from 108 to 112°, as an example) will increase top-end power at the expense of mid-range torque. Tightening lobe separation will have the opposite effect. Generally, that proves to be true, but the amount of variation can be significant. To see just how dramatic, or undramatic a change in lobe separation can be, glance over the accompanying

| | Camshaft 1 | | Camshaft 2 | |
rpm	CBT	CHp	CBT	CHp
2750	346	181	359	188
3000	362	206	372	213
3250	373	231	382	236
3500	381	254	392	262
3750	387*	276	396*	282
4000	384	293	393	299
4250	385	311	391	316
4500	379	325	389	333
4750	384	347	387	350
5000	378	360	382	364
5250	369	369	369	369
5500	358	375*	358	375*
5750	342	375	333	365
6000	313	357	304	347

dyno test results. Notice that in one instance, the differences were significant while in another, they are considerably less impressive. Much of the effect of a change in lobe separation is dependent upon the rest of the engine combination. Typically, a change in lobe separation will not have a drastic effect on peak horsepower, (aside from raising or lowering the rpm at which peak horsepower is produced) but it can significantly alter low speed and mid-range torque.

TEST A

Engine Specifications: 355 cid small block with street-ported 492 cylinder heads, 2.02/1.60" valves, 11:1 compression ratio, single-plane intake manifold and Holley 650 cfm carburetor, 1-3/4" headers

Camshaft Specifications: hydraulic, 222° at .050" lift, .467" valve lift. Camshaft 1, 114° of lobe separation; Camshaft 2, 110° lobe separation

This test is interesting because both cams produced the same peak horsepower while the one with 110° lobe separation pumped out 9 lbs-ft. more peak torque. Above the horsepower peak, the cam with 114° lobe separation made 10 more horsepower. Both of these cams were too short in duration to allow the engine to develop the maximum horsepower potential as determined by the flow capacity of the cylinder heads and intake manifold. If they were, the difference at higher rpm levels would have been greater. However, the shift in the power curve is obvious and graphically demonstrates the effect of altering lobe separation. It should also be apparent from these tests that for racing applications, it makes sense to specify a particular lobe separation to optimize the power curve.

higher rpm). That same person also determined that a wider lobe separation (112-114 degrees) produced more top end power.

In the real world, tighter lobe separation closes the intake valve earlier, resulting in higher cylinder pressure, which in turn produces more torque. Wider lobe separations result in later intake valve closing and less cylinder pressure, a reduction in mid-range torque, and an increase in top end horsepower. So although lobe separation receives the credit for either increasing or decreasing torque, it is actually the intake closing point that is the controlling factor. A similar effect can be achieved by altering cam phasing; advancing closes the intake valve sooner, resulting in more torque; retarding a cam has the opposite effect.

Street Cams—Most high performance street cams are ground with a lobe separation of 108° to 114° Opinions vary as to what constitutes the ideal amount of lobe separation, particularly for high performance street engines. Wider lobe separation—112° to 114°—allows a smoother idle and higher idle manifold vacuum, but it also reduces mid-range torque, while increasing top end horsepower. Closer lobe separation—106° to 110°—has the opposite effect.

rpm	Camshaft 1		Camshaft 2	
	CBT	CHp	CBT	CHp
1750	295	98	337	112
2000	284	108	320	122
2250	313	134	343	147
2500	321	153	360	171
2750	334	175	372	195
3000	348	199	374	214
3250	352	218	380	235
3500	366	244	384	256
3750	369	263	388*	277
4000	372	284	385	293
4250	365	296	378	306
4500	360	309	370	317
4750	349	316	360	326
5000	333	317	347	330
5250	332	332*	337	337*
5500	314	328	319	334
5750	304	332	301	329
6000	288	329	285	325

TEST B

Engine Specifications: 355 cid small block, 882 cylinder heads (76cc chambers), 1.94/1.50" valves, 9.5:1 compression ratio, dual-plane intake manifold and Holley 650 cfm carburetor, 1-5/8" headers.

Camshaft Specifications: hydraulic, 216° duration at .050" lift, .454-in. valve lift. Camshaft 1, 112° lobe separation; Camshaft 2, 108° lobe separation.

Obviously, this combination loved the tighter lobe separation. If you just look at the peak figures, the difference isn't particularly impressive--one cam produced 16 lbs-ft. more torque and five more horsepower. But look at the torque difference between 1750 and 2750. The cam with 108° lobe separation recorded at least 30 lbs-ft. more torque at every data point. From 3000 to 4000 rpm, tighter lobe separation bumped torque output by 13 to 26 lbs-ft. In this instance, the cam with wider lobe separation didn't gain power superiority until well past the power peak. These power curves demonstrate that cams with very similar specifications can in fact have widely differing power output. However, it should be noted that whenever lobe separation is tightened, there is some loss of idle manifold vacuum. With these cams it was only .5" to 1"/Hg. With longer duration cams, the difference in manifold vacuum tends to be greater when lobe separation is altered.

Don't read anything into these test results that isn't there. Judging from these figures, it would appear that 108° is the ideal lobe separation for a street cam. However, when a similar pair of cams with 10 less degrees of duration were tested, results were far less dramatic. Maximum difference in torque was only 12 lbs-ft. and the cams were within two horsepower at the peak. Again, 108° lobe separation proved to produce more power than 112° lobe separation, but in this instance, idle manifold vacuum was down by a solid 1"/Hg.

Although the degree of change varies according to the specific camshaft and the engine in which it's installed, the comparison in the sidebar on pages 78 and 79 provides a relative indication. The two cams compared in that sidebar are identical except for the noted differences in lobe separation.

Drag Racing—Drag race cars obviously have their own unique requirements, which translates into specific lobe separation specifications. Depending upon vehicle weight, engine size and transmission type, lobe separation typically ranges from 104° to 118° Generally, drag cars with automatic transmissions respond best to camshafts with 104° to 108° Powerglide transmissions, with only two gears (Low and Drive), rely heavily on the torque converter for torque multiplication. Powerglide-equipped engines therefore operate over a relatively narrow and low rpm band. In essence, during acceleration in Low gear, the engine remains at a constant rpm while the rest of the driveline tries to catch up. Shortly after the torque converter's input and output speeds equalize (that is when converter lock-up speed is reached) the transmission is shifted into Drive and the output stage of the torque converter plays "catch-up" again. Consequently, an engine linked to a Powerglide will typically run a cam with tighter lobe separation than a powerplant connected to a three- or four-speed automatic, where dependency on the torque converter is much less. Similarly, when a clutch and a four- or five-speed manual transmission (or clutch-assisted automatic) is employed, lobe separation is wider yet, as the engine's operating speed range tends to be

Depending on the division, an oval track engine may be fitted with a hydraulic, mechanical or roller camshaft. Each type of camshaft is usually mandated by the rules and other engine components must be carefully selected to achieve maximum performance.

higher. Most Pro Stock engines run cams with a lobe separation of 114° to 120°, (sometimes more) which is the reason they idle surprisingly well even though duration at .050" lift may approach 300°.

Oval Track—As might be expected, builders of oval track engines also have specific lobe separation preferences. Most engine builders prefer 106° for engines installed in cars that will only turn left. For this application, torque coming off a corner is the most important consideration and 106° lobe separation appears to put the torque

peak at the proper rpm for this type of racing. However, it's interesting to note that virtually all oval track engine builders install cams with the intake maximum lift point at 102° Some cam designers feel that it would be more advantageous to use 108° or 110° lobe separation for a broader torque curve—and advance the cam to build more mid-range torque. Engine builders seem reluctant to alter their thinking, so either no one knows the validity of the wider lobe separation theory, or no one is talking.

As noted, for further details on the effect lobe separation has on performance, see the sidebar on pp. 80 and 81.

Intensity

Camshaft lobe intensity is computed by subtracting net duration (computed at .050" lift) from gross or advertised duration which is computed at .004" lift in the case of a hydraulic and hydraulic roller cams, and a .020" lift for mechanical flat-tappet and roller cams. A hydraulic cam with a gross 278° and a net duration of 222° has a hydraulic intensity of 56°. When it comes to performance, less is unquestionably more—and for very logical reasons.

The ideal cam profile would raise the valves to full lift instantly, hold them open for a specified duration and then close them instantly. The laws of physics make it impossible to achieve instantaneous valve opening and closing, but recent advancements in design technology have made it possible to open and close the valves at higher maximum velocities. By so doing, engine efficiency is improved because the valves spend less time at very low lift where they bleed off cylinder pressure, but do not permit any appreciable airflow.

In practical terms, if two cams with similar lobe designs have the same net duration, same lobe separation and same lift, maximum torque and horsepower will be almost identical. But the cam with the smaller intensity figure will have a smoother idle, better off-idle response, superior low-speed driveability and a broader power curve. Viewed from another perspective, a lower lobe intensity number translates to more low end power without any loss of top end power. It also means that with a highly modified engine, it may be

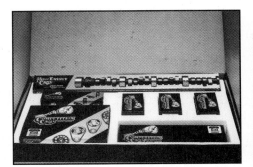
Cam and lifter kits offer a cost savings over the price of the individual components purchased separately.

practical to install a cam with longer duration at .050" lift than might otherwise be possible. This is possible because problems with poor idle quality and compatibility with torque converter stall speed are minimized.

State-of-the-art lobe designs therefore deliver "more cam" per dollar because they produce more power over a wider rpm band.

The effect of lobe intensity can be seen in the comparison between the highly regarded Chevrolet 3863151 (originally used in RPO L-79 350 hp 327 cid engines) and an aftermarket cam shown in the sidebar on p. 80 and 81.

The aftermarket cam has a lift of .454/.480" intake and exhaust; a duration at .004" of 272/284; a duration at .050" of 216/228; and a lobe intensity of 56.

For the Chevy cam, the lift is .447/.447; a duration at .004" of 290/290"; a duration at .050" of 222/222"; and a lobe intensity of 68.

At almost every test point on the dyno, from 1750 to 5750 rpm, the aftermarket cam produced more torque and horsepower than the Chevrolet high performance cam. Where the 3863151 registered maximum readings of 323 horsepower at 5000 rpm and 369 lbs-

Roller camshaft bearings are used by a number of Winston Cup engine builders to reduce friction. Special block machining is required.

ft. of torque at 3500 rpm, the aftermarket cam clicked off 335 horsepower at 5500 rpm and 383 lbs-ft. of torque at 3250. Without doubt, much of the power improvement was due to the difference in lobe specifications. Also, in combination with the duration and lift differences, the reduced intensity produced improved idle vacuum—17.5 in/Hg for the aftermarket cam, but only 16 in/Hg for the 3863151. In this instance, the aftermarket cam delivered more top-end horsepower, more low-end torque and smoother idle.

This comparison demonstrates the effects of the improvements made in cam design over the years. Chevrolet's 3863151 was designed in the early Sixties; the aftermarket cam was created in the late Seventies. So while some of the old standbys in high performance camshafts may have great nostalgic value, they don't produce as much horsepower and torque as newer designs. And that becomes immediately apparent on the dyno, on the track and on the street. So before you decide on a particular camshaft for your small block, make sure you look at all the pertinent specifications.

Overlap

Overlap is another commonly used camshaft term. It is used to describe the period of time when a cylinder's intake and exhaust valves are both open. Valve overlap occurs as a piston approaches and leaves Top Dead Center, extending from the exhaust stroke of one cycle to the intake stroke of the next.

Although the term overlap is still used, it has been largely replaced by "lobe separation" as a means of evaluating a camshaft's performance characteristics, and for good reason; lobe separation can remain constant when duration is altered, overlap typically does not. So comparing the overlap of Cam "A" to that of Cam "B" may or may not indicate a significant change in performance potential, depending upon the difference in durations.

Another consideration is that from the design standpoint, lobe separation is a cause, overlap is an effect. When a cam designer wishes to fine tune the power curve produced by a cam, he will frequently alter lobe separation while leaving lift and duration unchanged. In some cases, two cams will have identical specifications except for lobe separation which has been altered to shift the torque curve to better accommodate specific applications. Overlap understandably changes when lobe separation is altered, but aside from being an outdated reference specification, overlap has little meaning in defining a camshaft's performance potential.

Therefore, you shouldn't use it as a basis for cam selection.

CAMSHAFT SELECTION

Swapping the cast-iron intake manifold for an aluminum high-rise model and scrapping the stock carburetor in favor of a performance-oriented four-barrel will perk up any engine. Installing a set of headers isn't a bad idea either. Of course, a tune-up never hurts. But without question, the best means of significantly increasing the performance of a stock engine is to replace the original camshaft with a high performance profile. With a race engine, a cam swap won't usually provide the dramatic power gains realized with stock powerplants (unless the original selection was way off the mark—a common occurrence), but the right camshaft will make a significant power difference.

But where this power is gained is an area few people take the time to think through. It is a characteristic of older cam design technology that whenever a camshaft is responsible for a dramatic horsepower increase, the

Most aftermarket cams have identifying numbers on either the front or rear face. However, sometimes the inscriptions are a code rather than an outright grind or part number. If you don't have a Captain Midnight decoder ring, you may have to check with the manufacturer to determine the cam's identity.

engine speed at which maximum torque occurs is pushed quite a distance up the rpm scale. In some instances, installation of a high performance cam can even result in a decrease in peak torque. But with horsepower being a function of torque and rpm, simply shifting the torque band to a higher engine speed will

In a race engine, the right cam can make all the difference. Excessive duration leads to sluggish performance, but if the cam is properly matched to the rest of the combination, great performance results. This roller cam-equipped 331 cid small block has all the suds needed to boil a pair of slicks in a burnout.

result in greater maximum horsepower—often at the expense of mid-range torque. While high horsepower numbers are impressive, trading off torque for a few extra horsepower is not a wise decision unless an engine is operated only within a narrow rpm band at the top of the scale, such as with a manually shifted drag race car. The best results, both on and off the track, seem to be achieved by engines with a broad, flat torque curve.

And that's just the type of torque curve state-of-the-art camshafts are designed to produce. Working with the latest engineering techniques, top cam designers have been able to develop street cams that boost horsepower considerably without moving an engine's torque peak above its stock rpm level—and race cams that greatly extend an engine's usable power range. Consequently, the road to higher horsepower no longer means that a detour must be made around mid-range torque.

The key to raising horsepower, without bringing low-speed and mid-range torque to its knees, lies in selecting the "right" high performance cam. That means more than playing the numbers game—it means matching the cam to the speed range in which an engine operates. Many people mistakenly believe bigger is better; however it is often true that less duration translates into more usable power.

Horsepower vs. Torque

Engine dynamometers measure torque. Horsepower, on the other hand, is computed based on an engine's torque output at a specific rpm. A look at typical torque and horsepower curves demonstrates that even though torque may be falling within a particular rpm band, horsepower can be increasing (as rpm is raised) because of the influence of engine speed in the equation (torque x rpm)/5252. As an engine's torque peak moves up the rpm scale, peak horsepower increases even if the maximum torque reading remains the same, or even drops somewhat.

Most people think a high performance camshaft improves engine performance because it increases horsepower. Actually, such a cam raises the rpm level at which maximum torque is produced and broadens the torque curve. It may also deliver a slight increase in torque, but even if it causes the opposite, horsepower will increase because of the movement of the torque peak to a higher rpm. Certainly, the net result is a higher horsepower figure, but that increase is a byproduct of changes in the torque curve. More often than not, whenever peak horsepower is significantly increased, low-speed torque is reduced.

Although the latest camshaft technology has the potential to minimize loss of torque at very low engine speeds, losses can't be eliminated altogether. That being the case, you're better off with a current camshaft design than an older one. But irrespective of the profile or the application, the key to unlocking maximum performance is to cam an engine so that the torque and horsepower peaks are within the rpm range that an engine sees in normal operation—on the street or at the track.

High Performance Camshafts

Traditionally, high performance

If you've always wondered why you shouldn't put used lifters on a new camshaft, or should use assembly lube and follow all the other standard installation recommendations, take a look at the lobes in this photo. Notice that the base circle area is still black (showing minimal contact with the lifter) while the flank and nose are excessively worn. By the way, in case you haven't guessed, this isn't a Chevrolet cam.

camshafts have not brought major increases in torque when installed in place of their stock counterparts. However, new technology developed during the Eighties has changed that to some degree. Cams designed using the latest concepts have relatively long durations at .050-in. lift compared to their advertised durations. As a result, with properly selected duration specifications, a state-of-the-art high performance camshaft can produce a measurable torque increase compared to a stock cam. However, except for highly unusual cases, this increase will usually not exceed 5% and there will be some loss of torque at extremely low engine speeds. By comparison, the same cam that boosts torque only 5% can easily result in a horsepower increase of over 20% due to the rpm multiplying effect.

Compression Ratio—Compression ratio must also be considered when selecting a high performance camshaft. Significant increases in torque are almost always the result of

This camshaft started life like most others, with properly shaped lobes. However, lack of adequate lubrication during initial start-up and run-in wiped out the lobes. So to avoid premature lobe failure, use assembly lube and pre-lube the engine before initial start-up.

raising compression. One way to achieve this is through bumping static compression ratio; another is through valve timing—specifically intake valve closing point—which affects cranking compression (also known as cylinder pressure). Obviously, static compression ratio must be taken into account when altering valve timing and valve timing must be considered when altering static compression ratio, or else cylinder pressure will be either too high or too low for optimum performance.

Even with the mildest of cams, the intake valve doesn't close until after the piston passes Bottom Dead Center. Consequently, with the piston rising and the intake valve open, some of the air/fuel mixture that was just drawn in, is pumped back out of the cylinder. With a later intake valve closing, there is less air and fuel to compress, so cylinder pressure is reduced. It is for this reason that cam duration and static compression must be carefully matched—a change in one very often requires modification of the other. Excessively long duration reduces cylinder pressure which

translates to less torque. Conversely, if duration is too short with respect to static compression ratio, cylinder pressure will be too high and detonation will result. This is the reason that many camshaft application notes include static compression ratio requirements.

However, some high performance camshafts are designed to function with stock compression ratios. This being the case, it would seem that performance increases would be slight because duration cannot be lengthened to a great degree if adequate cylinder pressure is to be maintained. But there's more to the story than duration. By definition, a high performance cam has more lift and faster opening and closing rates than an original equipment (OE) cam. So with nothing more than factory duration specs, an aftermarket performance cam will deliver increased power.

Dual-Pattern Cams

In addition to providing acceptable durability, a street cam must also offer low-speed driveability. A high

performance cam should make a car fun to drive, not a chore. One method used by cam designers to generate profiles that have both a broad torque curve and strong top-end power, is to use profiles of different durations and lifts on the intake and exhaust lobes. Known as dual-pattern cams, they typically produce more power than their single-pattern counterparts when installed in an engine that's equipped with a carburetor or throttle body injector and a conventional single- or dual-plane intake manifold. By comparison, it appears that engines with Chevrolet Tuned Port Injection systems derive little, if any, benefit from a dual-pattern cam compared to a single-pattern design with similar specifications.

The need for a dual-pattern cam arises from the fact that the breathing capacity of most engines is limited by the exhaust port. With an original equipment type engine, restricted exhaust flow is fine because engine operating speeds aren't high enough to cause problems.

But with high performance and race engines, that isn't the case. The restriction imposed by the exhaust valve, port, manifold and pipe limits horsepower. One way to compensate for this is to lift the exhaust valve higher, and keep it open longer than the intake valve. Within a family, most cam manufacturers offer profiles that vary by 2° or 4° of duration. Consequently, when two profiles are selected for a camshaft, exhaust duration is typically 6° to 12° longer than that of the intake lobe.

If an engine has a highly modified set of cylinder heads, and the exhaust port has flow capacity sufficient to generate an extraction effect, it's possible to use the same lobe for both

Be generous with the cam lube, adding a big glob of on each lobe and spreading it so it coats the entire lobe evenly. This should only be done after the cam has been degreed-in and you're installing it for the final time. Use motor oil for degreeing-in, otherwise the lube could affect your readings. For more details, see the chapter on assembly.

the intake and exhaust. However, current Pro Stock technology makes use of cams with intake and exhaust durations that vary as much as 22°; there are cases where Pro Stock engines have been equipped with cams having 290° of intake duration and 312° of duration on the exhaust side (at .050-in. lift).

In a sense, the most highly modified race engines respond best to the type of intake/exhaust duration patterning used to maximize the power of high performance street engines. The big split in durations of a Pro Stock camshaft are necessitated by the huge dimensions of the intake valves, ports and intake manifold which generate excellent cylinder filling. Like a stock engine, the exhaust ports, no matter how extensively modified, cannot dump the waste gasses as efficiently as the intake system brings in fresh air/fuel mixture. But if a Pro Stock engine were topped off by a single, rather than dual four-barrel carburetor, and a conventional, rather than ram-type intake manifold, less exhaust duration would be warranted. Pro Stock-style, single four-barrel, small-

block engines commonly have exhaust duration that is 4°, 8° or 12° longer than intake (8° is the most common).

How Much is Enough?—With each engine being unique, the obvious question is, how do you select intake and exhaust durations for maximum performance? One method is to order a number of camshafts with different intake/exhaust duration combinations and test them. That's extremely expensive and time consuming, but with hydraulic lifter grinds, it's the only option. For street applications, the performance improvement to be gained from lengthening or shortening exhaust duration (compared to intake duration) isn't sufficient to justify the expense. Most cam manufacturers have learned which combinations are effective for popular engines so it's hard to improve on cataloged grinds—especially those offered for the small block. Cam grinders have been designing cams for this engine for well over 30 years, so there's very little that hasn't been tried in terms of intake and exhaust duration combinations.

Lash Loops—With mechanical lifter cams, it's a little easier to determine what an engine likes. It's possible to run a "lash loop" as a means of determining the optimum intake and exhaust durations. In most cases, if cam duration is in the ballpark, running a lash loop will not pay off with major performance improvements. But it will produce measurable power increases that just may spell the difference between a win and a loss at the race track.

Running a lash loop involves adjusting the intake lash to what appears to be the optimum setting, then altering the exhaust lash in .004" increments. Results are gauged by on-track or dyno testing. If the engine has more torque or mid-range power with the lash loosened .004", chances are the cam has too much exhaust duration; the exhaust lobe should be shortened by about 4°. The reverse is also true. If tightening exhaust lash .004" causes the engine to run better, more exhaust duration is called for.

Once the exhaust lash loop has been run, use the same procedure on the intake side. If the engine runs better with more lash, intake duration should be shortened; if tighter lash brings about improved performance, intake duration should be lengthened. Whenever working with intake lash, do not alter exhaust lash at the same time, and vice versa.

There are a few things to beware of when running lash loops. A single test at each setting will not provide conclusive results; a series of tests should be run and the results averaged after throwing out the high and low times—kind of the Olympic scoring method. It's also essential to be very careful when running lash loops with any cam which has specified lash

Since roller lifters don't preload the camshaft towards the rear of the block, roller cams have a tendency to "walk" forward. Cam buttons, which fit between the front of the cam and the timing cover, are used to ensure that camshafts don't take an unauthorized stroll. Although not usually necessary with a flat-tappet cam, cam buttons are occasionally used as insurance.

settings of about .012". When widening the lash, be very careful that the engine doesn't get into valve float as parts breakage will very likely result. Some reduced lash cam designs which call for .012" lash should be run at settings of no more than .014". However, lash can be reduced all the way down to .001" or .002". The only requirement is that some clearance must exist so that the valve firmly contacts the seat.

Another point to keep in mind is that any changes in the intake or exhaust systems will invalidate previous test data. For optimum performance, it's necessary to run a lash loop any time a change is made to the cylinder heads, intake manifold, carburetor or headers. And of course, internal engine modifications also call for a rerunning of the lash loop. Obviously, lash loops are warranted only for serious racing efforts.

Valve Lash—Close or Wide?

Close lash is a relatively recent development in camshaft design which was pioneered by Harvey Crane, of Crane CamDesign, a business that designs and analyzes camshafts for other cam manufacturers. Although he has not been associated with Crane Cams since 1989 (and therefore his opinions expressed here do not necessarily reflect or apply to camshafts produced by Crane Cams), he is considered to be a leading authority on camshaft technology. On the subject of valve lash, he states:

"Valve lash is a function of the ramp design. Why put all that ramp on a cam lobe, which is intended to take up the 'shock' of opening and closing the valves, if less ramp and less lash will accomplish the same thing? This philosophy comes from hydraulic lifter cam design. Theoretically, you don't need a ramp on a hydraulic cam because there's no clearance to take up. But you better have some ramp there, especially on the closing side, because the lifter is shorter at certain points. But with a hydraulic cam, it is possible to design the ramps so that they appear to be somewhere between very short and non-existent. Now if the average person looks at some of my hydraulic lobe designs, it will look like they have no ramps. But there are very carefully designed ramps in place. The success of these cams made me wonder why I couldn't apply the same technology to mechanical lifter cams. The problem was that I couldn't design the lobe with the existing computer software. So we developed some new mathematics and wrote some new software and that

enabled us to design mechanical cams with tight lash specifications. At first, a lot of engine builders looked at the .012" lash and said it wouldn't work, but we've proven otherwise. The thing you've got to keep in mind is that the more lash you have, the less lift you get at the valve. If you've got .030" valve lash, you've lost .030" lift."

The original impetus for wide lash was to reduce maintenance problems on stock engines. With a lash of .030", if an engine is run for 30,000 or 40,000 miles, some of the valves will have lash of .010" and others will be at .045" That really won't hurt anything. But if the lash were tighter—.012" to .018", as with the original Duntov Corvette cams—it was possible, over a period of time, to wind up with zero lash which inevitably causes engine problems. Designing cams with relatively wide lash settings simply provided more latitude for lash changes between settings. This resulted in fewer burnt valves and also reduced the frequency of valve adjustment. With a race engine, the valve covers are off as much as they're on. Valve lash is monitored very closely and frequently, so there's no need to design for long maintenance intervals.

As noted, it's critical that lash be set at no greater than .014" with cams specifying .012" lash. At wider settings, the valve is moved at extremely high velocities because the lifter is off the ramp and well up on the flank when the clearance is taken up, and when the valve is closed. These extreme velocities will result in parts breakage.

CAMSHAFT POSITIONING

Selecting the proper camshaft is only one of the steps along the road to maximum performance. One other is how the cam is installed. Anyone who has done much bench racing has heard the terms advanced, retarded, straight-up and split overlap used to describe the positioning, or indexing, of the camshaft relative to crankshaft position. But as is the case with most terms that are casually bandied about, these words are wrapped in a cloak of misunderstanding.

One reason is that both camshaft degrees and crankshaft degrees are used in referring to various cam timing events. Valve opening and closing points, camshaft advance or retard, intake centerline (or maximum lift point), exhaust centerline (or maximum lift point) and duration are always referenced in crankshaft degrees. Lobe separation is always referenced in camshaft degrees.

A crankshaft makes two revolutions for each single revolution of the camshaft. That means a crankshaft rotates 720° while a camshaft rotates 360°; that relationship explains the existence of camshafts with over 350° of gross duration. If duration were measured in camshaft degrees, a cam with 350° of duration would keep the valves open almost all the time. But within a 720° cycle, 350° represents slightly less than half the entire cycle.

Straight-Up—"Straight-up" is one of those terms that has been in use since the days of the flathead Ford. However, it is not universally applicable because it is meaningful only with reference to single-pattern cams which have identical intake and exhaust durations. When a single-pattern cam is installed "straight-up," the intake and exhaust maximum lift points (which are specified in crankshaft degrees) are the same as the lobe separation (which is specified in camshaft degrees). That is, if a camshaft is ground with 112° of lobe separation, it is installed "straight-up" if the intake maximum lift point occurs at 112° after TDC and the exhaust maximum lift point occurs at 112° before TDC.

Split Overlap—It is also true that when a single-pattern cam is installed "straight-up," a condition known as split overlap exists. At "split overlap," both the intake and exhaust tappets for any given cylinder are raised an equal amount when the corresponding piston is at Top Dead Center.

Indexing—One method of indexing a single-pattern camshaft is to rotate the crankshaft until number one piston is at Top Dead Center. Then the cam is positioned (by using offset bushings or keyways) so that the lifters for number one cylinder are at equal heights. But this method will do nothing but cause trouble when used with dual-pattern camshafts. The correct method of indexing or degreeing-in a dual-pattern cam is described throughout the rest of this chapter.

Advancing the Cause

Many cams are ground "advanced" from "straight-up." Crankshaft degrees are always used when referencing camshaft advance; offset bushings and keyways are always marked in crankshaft degrees. This means that the intake maximum lift point and lobe separation figures will not be equal. Most high performance cams with lobe separations of 108° or more are ground 3 to 5 crankshaft

Although properly torqued cam bolts rarely back out, installation of a bolt retaining plate is good insurance. The plate is also required to hold a cam button in place.

degrees advanced from "straight-up." That is, with a 108° lobe separation, the intake maximum lift point occurs at 103° after TDC and exhaust maximum lift occurs at 113° before TDC. With dual-pattern cams, intake maximum lift point and lobe separation figures determine the amount of advance ground into the cam.

Camshaft advance is a bit confusing because there are two reference points. One is the amount of advance (from split overlap) ground into the camshaft by the manufacturer; the other is the amount of advance or retard that may be added during installation. When a cam is degreed-in, valve timing can be advanced or retarded—from the specifications listed on the spec card—through the use of offset bushings or keyways. So it would be correct to say that a cam

Randy Dorton of Hendrick Motorsports doesn't leave anything to chance. That includes camshaft phasing. Even though he uses the best available components in every Winston Cup engine he builds, degreeing-in the camshaft is an operation that is never overlooked.

was advanced 4° because a 4° bushing was installed in the cam sprocket. If the cam was already ground 5° advanced from "straight-up," it would then be advanced a total of 9° (from "straight-up").

Similarly, if an offset bushing or keyway is employed to retard a cam 4°, it is being moved with respect to the opening and closing figures listed on the spec card. A cam ground with 5° of advance, if retarded 4°, is then advanced only 1° from "straight-up." So even though it has been retarded, it's still advanced.

The important point to keep in mind is that advance is relative, so whenever dealing with the subject, keep the reference point in mind—you're either referencing advance from "straight-up," or comparing it to the timing numbers listed on the specification card. Many engine builders make it a practice to "advance the cam two degrees" to compensate somewhat for timing chain stretch. In this case, "advanced two degrees" is in reference to the

valve timing figures, not to "straight-up." So to avoid excess confusion, whenever discussing camshaft advance, ask, "Advanced from what?" There are pros and cons to installing a cam either with advance or retard, which we will discuss shortly.

Degreeing the Camshaft

When you install a high performance camshaft, you can do it one of two ways—just stick it in the engine and button everything back up, or you can do it the right way. Without exception, the right way means degreeing it in (also called phasing the camshaft) to assure that valve timing events occur at precisely the right time with respect to crankshaft position.

The degreeing-in operation is simply a matter of checking an engine's real life valve opening and closing timing against the figures on the specification card that accompanies each camshaft. It is accomplished by mounting a degree

wheel on the front of the crankshaft and utilizing a dial indicator to check cam lobe lift. However, even though cam timing is being checked, erroneous readings are usually not caused by the lobes themselves. Mismatches between specifications and actual measurements are usually the result of errors in crank sprocket keyway positioning, cam sprocket dowel pin hole placement or an excessively stretched timing chain. Additionally, the dowel pin in the camshaft may be improperly located.

Finding TDC—But before cam timing can be checked, Top Dead Center must first be accurately determined. In many cases, the mark scribed on the vibration damper is not accurate. If the cylinder heads haven't been installed, simply bolt a positive piston stop over cylinder number one and follow the pertinent steps that follow. With the cylinder heads in place, the search for TDC can be conducted as follows:

1. Remove all the spark plugs to make engine rotation easier and bring number one piston to approximately Top Dead Center—just to get in the ballpark.

2. Mount a degree wheel on the crankshaft snout and rotate it so that the TDC mark is aligned with the pointer. Don't turn the crankshaft with the same bolt used to attach the degree wheel as this can move the wheel and cause incorrect readings.

3. Turn the crankshaft so that the piston moves an inch or so down the bore. Install a positive piston stop in cylinder number one spark plug hole.

4. Rotate the crankshaft clockwise

until the piston just contacts the stop. Don't use excessive force—you want a positive stop, not a hole in the piston. Note the reading on the degree wheel.

5. Spin the crankshaft in the opposite direction until the piston once again contacts the stop. Note the reading on the degree wheel.

6. Split the difference between these two readings to determine true TDC. As an example, assume that the readings obtained by rotating the crank clockwise and counter-clockwise are 22° and 18° respectively. These two figures total 40°, an indication that the piston is actually being stopped at 20° (1/2 of 40) before and after TDC. Therefore, the degree wheel is 2° off. With the piston still against the stop, rotate the degree wheel until it and the 20° mark are aligned. Re-tighten the degree wheel and check again. Each time the piston comes up against the stop (after being rotated in both directions), the pointer should indicate the same reading, in this case 20°. If it doesn't, correct it and check again. If it does, TDC on the degree wheel will correspond to the true TDC of the engine.

Once TDC has been established, remove the piston stop, install a dial indicator so that it measures lift at the pushrod or cam and check the intake and exhaust lobes of number one cylinder. Make sure that the indicator reads zero when the lifter is on the heel of the lobe. All duration specifications are tied to a specific amount of lobe (not valve) lift, hence the need for a dial indicator—it records lift while the degree wheel is read to check duration. All the necessary information can usually be found on the specification card that accompanies each camshaft. To ensure accuracy, it's a good idea to spin the engine over completely to verify that the dial indicator returns to zero when the lifter is back on the base circle. Many times the indicator mount will move, making the reading inaccurate; an apparent problem with the cam may in fact be a problem with the indicator mounting.

Cam Lift—Before you actually start looking at cam phasing, check cam lift. If measured lift does not match up with the specs on the cam card, the dial indicator may not be positioned properly. Should that be the case, opening and closing points cannot be accurately related to a given amount of lift because lift is not being measured accurately. To avoid these problems, make sure that the dial indicator is mounted exactly in line with the tappet or pushrod.

Example—As an example of a degreeing-in operation, assume that you've installed a hydraulic cam and the accompanying specification card lists gross valve timing at .004-in. tappet lift as:

•Intake opens 36° Before Top Dead Center (BTDC).

•Intake closes 74° After Bottom Dead Center (ABDC).

•Exhaust opens 80° Before Bottom Dead Center (BBDC).

•Exhaust closes 30° After Top Dead Center (ATDC).

You could use these as checking dimensions, but at those points, the

When degreeing-in a cam in an engine with cylinder heads installed, position the dial indicator so that it appears to be an extension of the pushrod. Excessive angularity can lead to erroneous readings. The degree wheel must also be securely mounted to ensure accurate readings. Note that an offset bushing was installed when this cam was degreed in.

cam is moving the lifter at such a slow rate that it is easy to be off by a few degrees. However, by the time the lifter has been raised .050" off the base circle, lift rate is pretty rapid so it is easy to see precisely when the dial indicator needle reaches .050" In the case of the camshaft used in the above example, the net valve timing figures (at .050-in. lift) are:

•Intake opens 10° BTDC.

•Intake closes 44° ABDC.

•Exhaust opens 54° BBDC.

•Exhaust closes at 0° ATDC (that is, right at TDC).

A large diameter degree wheel, like this one from Powerhouse Products is economically priced yet offers enough definition to accurately degree-in a camshaft.

The actual checking procedure entails mounting the dial indicator so that it measures the lift of either the intake or exhaust lobe of cylinder number one. Then the crankshaft is rotated in the direction it normally spins, while the dial indicator is closely monitored. It's a good idea to rotate the crankshaft through a few complete revolutions to ensure that all critical dial indicator readings are repeatable.

Timing Check—When making the actual cam timing check, begin with the lifter on the cam's base circle and the dial indicator needle on zero. Rotate the crankshaft in its normal direction and as the needle swings by .040" lift, slow the rotation rate so that the needle sneaks up on the .050" figure. You should always arrive at .050" lift by spinning the crankshaft in its normal direction. Going past the desired point and then backing up until .050" lift is indicated will result in erroneous opening and closing point readings (due to lack of preload on the timing chain). Once .050" lift is

achieved, note the reading on the degree wheel—it should correspond to the appropriate specification on the cam card.

With the opening point noted, crankshaft rotation continues in the normal direction of rotation, until the tappet begins descending. As already noted, reversal of direction will indicate erroneous opening and closing points. Once again, a slow turning rate is used to "sneak up" on .050" lift and when it is reached, the degree wheel reading is once again recorded. The entire procedure is then repeated to verify the results, then the other lobe of the pair working the valves of cylinder number one is checked.

Generally, if there is a disparity between listed and actual specifications, it is not that duration has been altered but that the entire opening/closing event is skewed a few degrees forward or back. With the cam referenced in the previous paragraphs, it wouldn't be at all unusual to come up with an intake opening of 8° BTDC and closing at 46° ABDC. This would indicate that the cam was two degrees retarded. And if, in the name of false economy, an old timing chain and sprocket set was reused, the cam could easily be as much as 8° or 10° retarded. In the latter instance, a new timing set would probably cure the discrepancy and if it didn't, either an offset bushing in the cam sprocket, an offset key for the crankshaft, or a multi-keyway crank sprocket could be used.

Some racers insist on checking every lobe, but this is a very time-consuming process and it usually isn't necessary. However, as a quick double-check, move the dial indicator to cylinder number six (this procedure

works on almost all American V-8s because cylinders one and six reach TDC at the same time so it isn't necessary to move the degree wheel) and repeat the check. If there is a problem with camshaft quality, you're 95% certain of finding it here. A more thorough check can be made by checking three intake and three exhaust lobes. If the cam, rather than a single lobe, is out of specification, the timing of all six lobes should be off the same amount. In any event, a camshaft should not be advanced or retarded unless both opening and closing points do not fall within specifications. If only the opening or only the closing point is off, there's a good chance that there's a mechanical problem with the cam rather than a phasing error.

Base Circle Runout—In the process of verifying opening and closing points, it's advisable to check base circle runout. Excessive runout is indicative of poor machining quality and will result in less than optimum performance. It will also make it difficult to check cam timing and establish proper lash or lifter preload. Most cam manufacturers strive to hold base circle runout to less than .001"; any cam with .002" or more runout should be returned to the manufacturer.

If the high spot is towards the opening flank, the valve will open prematurely and the engine will idle rough and have poor idle manifold vacuum. If the high spot is towards the closing flank, idle quality will be acceptable, but torque will be degraded because valve closing is delayed. These problems are especially noticeable with a hydraulic lifter cam. In most instances, an engine never "sees" base circle runout with a mechanical lifter cam (except for extreme cases) because valve lash is usually greater than the amount of runout. Consequently, when a lifter is bumped by a high spot on the base circle, the only effect is that clearance is momentarily reduced, and that has no impact on performance.

However, before packaging up the cam, make sure that both the lobe and lifter surfaces are clean. In an effort to save time, runout and cam timing are often checked after moly assembly lube has been applied to the cam and lifters. This lubricant contains small flecks of moly which will "bump" the indicator needle when they pass between the lobe and lifter. These moly flecks may make it appear as though runout is excessive, and may also alter timing indications by one or two degrees.

Advance vs. Retard—Even if a camshaft checks right on the numbers, it may be desirable to advance or retard it to enhance certain performance characteristics. Advancing a camshaft increases low-speed and mid-range torque at the expense of top-end horsepower; retarding has the opposite effect. Translated into drag strip performance, advancing the cam tends to improve elapsed times while retarding cam timing tends to boost top speed. In an oval track engine, a cam is advanced to make a car come off the corners harder and it's retarded to produce higher straightaway speeds. However, before cam phasing is changed, baseline performance should be established with the cam installed "on the numbers."

Intake Centerline—Which brings up another point—checking cam phasing according to intake centerline. Intake centerline is defined as the point at which the intake lobe reaches maximum lift. Typically, high performance and racing camshafts reach intake maximum lift at 100° to 114° ATDC. The shortcoming of using the centerline method is that actual opening and closing points are not checked, so machining inaccuracies go undetected. However, some engine builders use intake centerline as a reference point when altering camshaft phasing to shift an engine's power curve.

By way of example, many oval track engine builders have found that an intake centerline of 102° puts the torque curve where they want it. Consequently, whenever they install a new camshaft, they degree it in using opening and closing points at .050" lift, then they adjust phasing as necessary to establish a 102° centerline. This way, performance can be accurately compared with that of existing camshafts. While intake centerline is useful for comparisons, it should never be used to establish camshaft position. Whenever the opening and closing points as listed on the cam spec card are not used for the degreeing-in operation, cam phasing probably may not be accurate. Many cams have asymmetric lobes which means that actual centerline of the lobe is not at the point of maximum lift. While these two points may only be separated by a degree or two, that's enough to affect phasing.

With a symmetrical lobe, one side is the mirror image of the other. Intake centerline can be calculated by dividing intake duration in half and subtracting the intake opening figure. If a symmetrical intake lobe has a net duration of 234°, and the intake valve opens at 10° BTDC, then its intake centerline is 107° (234/2=117-10=107).

Suppose a cam's maximum lift point cannot be calculated and consequently can't be checked? Using the calculated intake centerline to determine camshaft phasing will most likely result in improper cam phasing.

In cases where it is useful to know the intake centerline, the cam should always be degreed-in using the opening and closing points at .050" lift. Then intake maximum lift point can be calculated (intake duration/2-intake opening), or the information can simply be read on the specification card that accompanies every cam.

A Word About Quality

The technology of both camshaft design and manufacturing had improved in quantum leaps over the past few decades. However, mistakes are still a part of life and shoddy workmanship can rear its ugly head at any time. It's for precisely these reasons that sharp engine builders check every component used in assembling an engine—even camshafts.

While absolute perfection isn't essential in a street camshaft, it's imperative in a race camshaft. The difference in acceptable quality latitude is due to operating environment. Junk parts don't belong in a street engine any more than they do in a race engine. But the latter operates primarily at maximum load and maximum rpm; the former loafs for most of its life and rarely reaches a camshaft's maximum rpm potential. Valvetrain stress is understandably much greater in a race engine hence the need for the absolute highest quality.

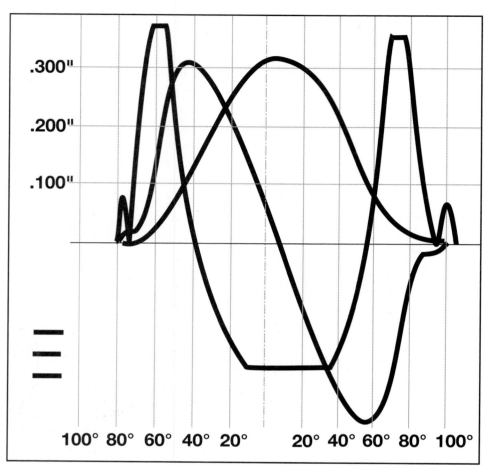

.300"

.200"

.100"

100° 80° 60° 40° 20°   20° 40° 60° 80° 100°

These lift, velocity and acceleration curves are representative of a typical high performance hydraulic lifter cam. In this case, the curves were generated by Chevrolet part number 3863151—the camshaft used in 350-horsepower 327 cid engines. The steeper the lift slope, the more aggressive the cam. A lift curve is only one aspect of lobe design. Note that velocity (the rate at which the lifter is raised and lowered) is greatest just after the lifter is raised off, and just before it's lowered back onto, the base circle. Acceleration curves say a lot about a camshaft's reliability and maximum rpm potential. Ideally, an acceleration curve should be smooth with rounded peaks, which in this case, it isn't. Harvey Crane was able to redesign this particular camshaft so that the acceleration curve was considerably smoothed out, providing maximum power potential throughout the rpm scale. This graph was created by Harvey Crane using special analytical software developed by Crane CamDesign, Inc. (904/760-4418). A Cam Doctor was used to acquire the data used to plot the curve.

Harvey Crane is adamant about the need to check camshaft accuracy before installation. He states:

"Anybody who assembles more than four or five engines a year should have a Cam Doctor, a cam-checking device made by Quadrant Scientific. An engine builder measures everything else when he blueprints an engine, yet most never look twice at the cam. They just take the manufacturer's word that it's all right. But I can tell you, the wrinkles in a camshaft can create a lot of problems in race engines. By wrinkles, I mean inaccuracy in machining. Sometimes you can even see small flats running across the lobe. You can see them when you hold a camshaft parallel with a fluorescent light bulb. Flat-tappet cams can only be inspected

after they've been run because the black of the parkerizing hides these imperfections. If you can see any flats on a lobe, don't even bother installing the cam. Send it back to the manufacturer. It may make good power, but it will eat up valve springs."

The subject of camshaft quality is an interesting one because many people think it relates directly to power output, but it doesn't. Many times a poor quality camshaft will produce more horsepower than one that passes a much more stringent quality check. But while it's making horsepower, it's also destroying valvetrain parts. When a camshaft of substandard quality is installed in a race engine, the gamble is whether the engine will last long enough to finish the race. Over the years, engine builders have discovered that the old canard rings true, "You can't win if you don't finish."

With a street camshaft, quality translates to durability. Poor quality control results in camshafts that develop flat lobes, worn lifters and/or broken valve springs after just 10,000 to 20,000 miles of driving. Dealing with a reputable cam company is one way of minimizing the possibilities of being the victim of inferior camshaft quality. Degree-checking a cam, not only for lift and duration, but for base circle runout, is another.

If questions still remain after checking a cam with a dial indicator and degree wheel, find someone with a Cam Doctor. You should be absolutely certain of camshaft quality prior to assembling an engine for the final time. ∎

7

VALVETRAIN

If you were standing on a solid floor, trying to hold a small piece of plywood firmly against the ceiling with a broom handle, you probably wouldn't have much trouble. Plywood isn't particularly heavy, so it doesn't take much strength to hold it in place for a few minutes. But suppose that instead of being solid, the floor was rolling like ocean waves. It would be almost impossible to hold the plywood firmly in place.

A valvetrain also needs stability if it is to allow the camshaft to produce maximum performance. Aside from performance considerations, an unstable valvetrain can cause any number of engine maladies, many of which are difficult to diagnose. The primary reason that camshaft manufacturers advise use of specific lifters, pushrods, valve springs and retainers is that they're attempting to ensure some degree of valvetrain stability. Parts from other manufacturers may work as well—or better—but they may also be inappropriate. If you do use all the suggested related components, troubleshooting is quite a bit easier when there is a problem, because the performance characteristics of those components is a known quantity to the cam manufacturer. On the other hand, if you've got a cam from one company, lifters from another, springs from a third and retainers from a fourth, how is the cam manufacturer to know whether everything fits as it

One of the reasons that late-model small-block engines produce so much horsepower while meeting strict exhaust emissions requirements is the use of hydraulic roller lifters. Even with identical cam profiles, roller lifters offer a measurable horsepower increase over standard lifters.

should and whether mating parts are compatible?

HYDRAULIC LIFTERS

Hydraulic lifters were originally designed in the Twenties as a means of eliminating the periodic valve lash adjustments that mechanical tappets require. With mechanical or "solid" lifters, some amount of clearance must exist in the valvetrain to accommodate the expansion and contraction that occurs as the engine heats and cools. This lash must be taken up gradually to avoid hammering the valvetrain, so even though only a few thousandths of an

inch clearance are required to handle expansion and contraction, valve lash typically ranges from .014" to .030", depending on cam design.

Components

Hydraulic lifters eliminate the need for valvetrain clearance because they automatically take up any clearance introduced into the system. Inside the body of a hydraulic lifter is a plunger that rests on a reservoir of oil. Engine oil is continually pumped through this reservoir, which is contained in a space called a compression chamber. When the lifter is on the cam's base circle, a check valve at the plunger's bottom is open so oil can flow into or

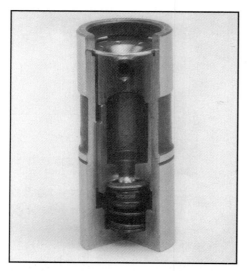

A hydraulic lifter is the most precisely fitted component in an engine. Plunger-to-shell clearance is critical because it effects leak-down rate. Several different types of check valves are used and each lifter manufacturer naturally claims that its mechanism is superior to others. In real life, performance is pretty much equal from one brand to another, provided the lifter is a quality part.

out of the compression chamber. When the cam lobe pushes the lifter up against the pushrod, the check valve closes, trapping oil in the compression chamber. Since oil is not compressible, upward movement of the lifter body is transmitted to the plunger, which raises the pushrod and rocker arm, thereby opening the valve (in the cylinder head). When the lifter returns to the cam's base circle, the check valve beneath the plunger opens again, allowing oil volume in the compression chamber to adjust to compensate for any clearance or excessive plunger preload that may have been introduced into the valvetrain.

Lifter Preload

As a general rule, hydraulic lifter preload should be set so that the plunger is .020" to .045" below the snap ring. This will allow the lifter to

compensate for normal valvetrain clearance and will not restrict rpm potential. The required amount of preload can be obtained by simply adjusting the rocker arm nuts 1/2 to 3/4 of a turn after all clearance has been taken up. This can be done most effectively by backing the rocker nuts off until there's measurable clearance between the rocker arm and valve stem. Then the nut should be slowly tightened while you twirl the pushrod between your fingers. Once all the clearance is taken up, the pushrod will become difficult to turn. At this point, an additional 1/2 to 3/4 of a turn of the rocker adjusting nut will set lifter preload correctly. Obviously, the lifters must be on the cam's base circle when this is done, so it's common practice to first warm the engine, then shut it off and spin the crankshaft until cylinder number one is at Top Dead Center on the power stroke. Lifter preload for cylinder one can then be adjusted, and the crankshaft rotated another 90° so the rockers for the next cylinder in the firing order can be adjusted. Proceed through the 1-8-4-3-6-5-7-2 firing order, rotating the crank 90° after each pair of rockers is adjusted, until all have been set.

On high performance and race engines equipped with hydraulic lifters, it is a common practice to set the rocker adjusting nuts 1/8 turn or less down from zero lash. This positions the hydraulic lifter plunger up against, or just a few thousandths of an inch below, the snap ring. With this setting, the hydraulic lifter is effectively functioning as a mechanical tappet because it can't take up any clearance in the valvetrain. On the negative side, running the plunger up against the snap ring is risky because the snap

ring may pop out and go flitting about the engine. If it does, serious engine damage is the typical result.

The practice of backing off the rocker nuts so that the plunger is up against the snap ring became popular in the Sixties when musclecar owners attempted to increase rpm potential with stock components. In some engines, valve spring pressure isn't sufficient to control the hydraulic pressure pushing against the plunger. At engine speeds above 5000 rpm, the hydraulic force is strong enough to overcome the valve spring pressure which normally prevents the plunger from moving upward to any great degree (unless there's clearance to be taken up). With the plunger "pumped up" (raised) from its normal position, the valve cannot close fully and the engine appears to be in valve float. Backing the rockers off so that the plunger is close to or against the snap ring eliminates lifter pump-up because the plunger can't move far enough to interfere with valve closure when hydraulic force overcomes valve spring pressure.

Lifter Pump-Up—As noted, this is the hydraulic lifter equivalent of mechanical lifter valve float. When an engine goes into valve float, the hydraulic lifter, which is self-adjusting, tries to compensate. A hydraulic lifter "sees" the extra clearance caused by the lifter bouncing on the flank, so it attempts to take some clearance out of the system. When it does that, it never allows the valve to close fully, because it takes up the clearance on the closing side of the cam lobe. Since the valves don't completely seat, the engine loses its compression (cylinder pressure) because pressure blows off through the open valve. Without

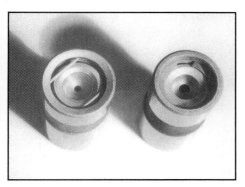

The lifter on the right is an "anti-pump-up" model, the one on the left is a plain vanilla version. About the only difference is the retaining ring and the depth of its groove in the lifter body.

compression, the engine can't make any power, so it effectively shuts itself off. The same thing happens with a mechanical lifter cam when it goes into valve float, only instead of the hydraulic plunger preventing the valve from seating, the lifter itself, being up off the cam lobe, is the culprit.

Anti-Pump-Up Lifters

What about anti-pump-up lifters? Actually, there's no such thing. The one true anti-pump-up design, which had a relief hole in the side of the lifter body to bleed off excess pressure, has never been available. The only difference between standard and anti-pump-up lifters is retaining ring style and sometimes placement.

Some anti-pump-up lifters are nothing more than standard lifters with a stronger retaining ring. In fact, one manufacturer made absolutely no changes in lifter design, but simply began calling its standard lifters "anti-pump-up" as a means of increasing sales and price. The "anti-pump-up" label is supposedly justified by the stronger clip, which has a better chance of staying in place if the lifters are adjusted so that the plunger rides up against the clip.

Other brands of anti-pump-up lifters have the retaining ring groove machined lower in the lifter body so the plunger's up and down movement is restricted. It can still pump up, but the plunger just can't move as far as it could if the ring were in the standard location. This is all well and good, but what usually goes unnoticed is that the revised plunger position calls for a longer pushrod. According to Steve Demos of Engine Systems:

"In the anti-pump-up lifters, the pushrod seat is .080" to .100" lower than in a standard lifter and that really messes up the valvetrain geometry if you don't use the correct length pushrods. If you just switch lifters and don't change anything else, the rocker won't be in the right position and you'll have problems with valve guide wear and parts breakage. I've had customers tell me that their engines don't run as well with anti-pump-up lifters. That's because they didn't use the right pushrods, so the rockers aren't positioned right, which means you don't get full lift out of the cam. But just sticking in a set of .100" long pushrods isn't the answer because that doesn't take things like block and head machining into account. Don't assume anything. Check for the exact pushrod length you need."

Selection

Surprisingly, all hydraulic lifters are manufactured by a handful of companies. While there are different styles of check valves, virtually all are widely available. So in spite of claims to the contrary, hydraulic lifter performance is pretty much the same regardless of design.

While it's hard to go wrong with brand-name lifters, some off-brands may be a teapot of trouble about to boil. Some companies purchase used lifters, remachine the bottoms and sell them as if they were new lifters. But if you buy brand-name lifters from a reputable supplier, it's hard to go wrong because hydraulic lifters are assembled to the highest precision standards of any engine component. To assure that leak-down rate (the rate at which oil bleeds out of the lifter between the plunger and shell) is within specification, the clearance between the plunger and lifter body is held to .0003". Both the lifter and plunger are machined to a tolerance of .001", then they are graded for size and separated into different categories. The plungers are also graded for size and then matched to an appropriate lifter body to obtain the nominal .0003" clearance. Tolerances are held to 200 millionths of an inch to assure that clearances are exact. If they aren't, the leak-down rate will be excessive and will result in valvetrain chatter.

Variable Duration Lifters

Leak-down is precisely what happens with so-called variable duration lifters. Either by virtue of increased plunger-to-lifter body clearance, or through a groove machined in the side of the plunger, variable duration lifters allow a higher volume of oil to leak out when the lifter is raised by the cam. As a result, the plunger doesn't rise with the lifter body (because the oil that would normally be trapped in the compression chamber is allowed to leak out). Ultimately, the bottom of the lifter contacts the plunger and that

Variable duration lifters look just like standard lifters externally. However, they shorten cam duration at low speeds because their relatively high leak-down rate allows the plunger to collapse. At higher speeds, oil flow is sufficient to overcome the leak-down so the plunger remains in its normal position. In theory, variable duration lifters are ideal for hot street engines; in practice, they're a band-aid for an improperly selected camshaft. Some brands appear to lead to premature valvetrain failure.

Roller lifters not only reduce friction, they allow for much more aggressive lift rates. Some type of link bar is required to prevent the lifters from rotating in their bores. The lifters shown are manufactured by Competition Cams.

causes it to rise. This lost motion (when the lifter body is rising, but the plunger isn't) delays valve opening so cam duration is effectively shortened, but lift is also reduced. At higher engine speeds, there isn't enough time for the oil to bleed off, so valve duration returns to its normal specification.

The concept of a variable duration lifter is appealing because in theory, it shortens duration at low engine speeds which increases idle vacuum and low-speed torque, without compromising top-end horsepower. And true enough, depending on design, a variable duration lifter will add from one to two inches of manifold vacuum at idle, but not without exacting a toll on component life. According to Paul "Scooter" Brothers of Competition Cams:

"We sell two different types of variable duration lifters. They do have their place—like in a race engine that must have a certain amount of idle vacuum to meet the rules—but they make more noise than a standard lifter. That noise means that two parts in the valvetrain are banging together that shouldn't be. I don't know that it would ever create a problem, but it sure doesn't seem like the best situation. Variable duration lifters won't turn the wrong cam into the right one and they don't deliver big power gains. However, they do help in some situations, but you have to be aware of what causes them to make noise; it's because there's some slack in the system that shouldn't be there, and two pieces of metal are banging together and shouldn't be."

Irrespective of lifter type, the best way to control pump-up is to switch to stiffer valve springs. This allows the establishment of proper lifter preload and minimizes the risk of engine damage caused by a snap ring that has been popped out of its groove and sent on a tour. Of course, if an engine is to regularly visit the other side of 7000 rpm, mechanical or roller

lifters are the logical choice. The only real drawback to these types of lifters is the need for periodic adjustment.

Hydraulic Roller Lifters

Hydraulic roller lifters are another option. Beginning in 1987, some small blocks were factory-equipped with hydraulic roller camshafts. The Chevrolet lifters differ significantly from aftermarket versions; they're also .63" taller than a conventional hydraulic lifter. Consequently, .63" shorter pushrods are used. Blocks designed to house original equipment hydraulic roller cams have taller lifter bores to accommodate the additional length of the factory roller tappets and contain a provision for a thrust plate (to limit forward movement of the camshaft).

Chevrolet hydraulic roller lifters cannot be used in a "non-roller lifter" block because the lifter bores aren't tall enough and there are no provisions for installing the lifter guide retainer. Several camshaft manufacturers offer kits for installing their hydraulic roller cams and lifters in blocks designed for flat-tappet camshafts.

Like other manufacturers, Chevrolet began installing hydraulic roller camshafts in production engines because they reduce internal friction, which translates into improved fuel economy. However, production hydraulic roller cam profiles do not have more aggressive timing or lift rates, so the only performance gains are a result of reduced friction. As might be expected, high performance camshaft manufacturers have addressed the situation and several companies offer replacement cams that deliver a significant horsepower increase. Many of these cams have

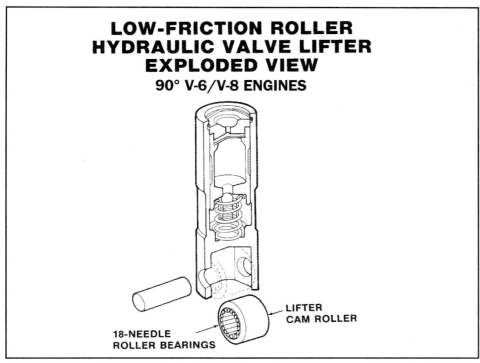

LOW-FRICTION ROLLER HYDRAULIC VALVE LIFTER EXPLODED VIEW
90° V-6/V-8 ENGINES

18-NEEDLE ROLLER BEARINGS — LIFTER CAM ROLLER

Use of hydraulic roller lifters in production small blocks began with the 1987 model lifters began with the 1987 model year. These lifters aren't compatible with cylinder blocks not originally equipped with hydraulic rollers.

Original equipment hydraulic roller lifters are designed with cost as a primary consideration. This method of retention (arrow) allows use of lifters that don't have to be fitted in pairs and can't be installed backwards–ideal for use on an assembly line.

been granted exemptions by the California Air Resources Board and are legal for installation in specific late-model vehicles in all 50 states. Check with the individual cam manufacturer for specific details regarding emissions-legal camshafts.

MECHANICAL TAPPETS

There isn't much to be said about mechanical tappets except that the standard caveats apply regarding the questionable quality of off-brand parts. However, it should be noted that oil flow to the rocker arms is affected by the lifter, and small-block Chevys turning high rpm have a tendency to flood the upper end with oil. One means of controlling the flow of oil up the pushrod is to install edge orifice lifters (available from some camshaft manufacturers or Chevrolet

part no. 5231585). With this style of lifter, oil is metered to the engine's top end through the clearance between the lifter body and its bore. Compared to a standard "piddle valve" lifter (carried by all high performance cam manufacturers and aftermarket suppliers, or Chevrolet part no. 5232695) the edge orifice lifter restricts oil flow by up to 20%. Edge orifice lifters are designed for use only on engines equipped with roller rocker arms; the restricted oil flow can cause galling when stock-type, stamped-steel rockers are used.

Restrictor Plugs—While edge orifice lifters unquestionably restrict the flow of oil to the "attic," (the rocker arm area) they don't restrict it enough for some applications. Depending on the intended use of an engine and the individual engine builder's preference, restrictor plugs

may be installed rather than edge orifice lifters. These plugs, which typically contain a .050 to .080" metering orifice, screw into the feed holes located in the rear cam bearing bore. Several companies, including B&B Performance and Moroso, offer restrictor kits with .080" metering holes. Obviously, restricting top-end oil flow is also a common practice when roller lifters are used. However, note that some roller lifters have built-in flow restrictions so installing restrictors in the block may be redundant and may limit oil flow too much.

Cautions—The degree of oil restriction to the top end is a function of oiling system flow volume and engine speed. The high rpm at which race engines operate in normal operation assures that sufficient lubrication will reach the rocker arms. However, in a street engine, installing oil restrictors or edge orifice lifters is like planting a time bomb. A street engine spends too much time idling and running at low speed to provide

Before installing a flat-tappet hydraulic or mechanical lifter, it's imperative that the bottom be coated with the same lubricant that's used on the cam lobes. Lack of adequate lubrication during break-in is the most common cause of cam and lifter failure.

adequate top-end lubrication.

Another caveat: When installing restrictors, check your silicone at the door. Some people think that an engine can't possibly be assembled correctly unless two or three tubes of silicone sealant are used. Then, when a gob of the stuff breaks off and closes up an oil passage, they wonder why they have an oiling system failure. It doesn't take much silicone to completely shut off an .080" oil metering restriction.

Mushroom Tappets

A unique type of mechanical lifter is known as the mushroom tappet, which has a standard sized (.842" dia.) body and a larger base or foot (.960" dia.). This type of lifter allows the use of specially designed race camshafts which move the valves at much higher opening and closing velocities (for increased horsepower) than would be possible with a standard .842" diameter lifter. Mushroom tappets are intended for use in racing categories that prohibit the use of roller tappets. Special block machining is required for mushroom

tappet installation.

Mushroom tappets are designed to circumvent the limitations placed on cam lobe design by the stock .842" diameter tappet. Lobes with the extremely high opening velocities required for maximum horsepower border on a condition known as edge riding; sometimes they go over the border. When a lifter is edge riding, it contacts the cam lobe at its sharp edge, rather than on its base—a situation that accelerates cam and lifter wear and instigates instability in the valvetrain. In some racing categories, mushroom lifters are illegal, but the lifter bores in Chevrolet blocks can be modified to accept the same .875" diameter lifters found in Ford engines. Installation of .875" or mushroom lifters is advantageous only if a camshaft designed to take advantage of the increased lifter diameter is also installed.

Roller Tappets

Viewed from afar, all roller tappets are pretty much the same. However, each manufacturer will be quick to point out the superiority of its

particular design. When examined up close, significant differences can be seen between various brands of lifters, but oddly enough, virtually all have been used successfully in a variety of race engines. Roller lifters differ primarily in their oil metering, link bar design and strength, needle bearing and axle diameter, overall weight and quality. Most of the larger high performance cam manufacturers produce their own roller lifters, so differences from one manufacturer to another can be significant. However, all of the better brands offer excellent strength and durability. As previously noted, some brands of roller lifters have built in oil restrictions, so check with the manufacturer to see if restrictor plugs will create problems.

ROCKER ARMS

When Chevrolet engineers unveiled the small-block V-8 engine at the beginning of the 1955 model year, many automotive "experts" criticized the individual stud-mounted rocker arm arrangement. At the time, virtually all rocker arms were shaft mounted and the small block's rocker

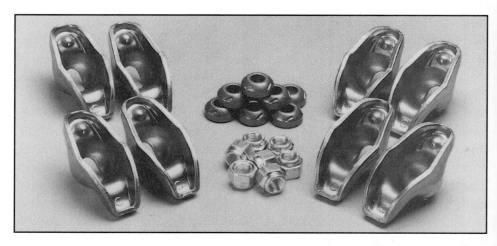

Stock type stamped steel rockers are available from several aftermarket manufacturers. Some offer longer slots to accommodate high lift cams. High ratio 1.6:1 rockers are also available. For race applications where stamped steel rockers are required, avoid the grooved pivot balls.

Several types of stock rocker arms have been manufactured by Chevrolet over the years. Those that are suitable for high performance applications have an identification letter, in this case an "O", near the tip.

Installation of aluminum roller tip rockers is standard procedure on race engines as stock-type rockers can't handle super high spring pressures. Contrary to popular belief, the roller trunions (pivots), and not the tips, are the primary advantage of roller rockers.

mounting appeared to lack the strength and stability to survive. Not only has it survived, it has prospered, as stud-mounted rocker arms have become the norm for all modern overhead valve engines. Without question, shaft-mounted rocker arms offer the ultimate in strength and stability, but they amount to overkill for all high performance and most race engines.

Stock Pivot Balls—One of the liabilities of stock stamped-steel rockers is their tendency to gall or split in the vicinity of the pivot ball when subjected to high rpm operation and extreme valve spring pressure loads. When an engine is built for a class that requires use of stock-type rocker arms, component selection is critical. Obviously, the rockers themselves must be checked for ratio accuracy, but perhaps of even greater importance is the selection of pivot balls. The most commonly found type of pivot ball has several grooves machined into the surface that contacts the rocker. In theory, these grooves are supposed to increase the

flow of oil between the ball and rocker. However, in virtually all grooved pivot balls, the grooves do not extend up to the top, so oil has just as much trouble getting between the ball and rocker as it would had no grooves been cut. Although the grooves can act as small oil reservoirs, any advantage this might offer is more than negated by the reduction in surface area. Consequently, for maximum effort race applications, a non-grooved rocker ball is preferable. Note that grooved rocker balls have proven to be a problem only when extremely high valve spring pressures are used.

Another limiting factor is the length of the slot through which the stud passes—it isn't long enough to accommodate the lift of many high performance camshafts. However, stock rockers are most commonly (and erroneously) faulted for their non-rolling tip. While the plain surface would appear to create high friction with the valve tip, it really doesn't. The radius of the contact pad is so large, the area is so well

lubricated and the amount of sliding movement is so small that friction between the rocker and valve tip is really insignificant. It's far greater between the rocker and the pivot ball.

Roller Rocker Arms

Aluminum and steel roller rocker arms, with needle bearings on the pivot trunions and at the tips, unquestionably reduce friction, but their primary advantages are strength and stability. Roller rockers are designed for high performance applications, so they obviously also have more than adequate slot length to accommodate the highest of cam lifts. Another advantage is that roller rockers for small-block Chevys are available for both 3/8" and 7/16" rocker studs. Any engine that's fitted with a healthy performance cam and stiff valve springs benefits from 7/16" rocker studs because the standard 3/8" studs flex too much. For race engines, a stud girdle is usually added to reduce stud flex to an absolute minimum. Several stud girdle designs exist and all do the same thing. Specifically, they reduce stud

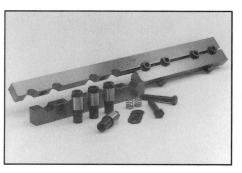

Individual rocker studs do move around, especially when super stiff springs are holding the valves closed. A stud girdle ties all the studs together which resists movement. Reduced stud deflection translates to more lift at the valve.

Rockers manufactured of stainless steel or chrome-moly are frequently used in endurance applications because they're stronger than aluminum and don't fatigue. Higher than stock, as well as lower than stock ratios are available. The latter types are used for cam break-in when super high pressure valve springs are installed.

ROCKER TIP-TO-STEM GEOMETRY

Zero Lift

Half Lift

Full Lift

Views showing roller to valve tip contact

With proper valvetrain geometry, the rocker should contact the valve stem as shown throughout its range of travel.

deflection by tying all the rocker studs on a cylinder head together. The primary differences in the various designs have to do with installation and ease of use. The latter consideration is pretty much a matter of opinion.

About the only drawback to roller rockers is expense—they cost three to five times as much as stock-type rocker arms. That's a moot point with a race engine (and some killer street engines) because rocker cost has no bearing on choice; cam lift and valve spring load demand the use of roller rockers. But for oval track racing in classes with rules specifying stock-type rockers, roller rockers aren't an option; for most high-performance street small blocks, they're not required. There's nothing wrong with installing roller rockers on a street engine, and contrary to some claims, durability is not a problem. However, some engine builders feel that aluminum's tendency to work-harden will lead to breakage and specify stainless-steel rockers for all endurance-type engines. On the other hand, an aluminum rocker will typically wear out its trunion bearings before the rocker body fails. There's no question that stainless steel is more durable, but it's also more expensive, so stainless rockers are typically used only in applications where spring loads and rpm are extreme.

Pushrod Seats—One of the methods that engine builders have used to extract unbelievable horsepower from small-block Chevy engines is to widen the intake port dramatically. Since the smallest "window" in the port is in the area that bends around the pushrod, extensive widening means that material has to be added to the outside of the port to prevent grinding completely through the port wall. As a result, the pushrod has to be angled away from the port and that creates a need for rocker arms with offset pushrod seats. Typically, the seats are offset between .050" and .225". Understandably, offsetting the pushrod seats creates a pretty healthy side load. The best way to handle these is with a shaft-mounted rocker such as those produced by Jesel. Rather than a single shaft for each head, most of the shaft-mounted rocker systems employ four shafts per head, which eases installation and maintenance chores.

Rocker Ratios

While stock-type rockers are only a fraction of the cost of exotic race pieces, you don't always get what you pay for; many stamped steel rockers don't deliver the proper ratio. Rather than the specified 1.5:1 ratio, some of these rockers only muster something in the area of 1.4:1 ratio. The only way to tell is by individually testing each rocker arm, which is precisely what racers do when required to use stock-type rockers. This type of diligent checking isn't necessary for street engines as the loss of a few horsepower due to reduced valve lift isn't critical. But for maximum performance, you need all the lift a cam can deliver, so the best procedure is to purchase name-brand rockers from a reputable supplier. Many camshaft manufacturers offer such rockers (with extra long slots) at surprisingly reasonable prices. Some companies also offer stamped steel rockers with a 1.6:1 ratio—an easy, inexpensive way to increase valve lift. Since these rockers look almost identical to those with a standard

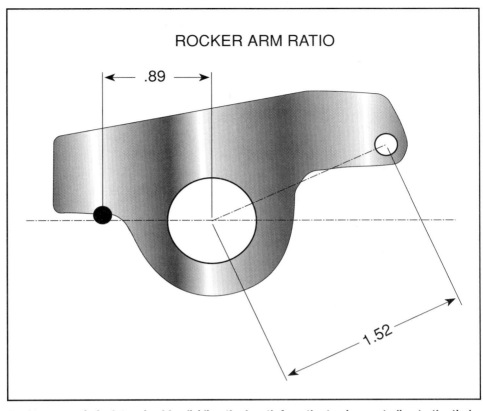

Rocker arm ratio is determined by dividing the length from the trunion centerline to the tip by the length from the trunion to the pushrod seat. Computed ratio will usually be higher than advertised ratio because compliance in the valvetrain reduces the rocker's effect.

1.5:1 ratio, they'll also slide by many tech inspectors.

Compromises—Rocker arm ratio is therefore a significant factor that influences valvetrain stability. It is also another area of compromise. Increasing rocker arm ratio increases power potential, but it does so at the expense of valvetrain durability. In most applications, the trade-off in favor of power is a good one because the increased valvetrain stresses aren't large enough to make much of a difference in durability. However, for some types of endurance racing, the possibility of premature valve spring failure cannot be tolerated, so rocker arm ratios are sometimes on the conservative side. In fact, some engine builders use ratios lower than stock. It's quite common for the big-

block Chevrolets found in off-shore race boats to be equipped with 1.6:1 rather than the stock 1.7:1 rocker arms. In such an instance, a bit of horsepower is traded for increased valve spring life.

Increasing Ratios—On the other hand, most drag race and oval track engine builders have developed their combinations around higher-than-stock rocker arm ratios and have experienced no problems. However, there's rarely a problem when an engine is assembled with higher-than-stock ratio rockers, because the valvetrain is thoroughly checked before the engine is ever fired. Trouble doesn't usually start brewing until an engine is already running and in a vehicle, and a switch is made to higher ratio rockers. The effect of

One way to significantly increase valve lift without changing cams is to install 1.8:1 or 1.9:1 rocker arms. These shaft mounted high ratio rockers are hard core race parts, but they've also been used on street engines for a dramatic (and expensive) performance increase.

rocker ratio on the valvetrain is the same as when one cam is swapped for another with greater lift. The valve spring stresses and the stresses coming back down the pushrods are raised.

Unfortunately, when rocker changes are made on a running engine, checks for coil bind, retainer-to-seal interference and piston-to-valve interference aren't done and that's what causes problems and failures.

Advantages—Significant horsepower gains can be achieved through experimenting with the rocker arm ratio because that's the only way you can raise or lower the lift—aside from switching camshafts. A change in rocker arm ratio also impacts effective duration—it makes the engine think the cam is more radical because the valve is opening more quickly. But the ratio that's right for one engine won't necessarily be right for another. All you can do is give the engine what it wants, and that's done by trying different ratios and seeing which one works out best. It may be "trick" to run 1.6:1 ratio rockers on a small block, but the

engine just may run best with a stock ratio. Much depends upon the aggressiveness of the camshaft. In a street engine, high ratio rockers typically pay a better dividend when used in conjunction with a stock-type cam; most high performance cams move the valve fast enough and lift it high enough that the increase in ratio doesn't have as much of an effect on airflow because the ports and manifold runners are a limiting factor. On a race engine, high-ratio rockers frequently bump up horsepower because the ports have enough airflow capacity to take advantage of the increased valve lift. Trial and error testing is the only way to be certain, but every time you change the engine combination, your trials and errors start all over again. While such experimentation is warranted in a race engine, the horsepower gains don't justify the expense for most street applications.

VALVE SPRINGS

Although the valve springs play the most significant role in maintaining

stability at high engine speeds, coordination of all valvetrain components serves to reduce the potential for problems. To assure valvetrain stability, you have to begin with adequate spring pressure, a consideration that's frequently overlooked when a high performance camshaft is installed in a stock or slightly modified engine. Stock valve springs are designed to handle the loads imposed by a mild camshaft rotating at relatively low engine speeds. Although some very mild high performance camshafts are compatible with stock valve springs, stiffer springs are generally required if the cam is to live up to its full potential. Not only does a performance cam open and close the valves more quickly, its power range is further up the rpm scale than its stock counterpart; higher engine speeds and higher opening and closing velocities require higher spring rates. But pressure isn't the only criteria that should be used when selecting valve springs.

Resonant Frequency

That point is well illustrated by a series of tests General Motors ran a number of years ago. A group of engineers testing a "Duntov 30-30" cam found that the engine's maximum rpm was lower than anticipated. To correct the situation, the engineers installed some "trick" valve springs from a Chevrolet "mystery" engine. But they still couldn't get the engine speed much over 7200 rpm. Then they installed a set of special aftermarket valve springs and very carefully set the open pressure exactly the same as it had been with the previous set of springs. The results were quite surprising—the engine ran

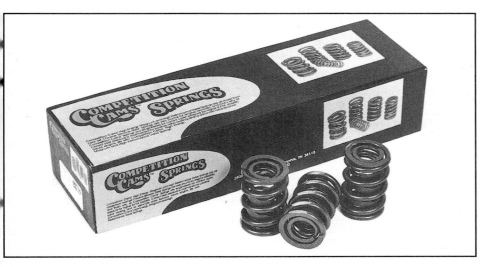

Valve springs play a critical role in determining horsepower, reliability and wear. Too much spring pressure and the cam and lifters wear out rapidly; too little pressure and rpm is limited, which affects horsepower. For best results, follow the camshaft manufacturer's recommendation for spring pressure and installed height.

1000 rpm faster. The reason? A change in the natural resonant frequency of the valve springs.

During engine operation, as speeds increase, the cam "excites" the valve springs as it spins through its opening/closing cycle. In turn, the springs begin to vibrate at a frequency determined by wire diameter and number of coils. When a spring's natural resonant frequency is reached, strange things begin to happen—most commonly, engine speed is abruptly limited because the vibrating springs can't control the valve.

Dual valve springs offer higher rpm potential because of their increased pressure, but that rpm potential is increased further if the inner and outer springs have vastly different natural resonant frequencies. On the other hand, if the inner and outer springs have a similar natural resonant frequency, much of the advantage is lost because both springs become "excited" and start to vibrate at approximately the same engine speed; the resulting spring surge will literally

shut off the engine. That was precisely what happened with the Chevrolet valve springs—they reached their natural resonant frequency at approximately 7200 rpm.

Aftermarket Springs—By comparison, the aftermarket springs were comprised of inner and outer coils with vastly different resonant frequencies; when one vibrated, the other was rock solid. Consequently, by specifically tailoring the resonant frequencies of the individual springs which comprise a dual or three-piece spring, vibration never becomes a built-in rpm limiter. Viewed from a different perspective, a single spring imposes a built-in terminal point for engine speed—once the spring's natural resonant frequency is reached, the engine will spin no faster. A damper helps the situation a bit, but dual springs are a better solution; dual springs with a damper are better yet. Although three springs offer maximum rpm potential, most engine builders stick with dual springs with a damper because they feel a three-

piece spring has too much coil-to-coil friction (which results in the generation of excessive heat). For more on dampers, see page 107.

You don't have to get up into race engine speeds to experience the effects of valve springs gone berserk. The typical passenger car engine will frequently run strongly to about 5000 rpm, but will run into trouble about 5200 rpm and absolutely cannot be coaxed up to 5300 rpm. The engine begins to miss because the springs are surging and not controlling valve movement.

Valve Float—Another rpm-limiting factor is valve float which occurs when spring pressure isn't sufficient to make the lifter follow the cam contour. What results is called separation—the lifter does not remain in continual contact with the cam lobe. Instead, it launches itself over the nose and bounces on the flank. Once valve float is reached, there is no way to further increase engine speed.

Rpm Upper Limits

Stories abound of Chevy small blocks equipped with hydraulic lifters turning 8000 rpm. In most cases, these tales should be taken with a grain of salt and about 2000 rpm. With an average high performance camshaft designed for 50,000 mile durability, and installed in conjunction with the valve springs recommended by the manufacturer, 5000 to 5500 rpm is a practical upper speed limit. Stiffer springs will increase the rpm ceiling, but to little purpose—the higher spring loads result in more rapid cam and lifter wear and most high performance hydraulic cams are designed to pump out peak horsepower at 5500 to 6000 rpm.

At first glance, these two springs may look identical. But if you're an experienced engine builder, the difference is obvious. On the left is a single spring with a damper. On the right is a dual spring. For a race engine, the best arrangement is a dual spring with a flat wire damper. All three pieces should fit together snugly.

Certainly, there are numerous grinds which will make peak power at 7000 to 7200 rpm, but these cams have too much duration to classify as legitimate street cams.

Consequently, for most street applications where engine speed rarely exceeds 5000 rpm, single valve springs with seat pressures of 85-100 psi are sufficient. For more aggressive engines and driving styles, stiffer dual valve springs will raise practical engine speed maximums to the 6500-7000 range. Some race engines, when equipped with a lightweight valvetrain, can be reliably turned as high as 8000 rpm with hydraulic lifters. But this type of rpm requires more than just stiff springs. Valvetrain weight has an effect and is especially critical on the valve side (as opposed to the pushrod side) of the rocker arm because of the multiplying effect of the rocker arm ratio—that means titanium valves and retainers.

High engine speeds are one thing, high power output at high engine speeds is another. If an engine is going to produce meaningful power at elevated rpm levels, the camshaft must have sufficient duration and lift and the induction and exhaust systems must be suitably tailored. It serves no real purpose to turn an engine 7500 rpm if its power peak is at 6000 rpm.

Coil Binding

Just as valve springs should be checked for coil bind whenever a cam with greater lift (than the one currently in place) is installed, they should also be checked when switching to higher ratio rockers. As a general practice, when an engine is being assembled, notes should be taken about where coil bind occurs. When this is done, it's possible to compute potential problems rather than waiting to be surprised after a cam or rocker arm change is made.

Checking Coil Bind—A common method of checking for this condition is to place a valve at maximum lift and attempt to insert a .060" diameter wire between the coils. That's an excellent means of getting into trouble. The fact that at least .060" of clearance exists between coils (with the valve at maximum lift) does not mean that the same amount of clearance exists between all coils in a spring. The coils near the top and bottom are closer together when the spring is in its extended state, and they're also closer together when a spring is compressed. So adequate clearance in between center coils doesn't guarantee that the end coils aren't in a bind. And it doesn't necessarily follow that the coils that reach coil bind are the ones that will break. In fact, springs usually break one coil up from the point of hardest coil bind. When a spring breaks right in the middle, it's usually the result of a bad piece of wire or extreme surging problems.

Avoiding Coil Bind—The best way to avoid coil bind is to follow the manufacturer's recommendations regarding installed height and valve spring part number to be used with a specific camshaft. As an example, one dual valve spring commonly used on high performance small blocks with a flat-tappet or hydraulic camshaft has a nominal seat pressure of 120 lbs. at an installed height of 1.875". Nominal open pressure is 395 lbs. at a compressed height of 1.175". That translates to .700" of valve lift (1.875-1.175 = .700"). This spring also has a nominal solid height of 1.080", which means that with an installed height of 1.875", the spring will be solidly in coil bind if valve lift is .795" or greater (1.875-1.080 = .795").

Installed Height—If you've been thinking that coil bind will only be a problem if valve lift approaches .795", you have been lured into the same trap that catches a surprising number of knowledgeable engine builders. The amount of lift that a spring will tolerate without reaching coil bind is partially dependent upon installed height. The spring described above is also suitable for roller cam applications, in which case the installed height is reduced to 1.750" as a means of increasing seat pressure to 165 lbs. With this setting, an open pressure of 426 lbs. is achieved at a height of 1.110". This translates into a valve lift of .640" (1.750-1.110 = .640".). The nominal solid height is still 1.080", which leaves only .030" between a maximum valve lift of .640" and coil bind at .670" Consequently, to retain the appropriate safety margin, this valve spring is recommended only for roller camshafts providing a maximum valve lift of .625" or less.

These unique conical springs from Competition Cams are wound to a 1.250" OD on the bottom and 1.460" on top. This design allows for higher spring pressures than would be obtainable with a standard 1.250" spring, but eliminates the need to machine the spring seats oversize.

But what happens when rocker arm ratio is bumped? If the .625" lift figure was achieved with a 1.5:1 rocker, a switch to 1.6:1 rockers will put lift at .667" and the springs in coil bind. Obviously, a change to 1.6:1 rockers necessitates installation of different valve springs that can tolerate higher valve lift.

Spring Options

Before venturing off into the land of high performance camshafts, it's advisable to take a long look at an engine's cylinder heads. All stock production small-block heads are machined for valve springs with an outside diameter of 1.250". That pretty much limits your choice to a single stock diameter spring. Most camshaft manufacturers offer a variety of special single springs that provide higher-than-stock pressures. But these springs are suitable only for relatively mild high performance cams. Once lift exceeds about .470" and/or duration exceeds 225° at .050" lift, dual springs are advisable. That means the spring pockets must be machined to a larger diameter because

dual springs usually have a 1.440 or 1.560" OD.

In most instances, the OD of the valve guide must also be machined (to a smaller diameter) to accept the high performance valve seals that are required to clear the ID of the inner valve springs. Machining tools that cut the spring seat OD and valve guide ID in a single operation are available from most high performance camshaft manufacturers. These machining operations must be done with the heads disassembled and removed from the engine, so plan ahead.

Dampers—Some, but not all dual valve springs contain a flat wire damper that fits between the inner and outer coil springs. This type of spring is definitely superior to dual springs with no damper. In all cases, it should require some amount of effort to pull the inner spring out. If you can set a dual spring on a bench, stick your finger into the inner spring, raise your hand and have only the inner spring come with it, the spring is either excessively worn, or wasn't properly assembled in the first place. Interference between the inner spring, damper and outer spring is essential to maximum pressure retention.

Unfortunately, when inner and outer springs rub against the damper, small particles of metal chip off and go traveling throughout the engine. Generally, the particles are too small to do much damage, but if nothing else, the thought of metal shavings working their way between critical surfaces is unsettling. To eliminate the problem, many race engine builders have valve springs coated with a dry film lubricant.

Although the amount of material chipped from the valve springs isn't

very much, it is a measurable amount. To demonstrate the point, one coating company tells its customers to weigh their uncoated springs before installation, and then again after the engine has run for a while. Each spring will actually lose a measurable amount of weight.

To date, most engine builders prefer dual springs with a damper to three-piece valve springs. The three-piece springs do not produce significantly more pressure than a top-of-the-line dual spring and seem to run hotter.

Spring Set-Up

Regardless of the type or brand of spring selected, the most important consideration is how well the springs are set up. Springs must be matched to the proper retainers so that excessive shimming isn't required to achieve the proper installed height. It's also advisable to ensure that the spring pocket OD matches the spring OD to prevent the springs from "walking." Spring cups can be installed if spring pocket OD is too large.

Retainers—For a time, aluminum retainers were all the rage for high performance street and race engines. But aluminum has a nasty habit of work-hardening and cracking, so aluminum retainers have gone on to the great recycling bin in the sky. Steel retainers are most commonly used, with titanium being the material of choice for killer drag race and oval track-type small blocks.

Except for some specially prepared race heads, small-block Chevy cylinder heads are machined to accept valves with 11/32". Consequently, the retainer/lock package must also be suited for an 11/32" stem. Most cam manufacturers offer several styles of

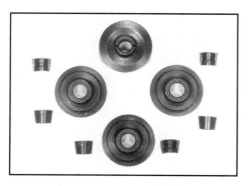

Retainers and locks (also called keepers and split keys) must be matched to each other with respect to angle. A 7° taper is used with stock and many high performance locks while a 10° taper is exclusively used in high performance and race engines. Either steel or titanium retainers and machined steel locks should be installed on a healthy small block. Avoid aluminum retainers at all costs.

retainers to allow for some latitude in installed height; a stepped retainer provides for more installed height than a flat version.

Another valve retainer variable is the lock angle. All stock-style retainers and many race types are machined for 7° locks; some race retainers accept 10° locks. Obviously, retainers must be installed with compatible locks to ensure that the valves stay in place.

Is a 10° retainer/lock combination better than a 7°? That depends upon who answers that question. Some engine builders swear by one style, others have the opposite opinion. For a street engine and most race engines, a 7° assembly, which is most economically priced, is more than adequate. Typically, 10° retainers and locks are used only in professional-caliber race engines.

Valve Locks—Also called split keys or keepers, valve locks fit between the retainer and valve stem and, as the name implies, lock the valves into place. The wedging action of the retainer clamps the lock against the valve stem; the small tang on the inside of the lock is for location purposes. While most locks utilize a standard tang location, some companies offer a selection with standard, .050" higher and .050" lower locations. This arrangement allows for relative quick and easy adjustment of installed height.

All top-quality valve locks are machined; the garden variety stock replacement types are stamped. Although failure of a stamped lock is rare, the cheapest insurance you can buy is to step up and buy machined locks. Most high performance engine builders make it a standard policy to use only machined locks—even on a stock rebuild. They feel that for the relatively small difference in price, it just doesn't pay to gamble.

PUSHRODS

Stock small-block Chevy pushrods measure 7.794" in overall length and 5/16" in diameter. However, you'll find that some manufacturers cite a slightly different length. Many race engines are equipped with longer or shorter pushrods, so some people have come to the mistaken conclusion that non-standard lengths offer some type of performance benefit. Nothing could be further from the truth. In fact, installing longer- or shorter-than-stock pushrods, when they are not required, can lead to serious engine problems.

Length

Legitimate use of special-length pushrods is called for only when standard length parts don't allow for proper valvetrain geometry. If longer-than-stock valves are installed (to achieve a desired spring installed height), if the block or heads have been milled excessively, if aftermarket cylinder heads or special rocker arms are installed, then standard-length pushrods are usually required.

Proper pushrod length places the rocker arm precisely in the middle of the valve stem when the valve is at half its total lift. If a cam provides total valve lift of .500", the rocker tip should be perfectly centered when the valve has been raised .250" off its seat. This should occur with very little movement across the face of the valve tip. Ideally, the rocker/valve stem contact point should be slightly to the intake manifold side of center when the valve is closed. As the valve opens, the contact point should move towards the exhaust manifold side of the tip and then should move back towards the intake manifold side as the valve reaches maximum lift. In all, there should only be a few thousandths of an inch of lateral movement. Excessive motion places a heavy side load on the valve stem and leads to rapid guide wear.

The quickest and easiest way to

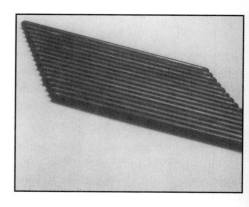

Race quality pushrods are available from a variety of manufacturers in just about any length desired. For maximum strength, these pushrods are manufactured of .083" wall seamless chrome-moly tubing. In addition to standard 5/16" diameter, 3/8" diameter pushrods are also available.

The quality of roller timing chain and sprocket sets varies dramatically depending upon the manufacturer. Many of the low-cost sets that are manufactured "offshore" have crank sprockets with keyways seemingly with blindfolded people. Name-brand sets are usually machined accurately, but if you degree-in a cam during installation, there's no doubt about valve timing accuracy. Some timing sets are supplied with a thrust washer to protect the block.

determine proper pushrod length is through use of an adjustable pushrod. Once in place, an adjustable pushrod is lengthened or shortened as required to center the rocker arm on the valve stem at half lift. Then its overall length is measured, giving you the proper pushrod length for the engine.

Most custom-length pushrods consist of a piece of steel tubing with hardened ends pressed into place. However, some manufacturers offer one-piece pushrods with wedged ends. These ends should be machined so that their radii match those of the pushrod seats in the lifter and rocker arm.

Heat-Treated Pushrods

Small-block Chevy engines not originally equipped with pushrod guideplates employ pushrods that are not heat treated; whenever guideplates are utilized, heat-treated pushrods are a necessity because the relatively soft

surface will wear very rapidly when it rubs against the heat-treated guideplate. Heat-treated pushrods are available from a variety of sources and in a variety of wall thicknesses, ranging from .049"-.083". Pushrods made from 3/8" diameter tubing are also available for race engines that require the ultimate in pushrod strength.

TIMING CHAIN & SPROCKETS

Much ado has been made of the difference between a silent type and roller timing chain. However, it has never been conclusively demonstrated that one type is clearly superior to the other. Since the beginning of time, Chevrolet has installed silent chains in all passenger car engines and roller chains in some truck engines. Both types of chains stretch and some engineers claim that a roller chain

actually stretches more than a silent type. The big advantage of a roller is that it will not jump a tooth when it gets old and feeble whereas a silent chain will.

The major objections to a stock chain and sprocket set are the aluminum gear/nylon tooth camshaft sprocket and 5/8" wide chain that has been in general use since 1967. While this piece of bean-counter engineering doesn't do much to inspire confidence, it is used in a surprising number of race engines. Some engine builders use a stock chain set because it's cheap and they simply replace it after every race or after a few races. Other people would rather pay a bit more and get a 3/4"-wide chain and sprocket set that will last longer. Whether that set is a high quality silent type with iron gears, or roller type is a matter of preference. There's even some controversy over whether a "true roller" is in fact superior to a plain roller.

Although LT1 engines are equipped with a link-type chain and sprocket assembly, the cam sprocket is considerably different than the one used on first-generation small blocks. A gear is machined on the back side of the sprocket to drive the water pump, And since the distributor is driven off the nose of the cam, the sprocket must accommodate the drive mechanism. In 1995 and later LT1, the distributor drive is simply a long camshaft dowel pin. Earlier versions of the engine used a coupler.

Roller Chains

All roller chains for small-block Chevys have two rows of rollers, but with some designs, the rollers or the pins on which they're mounted don't actually spin; by virtue of their being

When installing a crank sprocket with multiple keyways, be sure to match marks properly. With the appropriate keyway positioned at 1 o'clock, the matching mark by the tooth should be at 12 o'clock.

What do you do in this case? The rectangular mark (arrow), which usually corresponds to a 4° retarded position, is barely visible near the tooth. To ensure proper positioning in cases like this, double-check the mark by tracing an imaginary line from the keyway to gap between teeth directly above, then move left three teeth—and align that tooth with the mark on the cam gear.

A triangle mark (arrow) corresponds with a 4° advanced position. As with the other marks, when the appropriate keyway is at 1 o'clock, the proper tooth will be at 12 o'clock, three teeth to the left.

round, they will roll over the sprocket teeth, but their position within the chain is fixed. With a "true roller" design, the individual rollers and pins are free to spin, so there's less friction. On the other hand, the pins in some standard roller timing chains are larger than those found in a "true roller," so they're also stronger. Another consideration is roller construction—some are seamless, others are seamed. The seamless versions are kinder to the sprockets, which help longevity. On the other hand, being more expensive, they aren't as kind to your wallet.

Recommendations—All this background is informative, but you may not care. What you want to know is which timing chain to buy. The answer to that is—a good one. Keyway accuracy is of prime importance. Many off-brand (and some name-brand) chain sets are manufactured in countries that are known for low cost and equally low quality. Some of these sets have keyway locations that are off by up to

8°. So the best advice is to purchase a name-brand, top-quality chain set and to degree-in the camshaft in all cases.

Amongst high performance and race engine builders, the consensus of opinion is that the best type of chain for a particular engine depends upon the intended use of that engine. For a drag race engine that will be serviced regularly (the operative word here is regularly) a stock-type silent chain—with aluminum/nylon cam sprocket—is often the "hot tip." This type of chain and sprocket minimize the transfer of torsional shock loads from the crankshaft to the camshaft, which results in more consistent valve and ignition timing. In dyno testing, these benefits have surfaced in the form of a more efficient fuel curve. However, with this set-up, the chain and sprockets are changed every time the engine is torn down—and it's usually torn down after every race.

For street, bracket, oval track,

marine or any other use where regular and intense maintenance isn't planned, a roller chain should be used, because in general, it will provide superior long-term durability. Gary Grimes of Grimes Automotive Machine offers this piece of advice:

"Before you install the chain, put it in a pan of oil with a little moly lube mixed. Then heat it up to about 200° Fahrenheit for an hour or so. You'll be amazed at the difference that will make—it almost totally eliminates chain stretch. It may sound strange, but it works."

Torrington Bearing—Some chain sets are supplied with cam sprockets that are machined to accept a Torrington bearing. Rear thrust of the camshaft is controlled by the cam sprocket riding against the front of the block. This arrangement is satisfactory with standard flat-tappet cams, but with roller and mushroom-tappet cams, thrust control is more critical, so use of a bearing is advantageous. Forward thrust must also be controlled and most cam manufacturers offer a needle-bearing "anti-walk" cam button that fits in the center hole of the cam sprocket, between the cam and front cover.

The crown shape machined on the bottom of a flat tappet, combined with a taper .001" across the cam lobe (both are difficult to detect with the naked eye), essentially eliminates the need for forward thrust control. However, that's not the case with a cam designed for roller or mushroom tappets, hence the need to prevent the cam from "walking" fore and aft.

Regardless of cam type, a thrust bearing reduces friction and block wear so it's always worth the investment. If you can't find a chain and sprocket set that includes a bearing, make your own with one Torrington thrust bearing (part no. NTA-3244) sandwiched between two thrust plates (part no. TRA-3244). Competition Cams offers one-piece thrust bearings (the bearing and thrust plates are "encapsulated" to form a single piece) which are listed as part number 3100 TB. In all instances, the back side of the cam sprocket must be machined to accommodate bearing width.

Gear Drives

Of course, the best way to eliminate chain stretch (which is really more a case of chain and sprocket wear) is to eliminate the chain—which is what a gear drive does. Like any other piece of automotive equipment, gear drives have their positive and negative aspects. On the positive side, gear drives eliminate valve timing variations caused by chain stretch and flex (on a small block, each .020" of stretch retards the cam approximately

Standard fare on stock engines is a silent-type timing chain and sprocket set. Many racers use these because they're relatively inexpensive so they can be discarded as soon as chain stretch becomes evident.

1°). Gears also last almost indefinitely.

On the negative side, gear drives are expensive, noisy and require exacting tolerances to keep the gear teeth meshing properly. Any time a block is align-honed, the camshaft-to-crankshaft distance changes so some compensation must be made. Some gear drives incorporate an adjustable idler that can be positioned as required. Also note that drives using only two gears spin the camshaft in the reverse direction (compared to a chain drive) so a special "gear drive" cam must be used. Drives with three gears incorporate an idler and rotate the camshaft in its normal direction.

The most significant disadvantage to a gear drive is its extreme rigidity, which is very efficient at transferring crankshaft torsional vibrations to the camshaft. Many engine builders feel that this leads to premature camshaft or valvetrain failure. Although this theory has never been conclusively proven, most top engine builders prefer a timing chain and sprocket. Or a Jesel belt drive.

Jesel Belt Drive

As the name implies, Jesel's system uses a rubber belt, rather than a chain or gears, to spin the camshaft. The belt-drive assembly needs no lubrication and mounts on the exposed side of a special timing cover. The cam sprocket is a two-piece affair that allows for quick and easy advancing and retarding of the cam. In addition to providing extremely accurate and consistent valve timing, the Jesel belt drive simplifies cam changes significantly because the timing cover doesn't have to be removed. ■

IGNITION SYSTEMS

8

Over the years, all types of ignition systems have been developed for the small block—some good, some not so good and some downright rotten. Fortunately, any small-block ignition system can be easily upgraded. However, before delving into the pertinent modifications, I'm duty-bound to lead you to the following disclaimer. Making any change whatsoever to an ignition system may be in violation of local, state or federal regulations governing vehicles of certain model years. This is especially true in California, where the California Air Resources Board has made just about everything besides opening the hood illegal. Check local emissions regulations before performing any ignition modifications.

BREAKER POINT SYSTEMS

One of the major advantages offered by an electronic system is the replacement of the breaker points with a non-mechanical triggering device (an electronic switch). This is desirable because point wear increases with mileage, resulting in a continual deterioration of ignition system performance. After 10,000 to 12,000 miles, a typical set of points is as worn as a 10-year-old pair of shoes and must be replaced.

The latest innovation is small-block distributors is the one used on LT1 engines. It mounts up front and '92-'94 models are driven by a small shaft that's connected to the cam timing gear. 1996 and later models incorporate an extra long dowel pin to drive the distributor. Behind the rotor is an optical trigger wheel that provides extremely accurate ignition timing.

Limitations

In spite of an excellent record for reliable performance, point-type ignition systems contain a number of built-in limitations:

• The breaker points must carry a relatively high amount of current (2-3 amps) which leads to erosion of the contact surfaces.

• As engine speed increases, the time available (dwell time) to build high voltage in the coil decreases, dramatically reducing spark intensity.

• Breaker point opening and closing timing tends to be irregular. As the rubbing block wears and the contacts erode, dwell time, and consequently spark timing, is altered. Distributor shaft bushing wear also leads to timing irregularity.

• At high engine speeds, the rubbing block may not stay in contact with the distributor cam with the result being "point bounce" which leads to misfire.

• Since both the point contacts and the rubbing block are subject to wear, point sets must be replaced periodically.

These are the major shortcomings

that prompted Chevrolet and other manufacturers to universally convert to electronic ignition. And while that conversion didn't occur until 1975, electronic ignitions have actually been available since the early Sixties.

ELECTRONIC IGNITIONS

A number of years ago, when electronics were first applied to the point-type ignition system, manufacturers devised a variety of displays as a means of demonstrating the worth of their products. The one most commonly used (variations are still employed) simulated a spark plug with an adjustable gap. A standard ignition was fired up and the gap gradually opened until the spark no longer jumped across. Then the electronic ignition was connected and the spark flitted across an opening as wide as the Grand Canyon. While the demonstration is impressive, with sparks flying about as if a thunderstorm had invaded the display booth, it illustrates but a single aspect of the superiority of electronic ignition—increased voltage output. Unfortunately, many people are misled by these types of demonstrations and come away thinking that voltage is the only criterion of ignition system performance. But thankfully for automotive journalists, there's a lot more to the story.

Pointless Triggers

Clearly, points were as outmoded as eight-track tape players and "vibrasonic sound." When connected to electronic circuitry, breaker points become nothing more than a pulse generator that signals the control module when it's time to discharge the

coil into the distributor. This being the case, there's no need to maintain a mechanical triggering device with all of its inherent problems. So magnetic, optic and Hall Effect triggers have become the devices of choice in electronic ignition systems.

While each of these devices offers a unique advantage, they also have drawbacks. Light emitting diodes can burn out (although they rarely do) or get dirty enough to interfere with light transmission. Hall Effect circuits can fail due to heat. Consequently Chevrolet, like other auto manufacturers, has relied on magnetic triggers in original equipment systems. Although the failure rate of aftermarket systems using LED and Hall Effect triggers has been well within the margins of acceptability, the automakers feel that only a magnetic trigger, consisting of a reluctor and a magnetic pick-up, offers an acceptable level of reliability—magnets and steel reluctors are virtually failure-proof.

Why Electronic?

One may wonder why, after over fifty years of successful operation, did point-triggered ignition systems suddenly become inadequate. The answer is simply that in the late Sixties, the high compression, high rpm engines that were available created energy demands that conventional systems could no longer meet on a consistent basis. In an effort to solve this problem, Chevrolet offered optional Delcotronic Transistor Controlled Magnetic Pulse Type Ignition Systems on some high performance Corvette engines during the Sixties. Although this system is highly revered by Corvette restorers, it isn't a particularly good ignition

Points are as out of date as the Flat Earth Society, but if you have to use a point-type distributor, or are too stubborn to change to electronics, invest in a good set of points. High performance points have higher spring pressures for improved high rpm stability, but lead to accelerated rubbing block wear. A little dab of lubricant extends rubbing block lift.

system by current standards.

When the performance craze was throttled back by concerns over exhaust emissions, the need for high-energy ignitions didn't evaporate. In fact, it became more critical. Igniting the exceptionally lean air/fuel mixtures necessary for reduced exhaust emissions requires at least as much spark energy (not just voltage) as demanded by a high performance powerplant.

One method of achieving this is to widen the plug gap so that more fuel is exposed to the heat of the spark. Another approach, and one that should be used in combination with the first, is to increase spark current and duration. With an excessively lean mixture, gasoline molecule density is low; the gap between the plug electrodes is therefore widened, and spark duration lengthened, to improve the chances of "zapping" a sufficient number of gas molecules. A conventional point-type ignition system could ignite the lean mixtures used in late-model engines, but its

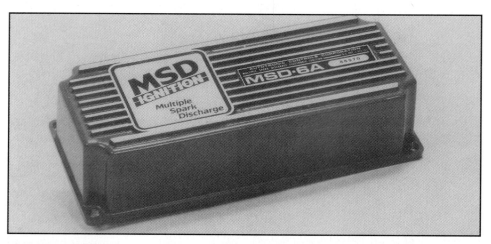

Multi-spark discharge systems can be connected to virtually any type of distributor. These systems put a fat spark across the plug gaps which not only makes for excellent power output, it also is very effective at preventing plug fouling when an engine is run a lower speeds.

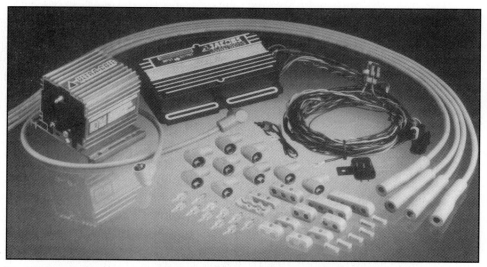

The Jacobs Ultra Team is a complete ignition system featuring high output coil, control module, plug wires and separators. Independent dyno testing has shown this system capable of increasing power output compared to other race type systems.

reasonably wonder about the need for other aftermarket ignition systems and whether they are of any advantage. As demonstrated by the name of the General Motors system—High Energy Ignition (HEI)—original equipment electronic ignitions do produce high levels of spark energy as compared to conventional ignitions. But GM has designed the HEI system primarily to meet the requirements of Federal new car emissions and fuel economy testing.

Since unit cost is a major consideration in a mass production environment, these systems aren't as powerful as they could be. But more importantly, their energy output falls off dramatically at engine speeds of 4000 rpm and above.

SPARK ENERGY SELECTION

The question that has yet to be answered is, "How much spark energy is really required for optimum performance or fuel economy?" It may come as a shock, but it appears that short of burning the electrodes off the ends of the spark plugs, there is no such thing as "too much." Obviously, there comes a point of diminishing returns where a doubling or tripling of energy levels becomes extremely costly and results in a barely measurable increase in operating efficiency. However, to take full advantage of a high energy spark, the entire system must be configured properly. The distributor cap and rotor and plug wires must have high dielectric strength to contain the spark energy and plug gap must be opened up to take full advantage of the system's fire power.

energy level would be so low that an inordinate number of misfires would result. Many of these would be barely detectable to the driver, but poor fuel economy would result and, under heavy load (as during full throttle acceleration or when climbing a steep grade), the engine would stutter badly since all cylinders would not be "giving their fair share."

So in addition to eliminating problems related to breaker points,

original equipment electronic systems fire a considerably "hotter" (increased voltage) and "fatter" (higher amperage) spark across the spark plug electrodes; voltage is sufficient to consistently ionize (jump across) gaps of .045 to .060".; amperage is high and burn time relatively long. Therefore, these systems produce considerably more spark energy than a conventional system.

This being the case, you could

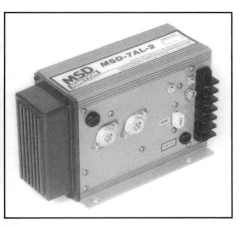

MSD's 7AL-2 is designed for drag racing and provides a tremendous amount of spark energy. The unit also includes a built in rev limiter; maximum rpm is controlled by a plug in chip.

Recommendations

For anything less than a maximum output, professional race engine, a high output ignition system such as an MSD-6 series or Jacobs Omni Pak is more than adequate. Systems with more spark energy might produce slightly more power, but considering the operating environment, the added expense isn't justified. Another point to be considered is that some super high output systems aren't designed to run for hours on end. They may prove to be unreliable when installed on a street, marine or oval track engine due to heat build-up.

As with most aspects of life around internal combustion engines, selecting the best ignition system for a particular application is a matter of making the best series of compromises. It's not so much a matter of right or wrong as it is a situation where some decisions are just more correct than others. As an example, most NASCAR Winston Cup engines come to life with an MSD-6T (which is also marketed through GM Performance Parts as Heavy Duty Ignition Control part no.

Inductive vs. Ignitions Discharge

Once all the marketing terminology is stripped away, there are essentially only two types of electronic ignition—inductive and ignitions discharge (CD). The problem with the inductive system is that it's subject to the same limitations as a standard point-type system—specifically, current is induced in the coil and therefore spark output is dependent upon the amount of time between firings. At high rpm, there is insufficient time to build up current in the coil, therefore spark output is reduced.

Conversely, in a capacitive discharge system, capacitors are used to store electricity which is discharged at a later time. The primary advantage of this arrangement is that a capacitor can be charged to maximum levels in a fraction of the time (known as rise time) required to induce voltage in a coil. Therefore, in a properly designed CD system, output is virtually unaffected by engine speed as high as 12,000 rpm—even though current still flows through the coil. This is possible because the coil is used as a simple transformer to step up the voltage fed to it by the CD unit. But instead of 12 volts, the coil will receive an input of 375-450 volts which places output in the 35,000 to 55,000 volt range irrespective of engine speed.

On the other side of the coin, inductive systems such as the GM HEI produce 50,000-55,000 volts at low speeds, but drop to less than 15,000 as the engine approaches 5000 rpm. The reason for this is quite understandable. As a means of determining whether a vehicle's exhaust emissions levels and fuel economy are acceptable, a variety of tests are conducted by the Environmental Protection Agency. Chevrolet, like other manufacturers, must therefore engineer their vehicles to pass these tests which are administered in a laboratory, not on the highway. That's one reason that EPA gas mileage figures seem as realistic as a science fiction fantasy. Since engine speed is kept quite low throughout the test series, there is no need for the ignition system to maintain its top energy output level at high rpm. Inductive ignitions appeal to auto manufacturers for another reason—they're cheaper to produce than capacitive discharge systems.

But when a vehicle is placed in the real world of highway driving, or used in a high performance or racing environment, it's necessary to use an engine's full rpm potential. This is where the original equipment systems come up short. However, basic capacitive discharge ignitions aren't the answer either. One of the most commonly heard criticisms of CD ignitions is that in spite of their ability to fire a plug under the most adverse conditions, spark duration is too short to reliably initiate complete combustion.

Multi-Spark—In the early Seventies, Autotronic Controls developed multi-spark discharge (MSD) ignitions. In so doing, they married the advantages of the CD system's fast rise time and the inductive system's longer duration spark. Multi-spark systems have been extremely successful and are widely used on all types of race and high performance street engines. Other manufacturers such as Accel, Jacobs and Mallory also offer high output ignitions that are suitable for high performance use.

Jacobs Electronics offers a number of Energy Pak ignition systems for street, race and marine applications. These patented systems tailor spark intensity and duration according to engine requirements.

The Ultra Coil from Jacobs is a take-no-prisoners unit that delivers up to 1950 watts of spark power.

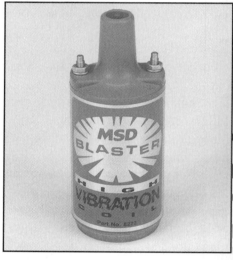

There are numerous models of high performance coils, but not all coils are compatible with all ignition systems. Be sure to verify compatability before installation and also make sure a coil is rugged enough for your application. This MSD coil is specifically designed to withstand a vibration intensive installation.

10037378). These engines have a displacement of 358 cid, produce in excess of 675 horsepower and run at 7500+ rpm for hours on end. If the MSD-6 circuitry is adequate for these engines, it is certainly more than capable of firing the plugs in a street, bracket race, marine, off-road or short track engine.

The 6A, 6AL and 6T all have the same output specifications; the 6T is the professional race version of the 6A and includes added internal bracing, rubber shock mounts and a special coating to protect the electronic components from shock and vibration loads. MSD-6T modules also include provision for hooking up a rev control. MSD-6AL modules have the rev control built in.

On the other hand, the MSD-10 and Jacobs Ultra Team have become the systems of preference for Pro Stock and similar hard-core drag race vehicles. Considering the differences in output specifications between race and street ignitions, it's understandable that the former offers somewhat more horsepower potential than the latter. If you're racing in a class where every last ounce of horsepower is essential, and can tune the engine to take advantage of a super high output ignition, there's no question which one to select. However, for most bracket categories, road racing, short track, marine and street engines, something less than a maximum output system is more than adequate. Such systems are also considerably cheaper than their super high output counterparts.

COILS

Aside from an electronic control module, the coil is largely responsible for ignition system energy output. As previously noted, most stock-type coils are capable of producing 25,000 to 30,000 volts; high performance coils generate 40,000 to 55,000 volts. While it may require only 10,000 to 15,000 volts to fire the plugs, the reserve capacity is good insurance against misfire. Reserve spark voltage (reserve being the amount of voltage above actual system requirements) will be tapped as plug gaps erode and as the electrodes wear and accumulate deposits, all of which increase voltage requirements.

Normal deterioration of plug wires, distributor cap and rotor also

From a performance standpoint, the principal drawback to an HEI system is that output falls off sharply above 4500-5000 rpm. A high output coil helps that situation somewhat. Accel's HEI Super Coil is unique in that it fits on the distributor cap, in place of the stock coil.

This is the back of a 1995 LT1 distributor. The extra long dowel pin fits in the wide grove located at the 12-o'clock position.

increases resistance, so after a time, voltage requirements may rise to 20,000 volts or more. This is still within the capability of a stock coil, so a stock ignition system can for some time continue to fire away when called upon. However, at higher engine speeds, there won't always be enough time between plug firings to allow a stock-type inductive ignition system to build maximum voltage. Even if the voltage does jump the plug gap, there may not be enough energy to initiate combustion. That's the reason that a high output coil

As a means of eliminating spark scatter and timing inaccuracies that come along with a distributor, many small-block race engines are fitted with a crank-triggered ignition. With this arrangement, timing is fixed at a particular setting unless a timing computer is included in the circuit.

alone won't suffice on a high performance engine.

DISTRIBUTORS

Prior to 1975, virtually all Chevrolet small blocks, like most other GM engines, were equipped with a conventional point-type distributor. The only exception to this was the Delcotronic transistor ignition system. The distributor used in this system appears identical to a standard point-type distributor externally—but there are no points inside. In their place is a magnet and an eight-toothed reluctor. These systems have always been comparatively rare, and although they eliminated the points, they didn't do much else to increase ignition system performance.

Unless you're doing a Concours restoration that calls for a Delcotronic distributor, there's no sense searching for one. Both the cast-iron and aluminum distributors that have been used as original equipment in small-block Chevrolet engines are suitable for high performance use. The cast-

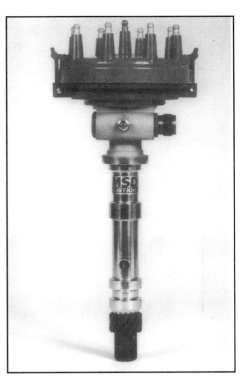

Special low-profile distributors are often used in a crank trigger system. These distributors have no advance mechanism, they're only for starting the engine (and driving the oil pump). Once the engine is running, the driver throws a switch and the crank trigger takes over.

iron models are stronger and more rigid, the aluminum ones are lighter. In actual use, there really isn't much operational difference and arguments can be made for the superiority of each type. It's not worth losing much sleep over the decision—either type will provide satisfactory performance. For engines operating at extremely high rpm, or under very heavy loads, the extra strength of a cast-iron or aftermarket aluminum distributor is advantageous.

Triggers—Of far greater importance than housing material is the triggering device used. Avoid points at all costs. Points, even dual points, are nothing more than a failure waiting to happen. If you have any doubts, just take a look at the top-

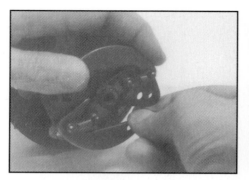

In both the older point-type and later HEI electronic distributors, (as well as MSD distributors) centrifugal advance is controlled by a spring and weight assembly that is located just beneath the rotor. Generally, it's only necessary to change springs and limit total travel when building a custom calibrated advance curve. For regular maintenance, it's a good idea to periodically remove the cap and rotor and pull out on the advance weights to make sure they move smoothly and reach full advance.

One of the best ways to improve the performance of a small-block equipped with an HEI ignition system is with a custom spark curve. The Super Curve Kit from American Speed Centers in York, PA includes special weights, pivot piece, springs and vacuum advance canister.

For street applications, once the centrifugal curve is set, the vacuum advance should also be dialed in. The easiest way to optimize the vacuum advance curve is with an adjustable canister (usually identified by the hex shaped area adjacent to the nipple. Turning the Allen wrench clockwise brings advance in quicker, turning it counter clockwise slows it down. Adjust it so that vacuum advance comes in as quickly as possible without causing the engine doesn't ping.

running race cars—from Pro Stock drag racing to Winston Cup oval track to SCCA road racing, electronic ignitions are used exclusively. Assuming you have a point-type distributor, the most economical way to eliminate points is with a conversion kit. Stinger and Mallory are a few of the companies offering conversion kits.

HEI Distributors

Another option is to substitute an HEI (High Energy Ignition) distributor. HEI systems first came into play on engines installed in 1975 model year cars. The integrated systems, which incorporate the coil and electronics in the distributor, were the sole source of small-block ignition until 1987 when a new small diameter distributor (3.9-in. dia. base plate) was introduced on the L69 (305 HO with 4-barrel carb), LB9 (305 TPI), LM1 and L98 (350 TPI) engines. The new system, with a separate coil, produces the same spark energy as the

integrated HEI systems, but it is considerably smaller and 46% lighter.

Although stock HEI electronics aren't up to handling the demands of a high performance engine, there's nothing wrong with the trigger mechanism. An original style HEI distributor also features a large diameter cap which offers a greater distance between terminals and therefore less chance of a crossfire within the cap. MSD also offers a Cap-A-Dapt kit which includes a large diameter cap and matching rotor and an adapter to mate it to a standard point-style distributor. With its small cap, the 1987 and later non-integrated HEI distributor doesn't seem to be optimal for high performance; the terminals are relatively close together and a high energy spark intended for one terminal could wind up jumping to an adjacent terminal inside the cap. At least that's the theory. In application, cross fire within the cap is rarely a problem.

HEI Modifiers—If you do use an HEI distributor, you have several options. One is to install a kit with an external coil and module, which

eliminates all the stock distributor components except the magnetic trigger, advance mechanism (if so equipped) cap and rotor. Jacobs, MSD and Accel all offer HEI conversion kits.

On the surface, it appears strange that after years of ignition systems with separate coils, GM developed an improved system with an internal coil only to have aftermarket manufacturers offer upgrades which eliminate the internal coil. (GM also reversed direction by returning to the divorced-coil arrangement, a process that began in 1987.) From a packaging standpoint, incorporating the coil inside the distributor cap makes sense. From an electronic standpoint, it doesn't. Coils build heat, and when the coil is inside the cap, heat dissipation is poor. Elevated temperatures certainly don't make a positive contribution to coil life, and they also have a negative effect on the control module that resides on the base plate of an HEI distributor.

Magnetism is another consideration. Where there's a functioning coil, there's magnetism in the air. Normally, it's of no consequence, when a magnetic field occurs near another piece of electronic equipment, strange things are bound to happen. In the case of an HEI system, magnetism generated by the coil can cause the control module to initiate "unauthorized" coil firings, which can make starting more difficult and cause detonation.

However, an internal coil doesn't appear to be a problem in some applications, so another option is to upgrade the HEI electronics with high output components such as those produced by Performance Distributors in Memphis, TN. Used extensively in oval track engines, Performance Distributors' Racing HEI unit incorporates a high output coil and heavy duty cap and rotor, along with a special control module to increase coil saturation. It produces a strong spark up to 8000-8500 rpm and is a completely self-contained system.

Aftermarket Distributors

Aftermarket distributors are another option. They're available from a

Performance Distributors of Memphis, TN offers a stock appearing HEI unit that's anything but. It contains a super high output coil and internal module that cranks out enough spark energy to light up a small town.

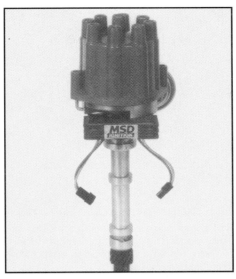

MSD offers a variety of distributors for small-block Chevys. This distributor contains an ignition module so the only other requirement to bring spark is a coil. The same basic distributor is also available with no ignition module attached, and a tach drive version is also available.

number of manufacturers, but MSD offers the widest variety. The basic MSD distributor (part no. 8461) has a cast aluminum housing, .500" steel shaft, reluctor and magnetic pick-up and centrifugal advance mechanism with extra springs for customizing the advance curve. Vacuum advance is not included, but can be added. A ready-to-run version of this distributor is also available. This unit (part no. 8460) includes an integrated high output inductive module, cap, rotor and vacuum advance canister. MSD also offers a race distributor with a housing machined from aluminum billet and ball bearings (as opposed to bronze bushings which are used in other models).

Other MSD distributors include a tach drive version and two low profile models—one with tach drive and one without—for use on race engines with Tunnel Ram-type manifolds (where distributor clearance is limited). Both

low-profile distributors are designed to operate with crankshaft triggered ignitions.

Accel—Accel is another company offering an assortment of distributors for the small-block Chevy. In addition to electronic distributors, Accel offers dual-point models. If you absolutely have to use points, you can choose from a 37-Series racing distributor or a 34-Series "Super Stock" model which is available with or without vacuum advance. All Accel high performance distributors use a Chrysler-style cap and rotor and the electronic Unispark models incorporate an HEI control module. Accel also offers a line of blueprinted OEM replacement distributors. Besides being completely remanufactured, these distributors incorporate high quality cap and rotor and adjustable vacuum advance canister. Point-type distributors include points with 32-ounce arm tension (for higher rpm potential) and electronic (HEI) distributors contain a new specially programmed control module.

Mallory—Mallory also offers both

On most Accel distributors, the advance assembly is located beneath the main body of the distributor. Although not as easily accessible as the assembly in a stock distributor, it's a bit easier to create custom advance curves.

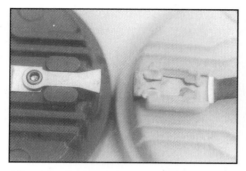

All rotors for small-block distributors may look pretty much the same, but there are big differences. The flimsy stock-type unit on the right doesn't inspire a lot of confidence. The high performance rotor on the left is made of better materials and more of them. The rotor tip is also longer and better reinforced for improved durability.

Can't remember which way to turn the distributor to advance timing? Just pull the vacuum advance canister toward the front of the engine (counterclockwise–the rotor turns clockwise). If that's too hard to remember, keep this book with you at all times so you're prepared for emergencies.

If you install a roller cam, which is machined from a steel billet rather than cast iron core, chances are you'll have to equip the distributor with a bronze gear. Some roller cams are manufactured with a cast iron distributor gear in which case no change is required. But for the most part, a bronze gear goes with a roller cam like double talk goes with a politician.

Many times, distributor gears fail because of inadequate lubrication. To minimize such possibilities, file a .030" by .030" slot on the base of the distributor housing with the slot oriented towards the camshaft. Some high performance distributors are supplied with a slot already in place.

dual-point and electronic distributors. The Comp 9000 series includes a large diameter cap and special rotor to resist arcing and carbon tracking, heat-treated aluminum housing and a screw-mounted plug wire retainer. In addition to the dual-point model, both optic and magnetic trigger electronic models are available. In the oval track version, (98 and 99 series) two magnetic pickups are mounted for use with two complete ignition systems. This provision allows the driver to substitute one ignition system for the other at the flick of a switch. Comp 9000 distributors do not have vacuum advance mechanisms. Mallory also manufactures lower cost Unilite and dual-point distributors with and without vacuum advance.

Distributor Gears

Regardless of the type of distributor you select, pay attention to the gear. Standard iron gears are acceptable if a conventional hydraulic or mechanical camshaft is in charge of valve timing. However, roller cams are machined from SAE 8620 billet steel and the gear on the cam isn't compatible with a cast-iron distributor gear. Whenever a roller cam is in residence, the distributor should be fitted with a high quality bronze gear—with one exception. Steel roller cams with cast-iron gears were developed during the very late stages of the 1980s. These cams can be used with standard cast-iron distributor gears.

Durability—In a high performance or race engine, distributor gear life isn't always what it should be. While bronze is compatible with steel, it doesn't have the strength of iron, so it wears at a higher rate. The situation can be particularly bad in Chevrolet small blocks because the splash lubrication of the distributor gear is inadequate at low engine speeds.

Things are even worse when a high volume oil pump is installed in an engine that doesn't really need one. High volume pumps are designed for use in engines with wide bearing clearances. With normal production clearances, oil doesn't flow as freely through the engine, so the oil pump is working against considerable back pressure. Since the distributor shaft turns the oil pump shaft, the load on the distributor gear caused by a high-volume oil pump can be substantial. That leads to accelerated wear—even with a stock iron gear.

Increasing oil flow to the distributor gear significantly improves gear life, primarily because of its cooling effect. This can be most easily accomplished by using a 3-cornered file to cut a .030"-deep notch in the lower sealing flange on the distributor housing. For maximum effectiveness, the notch should be oriented so that it is aimed towards the camshaft when the distributor is installed in its normal position.

Distributor housings should be notched—irrespective of the type of distributor gear used—in all engines operating under high loads and/or at relatively low rpm, especially if a high-volume oil pump is in place. True race engines rarely experience a distributor gear wear problem because their higher operating rpm provides sufficient lubricant flow, and proper matching of oil pump volume and bearing clearance eliminate excessively high lubrication system back pressures.

SPARK PLUG WIRES

Listen to a bunch of old-time Chevy racers talking, and you'll probably

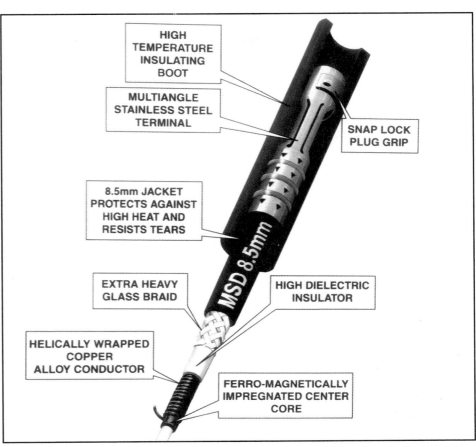

Spark plug wires look simple enough, but it takes careful selection of conductor, insulating and jacketing materials to ensure that wires survive in the hot and hostile underhood environment. Exhaust heat is a plug wire's biggest enemy.

hear about Packard 440 wire which had a silver-plated copper core. Solid, metallic core wires used to be the hot tip, but like many pieces of automotive legend, they've been replaced by something better.

Resistance Wires

At one time, metallic core wiring was the only alternative, but it wasn't the proper solution. Dependable resistance-type wire is the answer. Such wire has been available for many years, but the poor reputation of the early resistance wire caused many people to stick with metallic plug wires. Then came electronics, and metallic-core wires became unviable because they interfered with the

operation of on-board computers and high energy ignitions. Consequently race cars, as well as street cars, are now universally equipped with high quality radio suppression wires, with the helical wound type being most prevalent.

Resistance wires are actually superior to their metallic core counterparts because most ignition systems are designed to operate with some amount of secondary resistance. Secondary refers to the part of the ignition system that transports the spark. The problem with cheap resistance-type plug wires is that after a short period of time, they offer too much resistance. On the other hand, solid-core wire allows current to flow

Magnetos contain their own energy source–a self-contained generator. Although not considered a "high tech" system, magnetos are favored in certain applications where it may not be practical to run a battery. One advantage of a magneto is that the spark intensity increases as rpm rises.

after the spark has jumped the plug gap. It's this "follow-on" spark that creates radio frequency interference (RFI) which plays havoc with radios, televisions and onboard electronics. What you need is a low resistance, helical wound RFI-suppression wire that doesn't deteriorate This type of wire is available from any number of companies including Accel, Jacobs, MSD, Mallory, Moroso and Taylor. As a general rule, solid-core wires, like ignition points, should be avoided—there's absolutely no reason to use them.

MAGNETOS

Any discussion of ignition systems would be incomplete without mention of magnetos. Like many pieces of

equipment used on small-block Chevy engines, there are both good and bad aspects of a magneto. As an ignition device, a magneto is about the least sophisticated type available. In fact, the lowly lawn mower engine is sparked on to feats of grass-cutting prowess by a magneto system. That doesn't imply that a magneto is unsuitable for anything but mundane applications. Quite the opposite— everything from sprint cars to Top Fuelers to aircraft engines are magneto equipped. In fact, until the advent of electronic ignitions, magnetos were the only systems capable of providing acceptable spark output at engine speeds above 7500 rpm.

The beauty of a magneto is that it generates its own electricity, so it's completely self-contained. That means neither a battery, coil nor alternator are required. Another attractive characteristic of a magneto is that its voltage output increases linearly with rpm. The flip side of this is that at cranking speeds, voltage output is very low, so starting can be a problem. Mallory Super Mag utilize a separate coil so they're more suitable for street and low rpm operation.

Currently, automotive magnetos are widely used only in certain types of race cars such as fuel and alcohol dragsters and Funny Cars, sprinters and the like. Vibration is severe enough in these types of cars to damage a battery, so being able to run without one is a definite advantage— not to mention the weight savings. And since sprint cars spend a good deal of time on their heads, elimination of the battery removes the potential hazard of battery acid dripping on the driver in the event of a flip or rollover.

Magnetos can be used in street engines, but they rarely are. Street cars have to be equipped with a battery for purposes other than operating the ignition, so a magneto offers no weight-savings benefit. And since a street engine spends most of its time operating at low rpm, it rarely spins a magneto fast enough to generate high spark voltage. A third drawback is that it takes a bit of horsepower to spin a magneto, and while it isn't a lot, it represents a power loss that electronic ignitions do not impose.

SPARK PLUGS

A spark plug performs a relatively simple function—it provides a gap, inside the combustion chamber, for electrical energy to spark across. The only way for this energy to jump the gap between a spark plug's center electrode and ground electrode is to arc across it. When it does that, a spark is created—hence the name spark plug. But as you might have guessed, it's not quite that simple.

Heat Range

Heat range refers to a spark plug's ability to transfer heat from the tip of the insulator into the cylinder head. In order for a spark plug to perform satisfactorily for more than a few miles, it must be of the proper heat range. If a plug is too hot, it will cause pre-ignition, but even if combustion is normal, excess heat can ultimately burn the center electrode completely away. On the other hand, a plug with too cold a heat range will have a tendency to foul and misfire and can reduce horsepower. Heat transfer rate is largely controlled by the distance the heat must travel through the spark

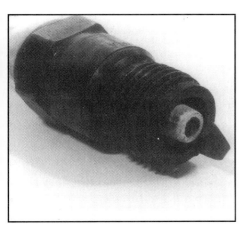

If a spark plug has too cold a heat range, it will foul. If it's too hot, the plug may self-destruct. This warm-up plug was accidently left in an engine during dyno testing and the center electrode was completely burned away.

plug body before reaching the head. Plugs that are considered "cold" have insulators that contact the metal plug shell very close to the threaded base. The insulators in "hot" plugs contact the shell towards the top, which makes for a longer path to the head surface. Keep in mind that the terms "hot" and "cold" are relative—a plug that's "hot" for one engine may be considered "cold" for another. That's because combustion chamber temperatures vary considerably depending upon an engine's state of tune and the conditions under which it is operated. When heat range is properly matched to requirements, insulator tip temperature will range between 700 and 1500° (F) under all operating conditions. This will provide maximum power and maximum plug life.

Recommendations—With a stock engine, it's best to follow the plug manufacturer's recommendation unless there's a good reason to deviate—such as a modified spark advance curve, poor fuel quality, extreme operating conditions or

experience with the recommended plug being inappropriate. With a modified engine, standard recommendations can be used as a basis for determining where in the heat chart to start. Raising compression ratio, leaning the fuel mixture, increasing initial spark advance or reworking the advance curve to come in quicker are all reasons to switch to a plug with a colder heat range.

Cam Duration—An often overlooked factor when selecting proper plug heat range is cam duration. If no other changes are made, swapping a short duration cam for one with longer duration decreases cylinder pressure, which has the same effect as lowering compression ratio. Shortening cam duration increases cylinder pressure, which has the same effect as raising compression ratio.

So even though a long duration cam is designed to produce more horsepower, at higher engine speeds, it will create a condition that calls for a hotter, rather than a colder spark plug under some circumstances. On the other hand, if a shorter duration cam is installed as a means of increasing low speed torque and smoothing the idle, a colder plug may be required because of the increased heat which is generated by higher cylinder pressure.

Octane—Another factor that influences heat range is gasoline quality. Lower octane fuels burn more quickly and create higher combustion chamber temperatures. In years past, when premium leaded fuels were widely available, octane was sufficient to meet the demands of virtually all high-compression street engines. But with the advent of unleaded gas, octane ratings of all

grades of fuel dropped. Consequently, pre-ignition, detonation and run-on became more prevalent problems. If you've been running the same heat range plugs for years, but have been plagued by detonation, pre-ignition or run-on for no apparent reason, it just may be that the plugs you're using are too hot because of lower fuel octane. Many times, a switch to colder plugs will eliminate those ugly knock and ping noises.

As you can see, the selection of spark plugs with a proper heat range isn't a cut and dried affair. So many factors enter into the equation, that some experimentation is usually necessary to optimize performance and plug life. As a general rule, if you're off on heat range, it's better to be too cold than too hot. Plugs that are too cold will foul more easily, build carbon deposits more quickly and slightly decrease power. Plugs that are too hot can cause pre-ignition, detonation and run-on—all of which can cause your engines to eat its own pistons and valves.

Plug Size

When selecting spark plugs for a small-block Chevy, another point to be considered is plug size. Prior to the 1971 model year, all stock small-block heads were machined to accept 3/8-in. reach plugs with 14mm threads and a 13/16-in. hex. These plugs are identified by a "J" prefix in Champion Spark Plug's numbering system.

Beginning with the 1971 model year, Chevrolet switched to "slimline" spark plugs with 14mm threads, .460-in. reach, a tapered seat (which eliminated the need for a washer) and a 5/8 in. rather than 13/16 in. hex. These plugs were formerly identified by a "BL" prefix in Champion's numbering system, but that has been changed to a "V" prefix.

L98 and LT1 aluminum cylinder heads (and some aftermarket castings) require a 14-mm slimline plug with 3/4" reach. In Champion's scheme of things, these plugs have a "C" designation and also feature a reduced installed height for additional header clearance.

Seat Style—While the hex size is the most obvious difference between these two types of plugs, the seat style is of most significance. Plugs with a 13/16 in. hex have a flat seat and require a gasket; plugs with a 5/8 in. hex have a tapered seat and no gasket is used.

Torquing—In cast-iron heads, 13/16 in. hex plugs should be tightened to 26-30 lbs-ft., which in educated wrench-hand terms translates to 1/4-turn past finger tight. In aluminum heads, tightening torque should be 18-22 lbs-ft. which is also approximately 1/4-turn past finger tight. Plugs with a 5/8-in. hex should be tightened to 7-15 lbs-ft. or 1/16-turn past finger tight (in either iron or aluminum heads). Some aftermarket heads require the use of 3/4-in. reach or .708-in. reach plugs. Tightening specifications are the same as for equivalent 3/8-in. reach plugs.

Although it is physically possible to screw a V- or BL-series plug into plug holes that were machined for larger J-series plugs, such a substitution should be done only on a temporary basis, when proper plugs can't be found. The tapered seat of the V-series plug doesn't have enough surface area contact, when installed in a plug hole with a flat seat, to properly transfer heat. Another potential problem with mismatched substitution is plug

depth—with its .460-in. reach, a V-series plug extends deeper into the combustion chamber than a .375-in. reach J-series plug. Consequently, the piston may smack the plug, close the gap or break the electrodes. Or you may avoid all that inconvenience and proceed directly to ventilated pistons.

Types of Plugs

Irrespective of size or heat range, two types of plugs are most commonly used in small-block Chevy engines—standard and projected tip. In a standard plug, the center electrode protrudes a minimum distance from the base of the plug. With a projected tip, the electrode extends considerably deeper. This is advantageous in most applications because it places the plug tip deeper in the combustion chamber and somewhat in the path of the incoming air/fuel charge. At higher engine speeds, the intake mixture has a cooling effect on the plug tip. Consequently, a projected tip plug has a wider operating heat range—it's designed to run slightly hotter at low speeds because it has less of a tendency to overheat at high speeds. However, in some endurance type racing applications, where an engine runs wide open for hours on end, a standard plug is often preferable because heat build-up can exceed a projected tip plug's dissipation capabilities. While projected tip plugs are clearly advantageous for most applications, there is one point to beware of; since they protrude further into the combustion chamber, piston to electrode interference is a distinct possibility when super high-compression pistons are used. If clearance is even a remote question, after installing projected tip plugs for

the first time, spin the engine over by hand—slowly—and make sure everything clears. Your pistons and your bank account will thank you for taking the time to check.

Retracted Gap—In engines fitted with pistons having obscenely large domes, it may be necessary to install retracted gap (R-gap) plugs. In a retracted gap plug, neither the center nor the ground electrode protrudes beyond the threaded shell. This type of plug is frequently used in supercharged engines because they are better able to withstand extreme heat and pressure. However, by tucking the gap up inside the shell, the electrodes are excessively shrouded and that imposes a power penalty. Need I say more?

Electrode Shapes—A relatively recent development in spark plug design is a series of unique electrode shapes. Champion manufactures fine wire and cut back electrode plugs; Accel offers a U-Groove plug; Bosch has a tapered electrode; and Split-Fire offers a Y-shaped ground electrode. AC also offers "Rapidfire" plugs with a multi-sided center electrode. All of these designs are intended to expose more of the spark by eliminating some of the shrouding that characterizes a traditional ground electrode. The question is, do they work?

At this point, the jury is still out. There's no question that unshrouding the ground electrode increases horsepower—racers have been cutting back the ground electrode of conventional plugs for years. Myron Cottrell of TPI Specialties, in Chaska, MN, states that in back-to-back dyno tests, he's seen cut-back electrodes deliver a solid five to eight horsepower increase. Tests of more

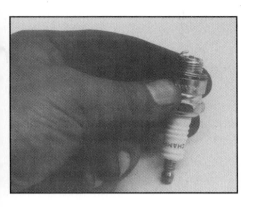

Want to pick up five horsepower free? Cut back the ground electrode, so that it covers no more than 1/2 of the ground electrode. The plugs won't last as long, but dyno testing has shown definite power increases.(Hand and photo by Myron Cottrell)

recently developed electrode designs have produced mixed results. These specialty spark plugs probably offer some advantage—the question is whether it's enough of an advantage to justify the added cost. Some people feel that special gap designs are worth the additional cost, others prefer to buy conventional plugs and file the ground electrode back.

Resistance Movement

Spark plugs with internal resistors are factory installed in newer vehicles to improve control of radio frequency interference (RFI). Although resistor-type plugs are widely used in passenger vehicles, they are generally not part of a high performance or racing ignition system. There's nothing inherently wrong with resistor plugs and contrary to popular belief, they have only slightly higher voltage requirements compared to conventional plugs. But if the heat, vibration and voltage levels encountered in a passenger vehicle make life difficult for the resistor element, imagine what racing conditions do to it.

Even if RFI suppression wire is in place, resistor plugs may be required to optimize radio clarity. So if you like music with your horsepower, you may have to install resistor plugs. You'll also get another benefit—the resistor reduces electrode erosion, so plugs can run longer before being regapped or replaced. These characteristics are advantageous in a street-driven vehicle, but in a race car, the resistor simply becomes another element that can fail at the most inopportune time. For that reason, you'll have to search long and hard to find resistor plugs with a cold enough heat range to suit a race engine.

CROSSFIRE & OTHER MYSTERIES

Once the distributor, coil and ignition module are all properly introduced and working together harmoniously, the next task is to ensure that the spark energy leaving the distributor cap reaches the appropriate spark plug at precisely the correct time. But there are several detours that can be thrown into the path of unwitting bands of sparks. Crossfire—the firing of one plug by the spark intended for another—can be deadly, especially in a high performance or racing engine. It usually occurs when the high resistance found in a cylinder during the compression cycle causes the current leaving the rotor to jump to an adjacent terminal (where resistance is lower) and fire the plug to which it's connected. Since that is usually the next one in the firing order, the cylinder has already started filling with an intake charge when the misdirected spark occurs. This charge is ignited and combustion takes place

while the piston is completing its intake cycle and transitioning to its compression cycle. The result of such extremely early lighting of the air/fuel mixture, which the upward traveling piston is trying to compress, is excess heat and pressure—and sometimes engine failure.

Some race engines, especially those with fixed timing, are prone to an entirely different type of crossfire. The errant spark will travel to the previously fired cylinder because the exhaust gasses in the cylinder provide a low resistance path. While this type of crossfire is not destructive, it does reduce power output. With the advent of high energy ignitions, the potential for crossfire has increased dramatically, but by taking the proper steps, such problems can be eliminated.

Spacing Things Out

One change necessitated by high energy ignition systems was in distributor cap configuration. Normally, the rotor tip is properly aligned with the distributor cap terminals when vacuum advance is at or near its highest level, as in a highway cruise condition. Under such conditions, the manifold vacuum causes the advance mechanism to rotate (advance) the magnetic pickup (or points in a standard system) such that when it triggers a spark, the rotor tip and appropriate distributor cap terminal are properly aligned. Since a typical passenger car engine spends most of its life in cruise mode, this arrangement is quite logical as it minimizes the distance the spark has to travel between rotor tip and terminal. But under full throttle or heavy load conditions, when manifold vacuum is too low to actuate the

With a conventionally sized distributor cap, ventilation (to allow ionized air to escape) may be necessary to eliminate crossfire. When drilling holes in a cap, be extremely careful or you may find yourself thumbing a ride to the parts store. Vented caps are available from MSD.

(vacuum) advance unit, and resistance at the plug gap is greatest, the rotor is no longer properly aligned (or phased) and crossfire can easily result if a distributor cap has closely spaced terminals. Improperly phased rotors increase the possibility of crossfire within the cap.

Solutions—This problem can be solved by fitting a larger diameter cap which allows the terminals to be spaced further from each other. Therefore, even if a rotor is out of phase, the distance between its tip and the adjacent terminal raises resistance to a point above that represented by the terminal to which current should be transferred. The path of least resistance then becomes the right one, and the potential for crossfire within the cap is all but eliminated—unless rotor misalignment is excessive.

Narrowing of the rotor tip is another means of reducing the possibility of crossfire within the cap. Grinding or filing the leading edge of the rotor tip increases the distance between it and the next terminal in the firing order. Filing a rotor tip's leading edge also delays the arrival of the rotor at the

desired terminal, so you'd do well to check spark timing if you modify the rotor tip.

In many instances, it isn't possible or desirable to install a large diameter HEI distributor. It is for such situations that the MSD Cap-A-Dapt was designed. In addition to the cap and adapter, the Cap-A-Dapt kit also features a special two-piece rotor which can be adjusted to obtain proper phasing. Cap-A-Dapt kits are available for standard Chevrolet, Accel and Mallory distributors. But regardless of the cap or rotor configuration, use high quality parts. High performance caps and rotors such as those available from Accel, Jacobs, Mallory and MSD have a higher dielectric strength than their stock counterparts, so they do a better job of spark containment.

Ionization

As a spark jumps the air gap between the rotor tip and distributor terminal (a small gap is normal as it allows current to be routed to each terminal without metal-to-metal contact), it charges or ionizes the particles of air through which it travels. Ionization of the air within the cap is usually a problem only with small diameter distributors. It can be reduced by installing an Alkyd cap (usually tan, brown, red or blue in color) keeping it clean and free of carbon tracks and ensuring proper rotor phasing. Rotors with fins on their top surface keep the air inside a cap stirred up and also tend to reduce ionization problems. However, it may be necessary to vent the cap by drilling holes in it. This allows fresh air to enter, displacing the charged air inside. But it is advisable only for race cars or vehicles rarely driven in

inclement weather, as moisture can easily enter the distributor.

Inductive Crossfire

Another form of crossfire, and one that is rarely understood, is caused by inductance. If you remember how a coil operates—current flowing through the primary winding creates a magnetic field that wraps itself around both the primary and secondary windings, inducing a voltage and consequently current though the two windings never touch—you're on the road to understanding inductive crossfire.

It usually occurs in the adjacent firing cylinders of a V-8 engine—numbers 5 and 7 on a small block Chevrolet—where the two plug wires in question run close together over a relatively long distance. Inductive crossfire is especially prevalent in wires with solid-metal cores.

In effect, the two wires become a transformer much like a coil. As current flows through the "primary" (the first of the two cylinders to fire) it builds a magnetic field that wraps itself around the adjacent wire and induces a voltage in the "secondary." This results in a weak spark reaching the plug in the corresponding cylinder. The cure is to maintain adequate spacing between wires (use non-metallic wire separators), avoid running wires parallel to one another over a long distance, and to install helical core plug wires. In a helical or wire-wound spark plug wire, the conductor is spiral or helical wound around a non-conductive core. By winding the conductor in a spiral, the magnetic field is disrupted, eliminating the possibility of inductive crossfire. ■

CUSTOM PROMS

The springs and weights are gone. Semi-conductors have taken over control of spark advance in late model computer-controlled small blocks. When an Engine Control Module is calling the shots, the only way to make changes is with a custom PROM. For stock and lightly modified engines, an off-the-shelf PROM is usually satisfactory. But if an engine has been extensively modified, a custom PROM is in order. There are a number of specialists across the country that can supply satisfactory custom calibrations, but it's also possible to do your own using a program called MasterTune from TTS Power Systems of Compton, CA.

But before you can evaluate the existing PROM to determine the required changes, you need another program to read and record the ECM's input and output readings. One such piece of software is Diacom from Rinda Technologies of Chicago, IL. Diacom records all sensor inputs and also displays selected outputs such as spark advance and the amount of knock retard. That information is used as the basis for the changes that will be programmed into a new PROM.

Whether or not you plan to do any experimenting with custom chips, if you race a vehicle with a computer-controlled engine, you need some type of device to record sensor inputs. It's the only way to know what the ECM is telling the engine.

VEHICLE TYPE: 1987 CHEVROLET	ENGINE TYPE: 5.0 Liter V8
ECM MODE STATUS: NOT LINKED	ECM PROM ID: 7961

Engine Speed	4475 RPM	Spark Adv Relative to TDC	34.9 DEG
Desired Idle Speed	600 RPM	Spark Adv Relative to Ref	27.5 DEG
Vehicle Speed	29 MPH	Knock Retard	1.6 DEG
RPM/MPH Ratio	159 :1	Spark Control Counts	0 #
Coolant Temperature	176 F	Integrator	128 #
Start-up Coolant Temp	169 F	Block Learn Multiplier	153 #
Manifold Air Temperature	88 F	Block Learn Cell Number	15 #
Throttle Sensor Voltage	4.02 VDC	EGR Duty Cycle	0 %
Filtered Load Variable	153 g/c	Canister Purge Duty Cycle	0 %
Oxygen Sensor Voltage	969 mV	Cooling Fan Duty Cycle	100 %
Oxygen Sensor Transitions	9 #	Battery Voltage	13.3 VDC
Air/Fuel Ratio (commanded)	11.6 :1	Fuel Pump Relay Voltage	13.5 VDC
Injector Pulse Width	9.6 mS	Engine Running Time	1 Min
Idle Air Position	87 #	Closed Loop Status	On
Air Flow Rate	140 GPS	Fuel Mixture Status	Rich

Configure Disk Exit Graph Info Link Mode Options Print Trbl_codes

Diagnostic data trace: Relative time frame -33

USE ←→ ARROW KEYS or SPACE BAR TO SELECT OPTION THEN PRESS "Enter"

RPUDYNE

Diacom records ECM data at a rate of approximately 16 frames pre second. The frame shown here pertains to a drag strip pass made in a 305 Camaro. Note that engine speed is 4475 rpm, vehicle speed is 29 miles per hour and spark advance is programmed for a total of 34.9°. Also note that 1.6° of knock retard is evident, meaning total advance was modified because the knock sensor heard something.

MASTERTUNE ELECTRONIC ENGINE TUNER		
0011	ECM CONSTANTS/SWITCH SETTINGS	DAVI

FUEL CUT OFF MPH	185
FUEL RESUME MPH	182
FUEL CUT OFF RPM	6500
FUEL RESUME RPM	6044
FAN 1 OFF (Deg C)	73
FAN 1 ON (Deg C)	80
FAN 2 OFF (Deg C)	73
FAN 2 ON (Deg C)	80
VATS SELECT	DISABLED
VATS DIAGNOSTIC, (Err 53)	ENABLED
KNOCK DIAGNOSTIC, (Err 42)	ENABLED
Vehicle Speed DIAGNOSTIC, (Err 24)	ENABLED
INJ FLOW RATE, SINGLE FIRE FIRE, #/HR	23.0
INJ FLOW RATE, DOUBLE FIRE FIRE, #/HR	23.0

In addition to allowing spark advance to be set according to engine rpm and load, the MasterTune program also provides the ability to alter the ECM's built-in rpm and mile per hour limiters. These limiters function by cutting off fuel rather than spark. This PROM has been set to limit top speed to 185 miles per hour. Want to go for a ride?

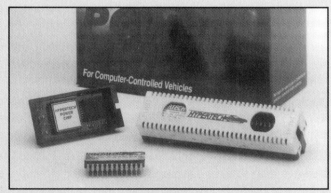

The small blocks installed in late-model cars and trucks are computer controlled, which means there are no springs or weights in the distributor. The spark curve (as well as air/fuel ratio) is controlled by a computer chip. High performance PROMs typically incorporate a more aggressive timing curve for wide opent throttle acceleration. These PROMS are from Hypertech.

NITROUS OXIDE & SUPERCHARGING

9

NITROUS OXIDE

Nitrous oxide is a chemical compound that comes bubbling along whenever two nitrogen atoms decide to tango with one oxygen atom. Technically known as N_2O, it contains 36% oxygen (by weight). Nitrous oxide won't burn by itself, but what it does bring to an internal combustion party is a lot of oxygen, which is an essential ingredient in the combustion process. Also known as "laughing gas," nitrous oxide has been used as an anesthetic for quite some time.

As opposed to more traditional engine modifications (cams, heads, carbs, headers, etc.), nitrous oxide requires no engine disassembly and has no impact on fuel economy or exhaust emissions when not in use. And should a nitrous-equipped car be sold, the basic system can be easily removed and transferred to another vehicle with the right adaptive hardware.

Basic Nitrous Systems

Although it doesn't pressurize the intake tract, a nitrous oxide system can be thought of as a "chemical supercharger." The most basic nitrous oxide system consists of an injector plate, a supply tank with manual on/off valve, the lines and fittings to

Nitrous oxide—it makes people laugh and engines growl. Also known as laughing gas, nitrous oxide injection functions as a chemical supercharger when fed into the intake tract. Nitrous vaporizes at -128° (F) and can drop temperatures in the intake tract by up to 70°. (Photo courtesy NOS)

connect the two, mounting hardware and electrical switches to activate the system. The injector plate contains two spray bars (nozzles) and is easily installed beneath a carburetor or fuel injection throttle body. In a basic system, calibration is fixed to deliver the precise amounts of nitrous oxide and supplemental fuel needed to boost horsepower a given amount. More sophisticated systems contain replaceable jets, which allow power output to be increased or decreased. Most adjustable single four-barrel

street systems offer power increases ranging from 100 to 175 horsepower. Race systems designed for single four-barrel small blocks deliver 150 to 200 extra horsepower.

Direct-port nitrous oxide injection systems can be mounted externally, or concealed beneath the intake manifold. These systems can be calibrated to provide up to 300 horsepower—provided engine displacement and port size are adequate for handling the required amount of nitrous oxide and

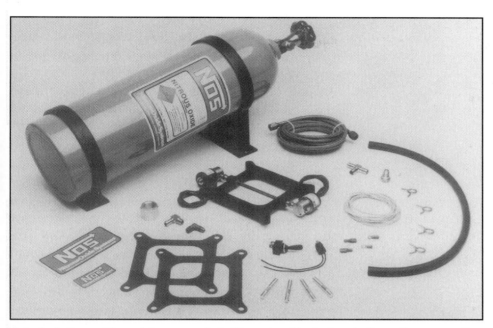

A typical nitrous kit contains a supply bottle, solenoids, fuel and nitrous lines, mounting hardware, activation switches and an injector plate that fits beneath the carburetor or fuel injection throttle body.

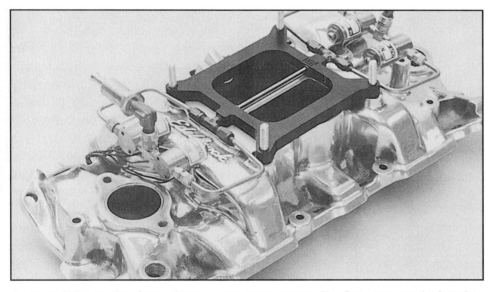

A new variation on the nitrous theme—a two-stage system. The first stage can be jetted to produce from 50-175 horsepower so the tires don't go up in smoke when a car is launched. Once everything is hooked up and traction isn't as much of a problem, the second stage is activated for an even greater power increase.

the liquid will vaporize, at which point there will be a severe drop in temperature; at the moment that liquid turns to vapor, nitrous temperature is minus 128° F. One of the reasons that injector plate systems (placed beneath the carburetor or fuel injection throttle body) work so well is that vaporizing nitrous cools the entire contents of the intake manifold. Port injectors, being located much closer to the valves, offer less of a cooling effect, but pump more nitrous oxide directly into the intake ports.

Increasing Horsepower

Nitrous oxide injection systems increase horsepower through two distinct means. As a gas flowing into the intake tract, nitrous oxide is an oxygen-bearing compound containing two parts nitrogen and one part oxygen. Since it's injected (under high pressure) directly into the intake manifold, an engine is force fed more oxygen than it could receive by drawing air through the carburetors or fuel injection throttle body. This is the chemical supercharging aspect of nitrous oxide; provided additional fuel is also brought to the party, increasing the amount of oxygen that an engine consumes translates into greater potential power output.

Cooling Effects—The second power-producing facet of nitrous oxide's personality is its cooling effect. Being at a sub-zero temperature when it enters the intake tract, nitrous cools everything around it, including the air and fuel that has been drawn in through the carburetor or throttle body. As the temperature of air drops, it becomes denser, thereby increasing the number of oxygen molecules in a given volume of air space. The number of nitrogen

complementary fuel.

Operation—Inside the storage tank or bottle (which must be properly mounted so that the internal siphon tube angles down), nitrous oxide liquid lives in a high pressure environment—approximately 900 psi (actual pressure varies according to ambient temperature). As it exits the solenoid, nitrous enters a low-pressure area (inside the intake manifold). At and/or below atmospheric pressure,

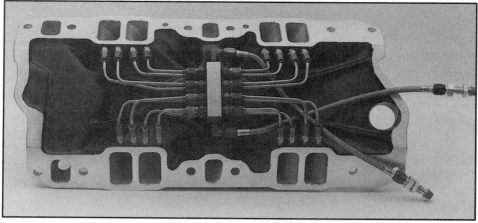

Direct port nitrous systems can be plumbed beneath the intake manifold and totally concealed. These systems are typically jetted to produce up to 250 discreet horsepower.

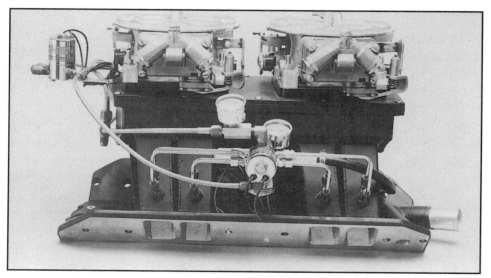

Most full-on race systems are of the direct port persuasion and are plumbed externally. This installation, on a tunnel ram, utilizes "Fogger" nozzles for improved atomization.

That's a serious problem, because a nitrous system is activated under maximum load conditions—the worst possible time to feed an engine a mixture that is either too rich or too lean (with nitrous, both can be deadly). Problems ranging from poor performance to severe detonation and terminal engine damage are frequently the result of nothing more than an inadequate fuel delivery system. The vehicle's fuel pump and plumbing must be capable of meeting the demands of the carburetor/fuel injection and the nitrous system simultaneously. To guard against lean mixture problems, a fuel monitor should be installed that automatically shuts off the flow of nitrous if fuel pressure drops below a predetermined level.

One way to accomplish this is with a controller like the Nitrous Mastermind from Jacobs Electronics (800/627-8800). One of the primary benefits of this controller is that it shuts off nitrous flow when fuel pressure drops below 4 psi. An optionally available adjustable pressure switch allows minimum fuel pressure at which nitrous is allowed to flow to range between 1 psi and 7 psi. But the Nitrous Mastermind also tailors nitrous flow to engine speed. Since an engine can safely ingest more nitrous as rpm increases, the "Mastermind" progressively increases nitrous flow as engine speed moves up the scale. Another safeguard is a circuit that prevents nitrous activation below a predetermined rpm point. And to make sure that nitrous isn't flowing when the engine hits the rev limiter, the system also cuts nitrous flow 50 rpm before it activates the built-in ignition rev limiter.

An adequate ignition also plays a

molecules is also increased, but is of no significance since nitrogen does not participate in the combustion process. So even if nitrous oxide did not support combustion, its cooling effect would still increase power output.

Fuel Requirements

The fact that nitrous oxide delivers a substantial shot of oxygen necessitates that fuel also be injected through a special circuit that is precisely calibrated. By weight, the theoretical optimum ratio of nitrous oxide to gasoline is about 9.5:1. But as a matter of practice, this ratio is usually altered to about 8.75 parts of nitrous for each part of gas. This slightly richer ratio helps prevent combustion temperatures from getting out of hand. It's rather obvious then that jetting of the nitrous system's fuel circuit is critical. If fuel flow is inadequate, the overall air/fuel mixture will be excessively lean.

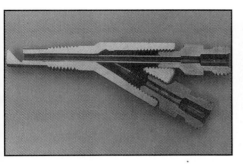

The "Fogger" nozzle exposed. It's really two nozzles in one. Fuel flows through the tube running down the center while nitrous is brought in around it. As the nitrous vaporizes it improves fuel atomization.

All solenoids are not the same. Internal passages can vary according to manufacturer and application and bigger ISN'T always better. If the passage on the supply side of the nitrous solenoid is too large, the solenoid may be prone to sticking closed because it can't overcome the nitrous pressure. Fluid enters through the outer passage and exits in the center.

It's not necessary with a street system, but on a race car, it's common practice to install two fuel pumps, one connected to the carburetors, the other to the nitrous system. Fuel starvation must be avoided at all costs to ensure proper system operation and engines that don't go boom.

Bottle pressure affects nitrous/fuel ratio and temperature affects nitrous pressure. When consistency is a major consideration, a bottle warmer is frequently installed to keep temperature constant. A bottle blanket can also be added to retain heat.

major role in the quest for maximum horsepower, especially with dual or triple stage nitrous systems. Any time you increase cylinder pressure, through any means, it increases the load on the ignition system. Any engine with nitrous—even a small 75-100 horsepower system—should have a solid high energy ignition system.

Although horror stories still abound, nitrous oxide injection systems offer safe and reliable horsepower—if they're properly installed. Fuel delivery is critical. The system needs to maintain at least 4.5 psi of fuel pressure under all operating conditions including maximum rpm in high gear. Some nitrous companies say that pressure can drop as low as 4 psi, and that's true—if your fuel system is absolutely perfect and your pressure gauge is dead-nuts accurate. But there are gauges that have been off by as much as a pound, and if they ever drop to 4 psi while the nitrous is activated, and the engine is under maximum load, the engine is history.

While a dependable high-volume fuel pump is an essential part of a nitrous system, it doesn't necessarily guarantee adequate fuel delivery. Some people install a high-volume fuel pump and connect it to a quarter-inch fuel line that has to run 15 feet to the engine and wonder why they have fuel delivery problems. That's one example of an improper installation. Even for a mild street engine, a 3/8-in. (or -6 AN) fuel line is needed at the very least; race cars call for a 1/2-in. (-8 AN) or larger fuel line.

Bottle Pressure

Nitrous bottle pressure is another factor that can cause problems. Although pressure usually isn't critical in a street installation (because things aren't being pushed to the limit) it can have a critical impact on a race engine. Surprisingly, even seasoned racers frequently overlook bottle pressure. According to Mike Hedgecock, pressure is most critical and has to be consistent because pressure and jetting are what control the amount of nitrous that goes into the engine. Normally, pressure will increase during the day as temperatures creep up, and drop at night when it cools off. Too many racers worry about (nitrous system) jet size and don't have the faintest idea what their bottle pressure is. That's like worrying about plug gap when you don't know where the timing is set. And it can be the end of your engine. If the pressure is up, and you don't adjust the fuel, you can get into a lean condition that's bad enough to cause severe detonation.

Camshafts

Another key to maximizing performance and minimizing problems with nitrous oxide is to use common sense when building or modifying the engine. The most

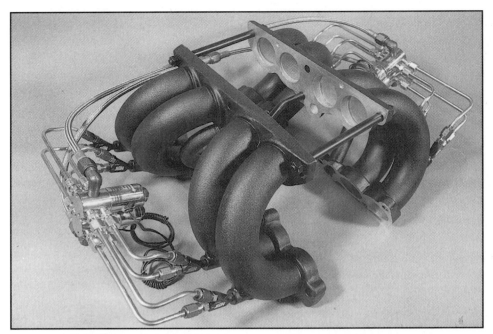

Nitrous oxide and late-model fuel injection engines are a marriage made in heaven. A nitrous system is self-contained and doesn't interfere with computerized engine controls. This is a rather "aggressive" system for a TPI engine. Milder systems are plumbed in at the throttle body. Plate-type systems are also available for TPI engines. The plate fits between the throttle body and plenum, making installation quick, easy and very effective.

sensible approach with a street engine is to select a camshaft that delivers strong low-speed and mid-range torque for everyday driving. That will ensure crisp throttle response, good fuel economy and driveability. Then the nitrous system can be called upon to really wake things up when it's needed.

Race Engines—Camming a race engine for use with nitrous also requires a bit of thought. If you plan to use "the bottle" only after the car has been launched (possibly in high gear only) a cam must be selected with that in mind. A car won't produce very impressive elapsed times if it's a slug until the nitrous system is activated.

Other Considerations

Beyond that, be sure to select a system produced by a reputable manufacturer; the money you save by

buying an off-brand can be real expensive if you destroy an engine because of a nitrous system malfunction. Installation is usually a simple matter of following the manufacturers' instructions. Be sure to mount the bottle properly (away from engine heat), keep the nitrous and fuel lines away from the exhaust pipes, and make sure your electrical connections are correct.

Limits—Being reasonable is another prerequisite; you can only put so much nitrous through any given engine because every intake port has a flow limitation. A given engine can be forced to consume only so much nitrous. Once the bounds of good judgment are exceeded, you've created an accident that's waiting to happen. Carburetors meter fuel in response to a vacuum signal that's communicated through the intake manifold to the discharge nozzles.

Injecting too much nitrous into the manifold can kill this signal, thereby reducing the amount of fuel metered by the carburetor, causing a lean condition. Racers using too many stages of nitrous set on "kill" have learned this expensive lesson the hard way—by destroying engines.

SUPERCHARGING

Even if a supercharger didn't add an ounce of horsepower to an engine, it would still have merit. If nothing else, a 6-71 GMC blower makes any small block look—and sound—like it's pumping out more horsepower than a big-block Pro Stocker. But as anyone who has driven a car powered by a supercharged engine can attest, blowers do a whole lot more than add looks and sound.

GMC

When General Motors Corporation (GMC) began manufacturing superchargers for its inline 6-cylinder diesel truck, bus and industrial engines back in the Thirties, no one had the faintest inkling that these units would one day be reworked for use on race engines. The first GM diesel was

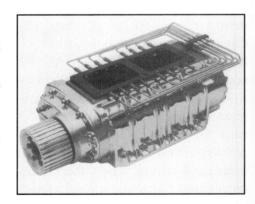

Nitrous can also be added to a supercharger. Most systems discharge through a plate that fits between the carburetor adapter and blower body.

Mounting a supercharger on top of a small block doesn't do anything but make a good thing better. The sound of a well-tuned small block with a blower on top will even send chills down the spine of Ford lover. There may not be a true substitute for cubic inches, but a blower comes mighty close.

the 6-71; the designation refers to six cylinders each with a volume of 71 cubic inches. Over the years, GMC has produced 3-71, 4-71, 6-71 inline and 6V-71, 8V-71 blowers, the latter two being used on V-engines.

The 4-71 and 6-71 are most commonly used on small-block Chevy engines. Some 8-71 and 10-71 blowers have also found their way onto drag-race-only small blocks. The 8-71 uses 8V-71 rotors mounted in an aftermarket case; the original 8V-71 case doesn't lend itself to use on an automotive V-8 engine. A 10-71 blower is built entirely of aftermarket components. The primary difference between each of these blowers is length; an 8-71 is one inch longer than a 6-71; a 10-71 is one inch longer than

an 8-71 and a 12-71 (used only in big block alcohol and fuel applications) is one inch longer than a 10-71.

Roots Type—All GMC-type blowers are of the Roots type; all Roots-type blowers are termed positive displacement. The basic design, which incorporates two rotors, was first patented by the Roots Brothers in the mid-1800s. GMC blowers are obviously a far cry from the original Roots configuration, but still share the label, as does any multi-rotor supercharger.

The first use of GMC blowers as a means of increasing the power of automotive engines dates back to the late Forties. Most installations were relatively crude affairs, but they worked—sometimes all too well.

Racers of the day didn't have adequate knowledge or fuels and many an engine expired as a result of too much boost and not enough octane. However, by the early Sixties most of the bugs had been worked out and GMC blowers (commonly called "Jimmies") had become fairly common sights at drag strips across the country. And by the 1980s, enthusiasm for the look, sound and power produced by "Jimmy" blowers had spread to all types of street cars and boats. The tremendous popularity of GMC blowers prompted companies like B&M and Weiand Automotive to develop their own positive displacement blowers specifically for street applications.

How It Works

Superchargers increase horsepower by literally forcing increased volumes of air and fuel into the cylinders. In a normally aspirated engine, power output increases as air temperature drops because the cooler the air, the more dense it is, which means that more air (and the oxygen it contains) is drawn into the cylinders than normal. Regardless of the way it's achieved, increased cylinder filling translates directly to increased power output. By mechanically stuffing the cylinders with air and fuel, a supercharger makes it possible to achieve power levels not possible with normal atmospheric conditions; the more air/fuel mixture that's rammed into an engine, the more power it produces—up to a point.

Drive Ratio & Boost

Boost is the determining factor. Whereas a naturally aspirated engine operates with some amount of manifold vacuum, a blown engine has

Blower drive ratio can be altered by changing the top, bottom or both pulleys. Top and bottom pulleys can be interchanged on most 6-71 drive systems, making it very easy to switch from underdrive to overdrive.

Weiand's street blower was designed to simplify installation. It's smaller than a 6-71, so it won't put out as much boost, but it is more than adequate for most street engines. It's size and drive arrangement are definite advantages in crowded engine compartments.

measurable positive pressure (stated in psi) in its intake tract once engine speed reaches a certain point. The drive ratio is largely what determines the amount of boost that a blower will produce. When a supercharger spins slower than the engine, it is said to be underdriven; if it rotates faster than engine speed, it's overdriven. Drive ratio is only one of the factors that determine boost. Valve timing, compression ratio and clearances within the blower itself are also part of the equation. Consequently, the correlation between drive ratio and the amount of boost pressure produced is not always consistent; 3% underdrive may result in 5 pounds of boost on one engine and 8 on another of the same displacement.

Pulleys—Most drive systems incorporate pulley sizes that allow drive ratio to be altered in steps of 3%; tooth count is used to determine drive ratio and each time the count is altered by one tooth, the ratio changes 3%. As an example, Weiand's small-block Chevy street supercharger kits are supplied with 33-tooth bottom and 37-tooth top pulleys which produce a 12% underdrive ratio. Switching to a 34-tooth bottom pulley alters the ratio to 9% underdrive. Whether it's the top pulley (on the blower) or bottom pulley (on the crankshaft) the effect on drive ratio is the same.

The beauty of this system is that top and bottom pulleys are interchangeable so a quick switch from underdrive to overdrive can be made by just swapping pulleys. Drive ratio is computed by dividing the number of teeth in the bottom pulley by the tooth count of the top pulley;

$$\text{Drive Ratio} = \frac{\text{Bottom Pulley Tooth Count}}{\text{Top Pulley Tooth Count}}$$

Using the Weiand kit mentioned above, you'd divide 33 by 37 which gives you .89. This means the top pulley spins at 89% of the bottom pulley speed or that it is spinning 11% slower. A figure of 12% rather than 11% is normally used for simplicity. When the pulleys are switched, the equation becomes 37 divided by 33, which translates to 1.12 or 112% or 12% overdrive (rounding will also alter actual ratios slightly). Generally, for each change in top or bottom pulley tooth count (which alters drive ratio by 3%) there's a one to two psi change in boost pressure.

Belts—Any particular drive ratio can be achieved through a number of pulley combinations. A 12% overdrive or underdrive ratio can be achieved with either a 32/36-, 33/37-, 34/38- or 35/39-tooth pulley combination. However, from a practical standpoint, wherever possible, it's preferable to switch to a larger pulley or pulleys (rather than

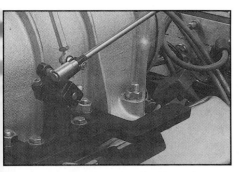

Whatever else you do, don't scrimp on carburetor linkage, especially with two four-barrel carbs. A good solid pivot mounting and a wide range of adjustment make set-up and adjustment easier and prevent slippage.

smaller) when making a ratio change because belt speed is reduced—thereby increasing belt life. As an example, if you wanted to switch from a 12% underdrive to 9% underdrive, the preferred choice is to install a 38/35 combination rather than a 37/34. However, if the existing combination for 12% underdrive was 37/33, it would only be necessary to change the bottom pulley to arrive at 9% underdrive. From an economic standpoint, that's a better choice. However, sometimes it isn't possible to change only one pulley unless a different length belt is also used so the economics of each situation have to be weighed. Fortunately, there's a good deal of belt tensioner adjustment on most drive systems so a wide variety of drive ratios can be accommodated with a single belt. Belt length for small block 6-71 blower installations is generally 54, 55.5, 56 or 57 inches; these lengths will cover total tooth counts (top and bottom pulley tooth counts added together) of 64-78.

When it comes to building supercharged street and race engines, Jim Oddy has a reputation that's hard to beat. Jim Oddy, who operates Oddy's Automotive (651 Bullis Road,

Elma, NY 14059, 716/674-2500) has the distinction of owning the world's quickest "doorslammer." His supercharged Pro Modified cars have recorded 1/4-mile elapsed times of in the 6.40s with a best-ever performance of 6.35 seconds at 219.88 mph.

Oddy also builds a number of blown small blocks for both street and race, and he's developed some interesting combinations. According to Oddy:

"You just can't beat a 6-71 for a street small block. You can make over 600 horsepower from a 350 on unleaded premium with 10 pounds of boost. But what we generally advise is for someone to start out with a combination that limits boost to 5 or 6 pounds. There's a learning curve that you have to go through to find the type of gas, gear ratio, timing, valve adjustment and converter the engine likes. By limiting boost to 5-6 pounds, you probably won't hurt anything if you're off because you won't be on the borderline of detonation. Then, after everything is right, you can bump the boost up and make more horsepower—safely."

Race Motors—Race motors are different; they're on kill all the time. So while Oddy limits the boost of his street engines to 10 psi or less, a race engine will crank up 22-25 psi. The extra boost may not do much for longevity, but it does wonders for horsepower. Blown small blocks fitted with 8-71 blowers are approaching 3-hp per cubic inch on gasoline. In a race engine, the advantage of the 8-71 over the 6-71 is two-fold. First, the larger blower can be run slower and still make the same amount of boost. Secondly, it builds

boost quicker, so it brings the power up quicker too. Total power potential is also greater with a larger blower (Oddy has also done some 10-71 small blocks) but as with anything, there are limits. By overdriving the blower to extremes, you'll gain power up to a point because the air will become heated too much. Also, the faster the blower is driven, the more torque is siphoned off the engine to drive it. So somewhere along the line you reach a point of diminishing returns. Air inlet temperature is a key thing that no one talks about, but it makes a tremendous difference. If the temperature of the air exiting the blower can be reduced by 70 deg., for example, an increase of 70 horsepower is possible. An intercooler is the only way to do that, but they've been banned by most racing organizations.

Fuel Systems—As a general rule, never go beyond a 1:1 drive ratio (into overdrive) if you're running pump gas; when you start cranking in boost, you need race gas in the tank. As with

Whether a mechanical or electric pump is to be used, it must have sufficient output to avoid fuel starvation. Installation of an electric pump is usually the best way to avoid problems.

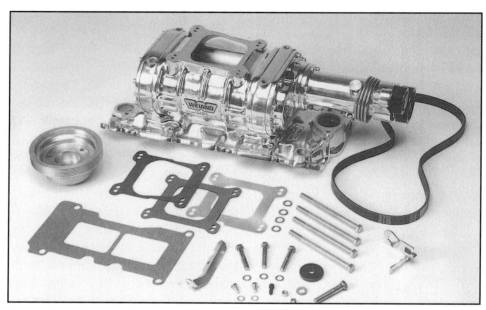

Believe it or not, some blowers are even emissions-legal. Weiand's small block blowers are 50-state legal when installed on 1962-1986 small blocks that were originally equipped with a carburetor.

nitrous, make sure the fuel system is adequate. Oddy recommends running -8 line (1/2 in.) from the fuel tank to the mechanical fuel pump, and -6 lines (3/8 in.) from the pump to the carburetors. It's also advisable to use both a high volume mechanical fuel pump and an electric pump (the electric pump pumps to the mechanical pump). If the electric pump fails, you won't get stuck because the mechanical pump will still be operating. Use a mechanical pump that is rated at about 11 psi and a regulator to maintain a constant 8 psi; to avoid fuel delivery short-fall, the system should be able to maintain 8 psi at the carburetors, under all operating conditions.

Ignition Timing—Ignition timing is also critical with a supercharged engine. Limit total timing to 28-30° because his research has shown that the blower builds so much cylinder pressure that the engine doesn't like a lot of timing. In his opinion, too much advance is the biggest engine killer on

the street—it just beats the bearing and rings to death. Every small block Oddy runs on the dyno makes maximum power with 28-30° Even on a race engine, running race gas, he rarely goes beyond 32°. That's one of the keys to making a blown motor live. If everything is done right, there's no reason that a blown street motor shouldn't last for over 100,000 miles. In reality, most street-driven vehicles don't get into boost that often. If you were driving on "kill" all the time, things would be different.

Even though street engines have boost limited, cylinder pressures and combustion temperatures get high enough to warrant extremely cold spark plugs. Oddy generally uses BL57 or BL60 Champion plugs. These are cold race plugs, so the ignition needs to be hot to avoid fouling. You will probably need an MSD-6A box at the very least to keep the plugs clean. A dual point deal just won't cut it because the engine won't stay running.

Dampers—Another component that Oddy feels very strongly about is the vibration damper. When a supercharged engine is operating under boost, it puts significantly higher loads on the crankshaft and bearings than a naturally aspirated one. Most blown race engines are notorious for getting only a handful of runs on a set of bearings. A number of years ago, Oddy was experiencing the typical short bearing life on his race engines so he began experimenting with the viscous vibration damper manufactured by Fluidampr. He noticed an immediate improvement in bearing life—instead of the bearings looking like trash after 10 runs or less, they lasted for over 30 runs and still looked like new. That experience prompted him to modify Fluidamprs specifically for supercharged engines. These modifications include drilling and tapping the necessary holes so a standard blower pulley (with six bolt holes) can be installed, and cutting a second keyway (1/4 in. wide). This is added to prevent the damper from

Since the drive pulley attached to the vibration damper, it's a good practice to install a high performance damper. As boost levels increase so does stress on the damper hub. Stock dampers have a tendency to crack.

B&M offers several versions of its street supercharger. The larger a blower's capacity, the more boost it can produce on a given engine.

blowers produce only 4-6 psi; even though these blowers are relatively efficient, their small size makes high drive ratios necessary.

The size relationship of a 6-71 compared to these smaller aftermarket blowers provides an insight into the reason for the extreme differences in drive ratio. A 6-71 has a displacement of 411 cid. Weiand's Pro Street small block blowers have a displacement of 144 cid; B&M's two standard Powerchargers for small blocks displace 144 and 162 cid respectively. But in spite of their size, the high drive ratios make it possible for these blowers to produce a reasonable amount of boost.

Limitations—Both the B&M and Weiand street blowers are designed to produce 5-6 pounds of boost on stock and mildly modified engines. They perform well in these type of applications, but problems frequently arise when attempts are made to push boost beyond design parameters. Both brands of blowers utilize a drive system that incorporates a ribbed, rather than a cog belt as found on a 6-71 installation. If you try to build too much boost, the belt will slip. The

spinning on the crankshaft in the event that the blower "sneezes" (kicks back).

Even on a street engine, a high performance damper should be used. Point one is that every engine needs a damper as opposed to a hub. Point two is that stock cast-iron dampers have a tendency to crack when used on supercharged engines. As horsepower increases, so does the need for adequate torsional vibration control, so just about every knowledgeable engine builder strongly advises the use of a high performance vibration damper on any supercharged engine.

Aftermarket vs. 6-71

The primary drawbacks of a 6-71 style blower are its expense and its size. Which is precisely the reason

that B&M and Weiand developed their own Roots-type blowers. B&M's Powerchargers (formerly called Forced Induction) and Weiand's Pro Street superchargers are smaller than a 6-71 and are designed specifically for use on automotive engines. These blowers have a carburetor mounting flange cast integrally in the blower housing and bolt to special intake manifolds which allow for a very low profile. The complete blower, with carburetor, will fit beneath the hoods of many cars and pickups.

Since the aftermarket blowers are relatively small, they must be turned at comparatively high rpm to develop boost. Both B&M and Weiand supply their street blowers with drive ratios in the vicinity of 2:1. In 6-71 parlance, that translates to 100% overdrive. But even at these drive ratios, these

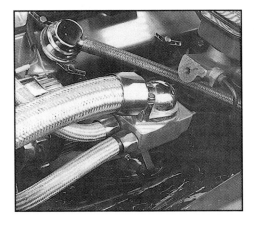

Depending on the blower manifold construction, it may not be possible to install a thermostat. Some people get around the problem by building a remote thermostat housing.

Several companies, including ATI, Paxton and Vortech offer centrifugal blower kits for late-model TPI engines. These kits offer very clean installation and some are even emissions-legal.

idler arrangement also contributes to belt slippage because the direction in which tension is applied pushes the belt away from the top pulley. Consequently, the belt doesn't get a good wrap around the pulley, which contributes to slippage. All blower drive systems have a similar idler mounting arrangement, but the larger blowers utilize a cog belt so slippage is never a problem.

That may sound like an indictment of these superchargers; it's not. When operated within their design parameters, the B&M and Weiand blowers both perform very well and can increase engine output by 75-100 horsepower (on stock and lightly modified engines). But forget about trying to get over seven pounds of boost, especially with a modified engine. If you really want to pump up the power, you have to step up to a 6-71.

Several companies offer 6-71 street blower kits, and a variety of 6-71 and 8-71 race blower assemblies. In addition to Weiand, Blower Drive Service (12140 Washington Blvd., Whittier, CA 90606, 213/693-4302), Dyer's Machine Service (7665 W. 63rd St., Summit, IL 60501, 708/496-8100), Littlefield Blowers (6840 Orangethorpe, Buena Park, CA 90620, 714/739-2275), and Mooneyham Blowers (13406 Lakewood Blvd., Bellflower, CA 90706, 213/634-5192), offer kits. B&M offers its own version of the 6-71, called the MegaBlower. As opposed to incorporating a remanufactured 6-71, the MegaBlower is built entirely of components designed and manufactured by B&M. The company also offers a 250 Powercharger which is just as long as a MegaBlower, but two inches lower.

Centrifugal Blowers—Centrifugal blowers, such as those produced by Accessible Technologies Inc., (14014 W. 107th Street, Lenexa, KS 66215,

913/338-2886), Vortech Engineering (5351 Bonsai Ave., Moorpark, CA 93021, 805/529-9330) and Paxton (1260 Calle Suerte, Camarillo, CA 93012, 805/987-5555) also offer interesting power augmenting possibilities. Centrifugal blowers take air in at their center and force it out an orifice in the housing. In operation, a centrifugal blower uses an impeller, rather than overlapping rotors, to create boost. Centrifugal blowers are relatively small, and fit easily beneath the hood of just about any car. That's an important consideration with late model Camaros and Corvettes, because there isn't much usable vacant underhood space.

While they don't offer the massive appearance and distinctive sound of a 6-71, centrifugal blowers are appealing for several reasons. They produce significant power increases, they're compatible with late model fuel injection engines and the larger models can produce more than enough boost to put a crankshaft right out of the bottom of an engine.

The only major drawback to a centrifugal blower is that it doesn't build boost as quickly as a Roots-type. Rather than quickly building pressure and maintaining it as rpm increases, a centrifugal blower builds boost at an exponential rate—doubling rpm increases boost by a factor of four. However, since a street engine can withstand only so much boost, blower drive ratio must be set to provide a particular boost level at a specific rpm. Consequently, at lower engine speeds, boost drops off significantly. On the other hand, this can be a blessing—limiting boost at lower speeds creates fewer traction problems. ■

EXHAUST SYSTEMS

10

HEADERS

It was more years ago than I care to admit when I first became aware of a highly sought-after, but mysterious piece of "speed" equipment known as a header. The introduction occurred shortly after I obtained a driver's license when, with water dripping from behind my ears, I pulled in for gas and happened upon a gathering near one of the Sinclair station's repair bays. Charlie, a local racer who was convinced he was about to break into the big leagues of drag racing (and wanted everyone to know it), was regaling his audience with tales of dash and daring behind the wheel of his 348 cid, 335-horsepower, 1959 Chevrolet Impala. One of the unique features of Charlie's car was its exhaust system; it was the first car in the area to have headers. With all those pipes weaving their way around the motor, the engine compartment had a race-ready appearance, although to the untrained eye, it looked somewhat like a snake pit.

Charlie went on and on (as he was prone to do), expounding upon the merits of "tuned racing headers." His audience listened, mouths agape, until someone asked the origin of these wondrous power-producing tubes of steel. "I got 'em from Jerry Jardine," Charlie stated, "I just called him up in California and said 'Jerry, I need some headers, I gotta run this weekend.' He got them right out to me."

To launch like this, a drag race car obviously needs a well-designed set of headers. Tubing diameter is critical and if it's too large, performance will be compromised as much or more than if it's too small.

That was many years ago, and during the intervening decades, Jerry Jardine has moved on to building specialized automotive and motorcycle products, Charlie has gone on to who-knows-what and headers have come of age. In Charlie's day, they were produced by small "backyard" companies and were exclusively within the province of dedicated racers; today, headers are produced in huge factories and routinely installed on all manner of vehicles, all in the quest for improved performance or greater fuel economy. Even Chevrolet has gotten into the act. Corvettes produced from 1985 to 1991 were fitted with tubular exhaust manifolds right on the production line. While the factory headers don't offer the ultimate in performance potential (proper headers are too expensive and too difficult to install in a production line environment), they are a step above cast-iron exhaust manifolds.

Tri-Y

When tubular exhaust manifolds (the formal name for headers), were introduced, they were generally of the "Tri-Y" design. In this configuration, four relatively short primary tubes are

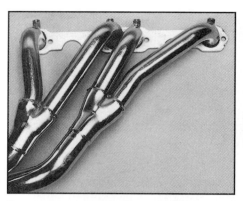

It may come as a surprise that Tri-Y headers are more expensive to produce than four-tube types. The Tri-Y design, saw widespread usage in the early sixties but interest slacked off as cheaper four-tube headers became readily available. Tri-Y's have been making a comeback of sorts because they can be more easily fit into crowded engine compartments.

Four-tube headers come in a variety of lengths and tubing diameters. Tubing wall thickness and flange thickness vary significantly—as does durability. These full-length headers are designed for 1982-92 Camaros that are not street driven—they contain no provisions for emissions-control equipment.

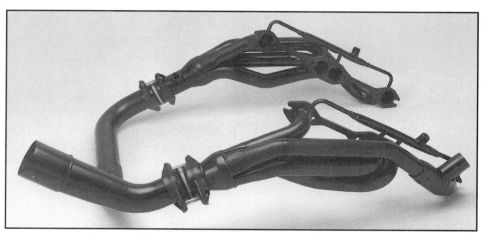

In order to be EPA- and CARB-approved for use on late-model vehicles, headers must contain provisions for connecting all original equipment emissions control equipment. These headers fit late-model Chevy trucks with 305 or 350 engines. Note threaded oxygen sensor hole in the collector.

connected in pairs, each of which leads into a larger diameter secondary tube. The two secondary tubes are then joined further downstream in a collector. As a result of primary tube pairing, adjacent firing cylinders are separated, at least until the exhaust gasses reach the collector. In fabricating a Tri-Y header, three individual "Y" connections are made, hence the name.

The stepped 4-2-1 arrangement of the pipes are especially conducive to increased horsepower in the lower and middle rpm ranges. The Tri-Y system was predominant well into the Sixties, until drag racing engines began peaking at considerably higher speeds. At this point, the four-tube, tuned, "equal length" header began to achieve more popularity. Although the Tri-Y arrangement, which bolsters low-speed and mid-range performance, is superior for most street and some race applications, it has been largely abandoned in the face of overwhelming demand for the individual tube variety. Tri-Y headers are harder to build and don't look as "racy" as the four-tube variety so they have two strikes against them. However, anyone looking for an increase in mid-range torque would do well to experiment with a set of Tri-Y headers (which may require jetting and timing changes).

Four-Tube Headers

Although some header companies still offer Tri-Y headers, the majority of commercially available tubular exhaust manifolds are comprised of separate tubes leading from a cylinder head port to a common collector. But from one manufacturer to another, there can be significant differences in the routes taken between the two termination points. Considering that all the tubes must end at a given length from the back of the block or other fore/aft reference point, it can be seen that the rear-most tube must travel a more tortuous route if it is to be the same length as the forward-most tube. With a true race header, the fabricator will do whatever is necessary to keep the lengths of all tubes within a very close tolerance. In fact, with some engine/chassis combinations, clearance is so tight that equal length can be approached only by routing a tube from one bank into the collector on the opposite side. Needless to say, installation of these headers are quite difficult, but fortunately, small-block Chevys rarely present such problems when installed in a production chassis.

Dedication to near-perfect equality of length may be appropriate for race car headers because race engines tend to operate over a much narrower rpm band than street engines. Length

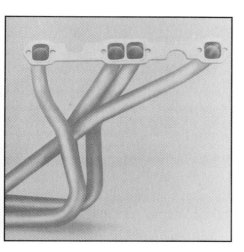

Race headers are typically fabricated from 1-3/4" or larger tubing. Use of this type of header on a street car isn't particularly wise as they will reduce power within the engine's normal operating range.

differences of much greater proportions are acceptable when an engine operates over a wide rpm range; so long as all pipes "tune" within the engine's normal rpm range length differences will not be particularly detrimental. In any event, much of the effect of tueffect is lost when an exhaust pipe and muffler are bolted to the output end of the collector.

Tubing Size

Diameter—Diameter is one of the most important factors with headers. If primary tube size is too large, both performance and fuel economy losses will be realized. In the days of oil "shortages," header manufacturers responded to the strong demand for mileage improving equipment by producing headers with primary tube diameters as small as 1-3/8". By comparison, in times when the demand for horsepower reigns supreme, street headers for small blocks are generally fabricated from tubing measuring 1-5/8" or 1-3/4" in

diameter. As a general rule of thumb, as engine size and/or normal operating rpm decrease, there should be a concurrent reduction in header tube diameter. It is for precisely this reason that some manufacturers list more than one part number (for a particular vehicle) when a single model would seem to be sufficient; each is designed for a particular application.

For example, early-model Camaros and Chevy IIs were available with a variety of small-block engines ranging in displacement from 302 to 350 cid. For race applications, a 1-7/8" or even 2" diameter might be appropriate, however, when the same engine/chassis combination is pressed into highway service, one would be better advised to install a set of headers with 1-5/8" or 1-3/4" tubes. And for pure economy driving, diameters of 1-3/8" or 1-1/2" might be in order. What all this means boils down to is that header tube diameter and length must be matched to a specific application for the best results.

BIBS—When selecting a set of headers, most people fall victim to BIBS—Bigger Is Better Syndrome. BIBS leads people to believe that if a set of 1-5/8" tube headers is good, a set with 1-3/4" tubes must be better and 1-7/8" header tubes must be pure heaven. Nothing could be further from the truth.

When primary tube diameter is too large, velocity is reduced and the header loses much of its scavenging capability. In a sense, this creates greater back pressure because the slight vacuum created by a column of gas moving at high velocity is absent. With properly sized primary tubes—or even tubes that are slightly too

small—exhaust gasses from each cycle help scavenge gasses from the following cycle. In turn, this action tends to improve the fuel metering signal that reaches the carburetor. So in spite of the commonly held belief that installing a set of headers requires a richer mixture, if the headers are correctly sized, a leaner mixture may be required to compensate for a stronger signal.

There's another reason to avoid installing race-type headers on a street engine. With headers having tubes measuring larger than 1-3/4" in diameter, installation may require special considerations. Placement of bolt holes with respect to the exhaust ports makes it impossible to bolt a set of 2" headers to a conventional small-block head. Large diameter headers are therefore installed in conjunction with an adapter plate. The plate is bolted to the head with tapered-head Allen bolts that are flush with the plate's surface and the headers are then bolted to a second set of more widely placed holes in the plate.

Late-model Camaros, Corvettes and pickups equipped with fuel injection obviously make concerns about carburetion irrelevant. While most of the headers produced for these vehicles incorporate 1-5/8" primary tubes, some feature 1-3/4" tubes. On the surface, these would appear to be too large, but these types of headers are typically very short, with the collectors being positioned near the cylinder block/oil pan junction. From there, a Y-pipe connects to the catalytic converter(s). In this type of installation, 1-3/4" headers often provide a performance increase over their 1-5/8" counterparts.

Length—What about length? Small-block headers vary from 15" to

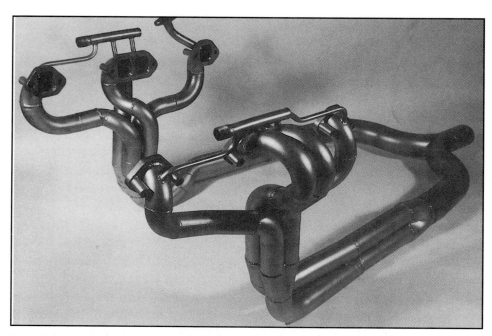

Material is one of the reasons that headers for late-model vehicles headers are made of stainless steel because it offers greater durability than mild steel. Emissions requirements for durability and higher under-hood temperatures require the use of materials like stainless.

over 40" in primary tube length; collector length ranges from 3" to 48". As with diameter, header length should be matched to engine size and operating rpm if possible. Even if tube and collector diameter are ideally matched to engine displacement, if the primary tubes and/or collectors are too short, maximum scavenging occurs at too high an engine speed to be of any use. On the other hand, if header tube and collector length are too long they'll restrict flow, particularly at higher engine speeds. So the key is to determine the ideal diameter/length combination for a particular engine operated within a specific rpm range. Whether it's a street machine, drag race or oval track car, truck, tractor or boat, the volume of exhaust produced by the engine is what determines header dimensions. A 302 cid race engine that turns 10,000 rpm will produce more exhaust gas volume than a 350 cid street engine that never sees the high

side of 5000 rpm.

Unfortunately, the ideal header may not fit the chassis in which the engine is installed; space limitations dictate that Corvette headers are shorter than Camaro, Nova or Chevelle headers. Side mounted exhausts can sometimes be used to extend header length, but there may be few other alternatives with an under-chassis exit aside from a set of custom-built headers. With emissions-controlled vehicles, placement of the catalytic converter is often the governing factor controlling header length.

Material

From the practical, as opposed to theoretical standpoint, material is a major consideration. In days of old, all header tubing was 18 gauge (.049") mild steel while the flange plate was cut from 1/4" thick material. A header so constructed usually offers sufficient strength and durability to provide years of good service, but in

the damper regions of the country, the effects of rust and general deterioration can end header life in a hurry. When improved durability is required, headers made of thicker (16 or 14 gauge) mild steel or stainless steel are available as are chrome-plated or aluminum coated models. Typically, headers manufactured with 5/16" or 3/8" thick flanges and 14- or 16-gauge tubing are noticeably quieter than those manufactured of lighter weight materials.

However, in many cases, "heavyweight" construction isn't applied across the board, so these types of headers may not be available for your particular application. Or they may not be desirable. If properly cleaned, and coated with high temperature paint, race car headers will last almost indefinitely. That being the case, headers made from heavy gauge material offer nothing more than extra weight—except in a few circumstances. Race cars that run for long periods of time may need heavier headers to avoid fracturing. In fact, reinforcing brackets may be required.

Tuning

Unquestionably, by tuning header length for maximum exhaust scavenging at a particular engine speed, there's a considerable amount of power to be gained. But before you spend a bunch of money, take a hard look at standard production headers. Some models offer adjustable primary tubes, and collector extensions can be easily made from appropriately sized tubing. Many times, a few modifications made to an existing header are all that's required for maximum horsepower. On the other hand, you may not be so lucky, and a

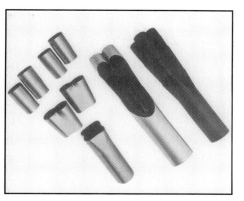

The best way to determine optimum header length is use the vehicle on which they'll be installed as a test bed. Several companies offer kits that allow primary tube and collector length to be easily adjusted.

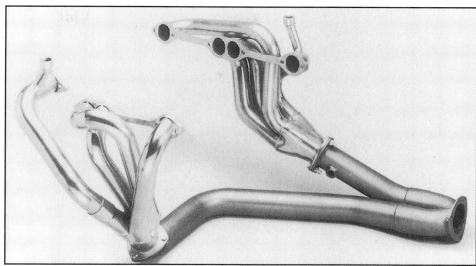

Fourth-Generation Camaros and Firebirds present an extremely challenging situation for header manufacturers because there isn't much clearance. Fortunately, high performance manufacturers usually rise to challenges. These '93-'95 Camaro/Firebird headers from Arizona Speed and Marine feature 1-3/4" primary tubes and a 2-1/2" y-pipe with a 3" flanged outlet.

custom set of headers may be the only way to handle the competition. In either case, do enough experimenting to get a handle on the dimensions of the ideal header for your car. Many custom header fabricators are excellent craftsmen, but don't know all they should about exhaust tuning. Their opinions may be of little value. However, a header maker who has built many different sizes of headers for your type of car can be invaluable.

Another consideration—on any vehicle equipped with a muffler, header length and diameter may not be all that critical. A muffler and exhaust system will negate much of any improvement derived from optimizing header configuration. This doesn't imply that such optimization is worthless, only that when a muffler is involved, the final performance achieved by optimizing header length and diameter will not justify the expense of designing and building a custom set of headers. A properly sized standard production header will deliver the best price/performance ratio. Any engine that will have its exhaust gasses routed through a muffler should be fitted with standard production headers.

However, some manufacturers offer headers that have been optimized for a particular engine/chassis combination—such as a stock-type 350 with Tuned Port Injection in a Corvette or Camaro. These headers will cost a bit more than standard "off the rack" models designed to accommodate everything from a bone stock to a highly modified engine—but they may offer enough of a performance improvement to justify the expense.

Diameter Guidelines—As a general guideline, stock or lightly modified street engines of approximately 350 cid should be equipped with 1-5/8" diameter headers; extensively modified 350's will benefit from 1-3/4" primary tubes; 283-307 cid engines call for 1-1/2" diameter tubes and 383-406 cid small blocks will benefit most from headers with 1-3/4" or 1-7/8" diameter tubes, depending upon the level of modification. In most cases, collectors that are 3" in diameter are the rule; the exception is when primary tube size is 1-1/2" or less, in which case a 2-1/2" diameter collector may be used. Following these recommendations may cost you a few horsepower at the top end, but power increases at lower speeds—where an engine spends most of its time—will more than compensate. Consequently, headers of the recommended diameter will produce better acceleration.

In fact, the recommended diameters will work surprisingly well on some race engines with limited rpm potential. The improved mid-range power will result in a better launch at the drag strip and more power off the corners of an oval track. Some experimentation with headers that are "too small" can pay handsome dividends at the track. However, fully developed race engines, which reach peak horsepower above 6000 rpm, require a header tube size ranging from 1-7/8" to 2-1/8", and 3-1/2"

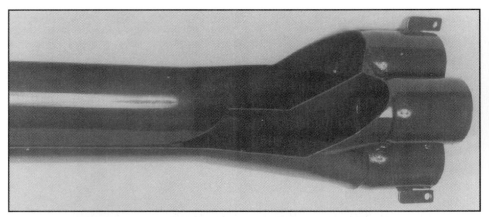

Several racers have found a performance improvement after installing a Flowmaster scavenger/collector. This four-two-one collector can be used on both race and street small blocks to improve mid-range torque.

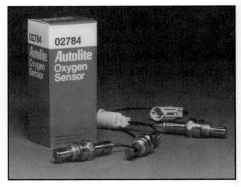

The exhaust gas oxygen sensor doesn't "light off" until it reaches normal operating temperature. When headers are installed, it may be necessary to replace the original EGO sensor with a preheated model; the further the sensor is from the cylinder head, the longer it takes to reach temperature.

collectors. Collector length can vary greatly depending upon the type of racing. Some 4- and 5-speed drag cars are equipped with headers having very short collectors, from 6" to 8", while oval track cars usually have collectors measuring over four feet in length. In all cases, a crossover pipe that connects the collectors will increase power.

One point to consider when choosing headers for a small block. With the advent of Tuned Port Injection, 350 cid engines have been coaxed into producing over 420 lbs-ft. of torque. Those are big block numbers, so a healthy TPI engine may require headers with larger diameter tubes than a similar carbureted engine.

Jetting & Timing—Any significant change made in the exhaust system brings with it a potential requirement to adjust the intake mixture and/or ignition timing. Switching from cast-iron exhaust manifolds to tubular headers results in less residual exhaust gas being left in the combustion chambers. This can result in the need for a slight change in jetting. Similarly, a change in header diameter or length may also require recalibration of the intake mixture.

Many times a "trick" set of headers is written off because it doesn't improve performance, or worse, decreases it. However, the real culprit may be the racer who failed to experiment with jetting and timing.

EGO—One of the advantages of computerized engine controls is that the exhaust gas oxygen (EGO) sensor "reads" the exhaust content and supplies the control module with the data necessary to correctly recalibrate the air/fuel ratio. In some vehicles, it may be necessary to switch to a heated EGO sensor because if the sensor is located too far from the cylinder head, the exhaust will cool off too much to bring it up to operating temperature. (Headers allow the exhaust to cool more quickly than cast iron exhaust manifolds.)

One way to keep the heat up for proper EGO sensor and possibly catalytic converter operation is to insulate the headers with a thermal coating or a special heat insulating fabric tape. Most of the top Winston Cup engine builders use one—or both—of these materials.

Headers that radiate less heat also make more power because as exhaust gasses cool, they lose velocity. One of

the advantages that cast-iron headers offer is that they retain more heat than tubular headers. Unfortunately, they have so much mass, that they become under hood heaters which which has a negative effect on power. Thermo-Tec of Berea, OH markets header insulating fabric in 50-foot rolls.

Building Your Own

If you decide to build your own headers—either out of desire or necessity—you've got to find a place to start when calculating length. Myron Cottrell of TPI Specialties offers this advice:

"Over the years, I've run a bunch of different headers and I've found that the ones that work well on a small block all have around 80 cubic inches of primary tube length. That figures out to almost double the cylinder volume, because each cylinder in a 350 has a displacement of just under 44 cubic inches. Once you determine the outside diameter of the pipe you want to use, then you can compute the area, divide it into 80 and that will give you the length. This formula may

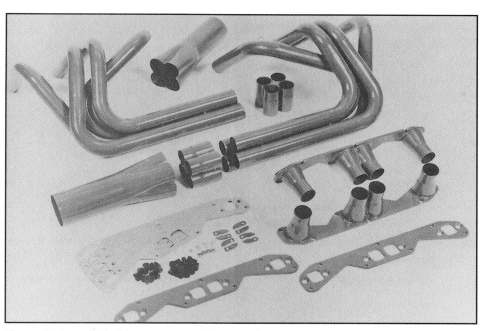

The easiest way to build your own set of headers is to start with a "you-weld-it" kit. This one is designed for an open wheel type oval track car and requires little more than welding. Other kits contain only straight lengths of pipe and "U" shaped bends. Each "U" must be cut at the desired angle and curved sections welded together to form a bend. Note the dual flange arrangement which is required by the large diameter of the pipes.

not give you the ideal length, but it won't be off by much. If anything, the pipes will be too long which is an advantage because it's easier to shorten than to lengthen a piece of tubing."

Alternative Designs

AR Headers—While header technology has largely remained unchanged over the years, anti-reversion (AR) and stepped headers are two relatively recent developments. Developed and patented by an engineer named Jim Feuling, the AR header is designed to improve mileage and economy by reducing exhaust dilution of the incoming air/fuel mixture. This is accomplished by inserting a cone at the point where the header tube meets the flange. Since reversion pulses travel along the wall of the tube, the cone, which is of slightly smaller diameter, traps them, thereby preventing entry into the combustion chamber. (AR headers were produced by Cyclone and Blackjack under a licensing agreement with Feuling, but are no longer available from those manufacturers.) Although they have performed well in a number of instances, it appears that they require different valve timing and air/fuel calibrations than conventional headers to produce maximum power. Consequently, they never achieved the widespread popularity that was expected when they were introduced.

One of the problems may be that the anti-reversion principle works too well. By killing the reverse pressure waves that normally invade the combustion chamber, the scavenging effect of the gasses travelling through the header tube is increased to the point that it can "vacuum" a portion of the incoming air/fuel mixture right through the combustion chamber. This problem is noticeable primarily with a dual-pattern camshaft with exhaust duration exceeding intake duration by 8 deg. or more.

By eliminating the flow of reverse pulses into the combustion chamber, AR headers keep the intake side of the engine "pure" (free of exhaust pulses). Consequently, a stronger metering signal is presented to the carburetor, necessitating smaller jets to achieve a given air/fuel ratio (compared to the same engine with conventional headers). Aside from tuning considerations, it should be noted that AR headers are designed to work with a crossover pipe connecting the collectors.

Some engine builders attempt to achieve an anti-reversion effect by installing headers with tube openings that are slightly larger than the port openings. One advantage to this approach is that conventional headers are cheaper than AR models and are also available in a wider variety of configurations. However, header flange/port mismatching does not function as effectively as AR cones.

Stepped Headers—Garden variety four-tube headers employ the same diameter tubing from the header flange to the collector. Stepped headers integrate two sizes of tubing. Depending on the design, the step may be up or down—1-3/4" tubes may step up to a 1-7/8" diameter, or 1-7/8" tubes may step down to 1-3/4" diameter. The direction of the step depends on the effect trying to be achieved. Headers that step up in diameter tend to function as extensions of the exhaust ports. As such, the velocity that exhaust gasses achieve in the port is maintained in the first part of the primary tube.

When tube size steps down, the first stage of the primary tube has a comparatively large capacity, so it will accept a large volume of exhaust gas. As the gasses move away from the cylinder head they cool, so they can be contained in a smaller diameter tube without it becoming a restriction. Stepping down in tube diameter allows the use of larger tubing at the port mouth than might otherwise be possible, if room limitations preclude the use of large diameter tubing all the way to the collector.

Most of the stepped headers in use are of the step-up variety. Compared to a conventional header, they tend to broaden the torque curve. Stepped headers are used on drag as well as oval track and road race engines.

180-Degree Headers—Another variation on the standard header theme is the 180° arrangement. Conventional headers, which bring the four tubes from the cylinders on each bank into a common collector, don't provide for even spacing between pulses. With the small block's 1-8-4-3-6-5-7-2 firing order, cylinder 1 (on the left bank) fires, then 90° later cylinder 8 fires, followed by another 90° before cylinder 4 fires. So the crankshaft has rotated 270° before the next cylinder on the left bank fires. By comparison, there's only 90° separating the firing of cylinders 4 and 8 on the right bank. Throughout the firing order, the interval between firings of cylinders on the same bank is inconsistent and can be 90°, 180°, or 270°.

Conversely, 180° headers bring primary tubes together based on firing order, not the side of the engine on which they're located. So the primary tubes from cylinders number 1, 4, 6 and 7 are brought into one collector

Ram's horn manifolds are the most popular because they provide the best performance to begin with. After porting and connection to a special two-into-one exhaust system these reworked manifolds deliver a surprising amount of power. Although designed for oval track use, they also provide a power gain for street cars in situations where the owner doesn't want to install headers.

while the tubes from cylinders 8, 3, 5 and 2 are brought into the other.

Although 180° headers do offer a performance improvement in some applications, they are so cumbersome to install, that they aren't widely used except in some classes of oval track and road race cars.

Stock Exhaust Manifolds—Now there's a novel idea—plain ol' cast-iron manifolds. As crazy as it sounds, they can be turned into respectable headers. Brzezinski Racing Products of Pewaukee, WI has been building cast-iron racing exhaust systems for many years. In classes where "stock" exhaust manifolds are mandated, a Brzezinski exhaust system can deliver over 20 horsepower more than stock manifolds. Corvette "ram's horn" manifolds are the basis of most systems since they produce the most horsepower. However, log and Chevy II type manifolds are also available. An important part of the Brzezinski exhaust system is a 2-into-1 collector which joins the exhaust pipes connected to each manifold.

Although engineered primarily for oval track racing, Brzezinski exhaust systems have also achieved popularity

Cast iron headers must be run in some oval track racing divisions so it's only natural that someone figured out how to improve their efficiency. As can be seen, Brzezinski Racing Products removes quite a bit material when opening up the manifolds for improved air flow.

with owners of classic Corvettes and other special interest cars; original appearance is maintained yet power is significantly increased.

Headers & the EPA

All was wonderful in the world of headers until November 1990, when the EPA added a few amendments to the Clean Air Act. These amendments make it illegal for anyone to make any changes to an engine if those changes involve disabling, removing or rendering inoperative, any emissions control device. Consequently, the only headers that can be legally installed on a 1968 or later (1966 or later in California) street-driven vehicle are those that have been certified by the EPA or exempted by the California Air Resources Board (CARB).

The EPA regulations pertain to virtually every piece of engine equipment that has anything to do with exhaust emissions. However, an exhaust system is an obvious focal point, for both regulators and inspectors. Consequently, most header manufacturers have done the necessary work and have been granted CARB exemptions (which the EPA accepts for the 49 other states). As time goes on, the number of legal headers will increase, but so will the price; "Smog" headers tend to be fabricated from heavier gauge tubing, and most also include fittings for connecting an air pump. This type of header is more expensive to produce which is reflected in the cost.

CATALYTIC CONVERTERS & MUFFLERS

Whenever headers are installed, it's standard practice to add dual exhaust (if the vehicle isn't already so equipped) and low-restriction mufflers. While you can pretty well do what you wish with the mufflers and exhaust pipes, the law requires that a catalytic converter must remain in place if the vehicle was originally equipped with one. In fact, a catalytic converter can be replaced with an aftermarket model only if the vehicle is over five years old, or has over 50,000 miles and the original converter is not operating properly. EPA regulations also require that the original converter configuration be maintained—vehicles originally equipped with a single converter cannot be converted to dual converters and vice versa. The only exception to this rule is in the case of an engine swap. If the engine being installed was originally equipped with dual converters, and is of a later model year than the vehicle, its exhaust emissions controls must be maintained.

Just because you're working on a race car doesn't mean you can kiss off the EPA regulations. The anti-tampering rules apply to all vehicles. If you purchase a car that was

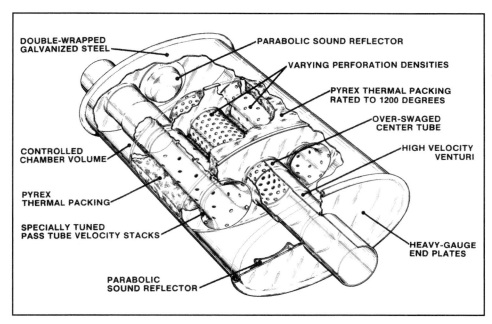

A typical "turbo" style muffler incorporates three tubes, perforated tubes and high temperature thermal packing to control sound. Some models also incorporate sound reflectors and oversized chambers to keep sound levels reasonable while maintaining maximum flow capacity.

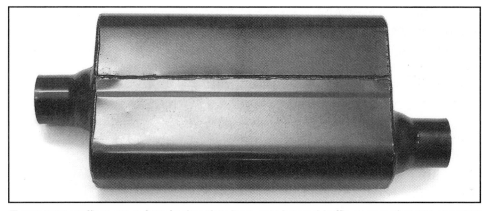

Flowmaster mufflers are unique in that they have only internal baffles separating one chamber from another. They use a patented design to reduce noise with minimal back pressure.

originally equipped with a catalytic converter, it is illegal to remove that converter or any other piece of emissions control equipment. To be completely legal, it's necessary to apply to the EPA for an exemption. Of course, a race car is never subjected to an emissions inspection, so the chances of being "apprehended" are pretty slim. However, you might be in for a rough time when you sell the car

if everything isn't perfectly legal with respect to the catalytic converter and other emissions-control equipment.

In spite of all the bad rap heaped upon catalytic converters, some really aren't all that bad. The monolith types, first used by Ford, are considerably less restrictive than the older pellet types so power losses aren't all that bad. In fact, Random Technology Loganville, GA (770/978-0264) offers

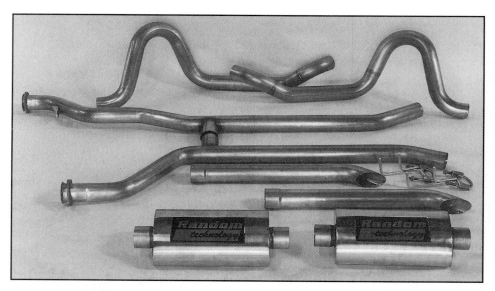

Complete exhaust systems feature bolt-on convenience and smooth mandrel bends. Many, like this '94-'96 Impala SS system from Random Technology, are made of high grade stainless steel. With 2-1/2" diameter pipes and straight-through mufflers, this system holds back-pressure to an absolute minimum which is just what's required for maximum horsepower.

High efficiency catalytic converters like the Random Technology Super High Flow converters reduce back pressure and comply with EPA and CARB requirements. This model fits '93 to '95 Camaros and Firebirds and features 3" diameter inlet and outlet.

Header bolts invariably shake loose or rust permanently into place. Stage 8's stainless steel groove lock bolts are designed to avoid both unpleasantries. After each bolt is tightened, a specially shaped washer and "C" clip is slipped into place to prevent unauthorized counter rotation. Being manufactured of stainless steel, rust isn't a problem.

Super High Flow catalytic converters that offer amazingly little flow resistance. The company's models with 3" diameter inlets and outlets flow 501 cfm at a test pressure of 28-in./H_2O. Numerous tests published in a variety of magazines show virtually no power loss when an engine is equipped with two Random Super High Flow converters (compared to a system with no converters).

With catalytic converters this good readily available, there's no reason to operate a vehicle with an illegal exhaust system. However, for a catalytic converter to function properly, it must reach its "light-off" temperature, which is around 600°, quickly. Location is obviously a consideration and the closer a converter is to the exhaust ports, the quicker it will light off. Once it reaches normal operating temperatures, a catalytic converter will operate in the vicinity of 1000 to 1200°. So in addition to location, heat radiance must also be considered to avoid causing under-car fires.

Another point to consider is that in addition to neutralizing environmentally harmful components of engine exhaust (hydrocarbons, oxides of nitrogen and carbon monoxide), a catalytic converter also dampens exhaust noise levels. Consequently, mufflers that might be too noisy for a conventional exhaust system may be acceptable when used in conjunction with catalytic converters. There have even been some cases where sound muffling was left totally to the converters.

But in most instances, a pair of low-restriction "turbo" style mufflers with either 2-1/4" or 2-1/2" inlets and outlets, connected to appropriately sized exhaust and tailpipes, are in order. The end goal is to devise the lowest restriction exhaust system that provides adequate sound control. Applied Technologies and Research, (ATR) Borla, Flowmaster, and Walker Dyno Max mufflers, with 2-1/2" or 3" inlets and outlets, are among the lowest restriction models available. ■

OIL & OIL SYSTEMS

11

Ask 10 different engine builders which brand or type of oil is best, and you'll likely get 10 different answers—and start an argument. But irrespective of brand or grade preference, everyone will agree that lubricating oil isn't much good unless it is delivered, at sufficient volume, throughout an engine. Oil has been called, among other things, an engine's life blood, so the system that delivers it must be adequate for whatever operating conditions are at hand.

Obviously, the next question is, "What's an adequate oiling system?" Again, individual opinion will vary, but there's something else to be considered; the specific engine and its intended application. The optimum system for a full-tilt drag race engine isn't necessarily the best bet for an oval track engine. And neither of these race systems may be particularly suitable for a street small block.

OILING SYSTEMS

One of the small-block Chevy's most notable strong points is its oiling system. Whereas many Brand X engines require all types of special paraphernalia for any type of high performance work, you have to get into pretty severe operating conditions before a small block needs anything very special to bolster its lubrication system. In fact, some milder race

Walk into any NASCAR Winston Cup engine shop and you'll see nothing but dry sump oiling systems. Most teams use a three-stage pump with one pressure and two scavenge stages; four-stage systems are also commonly used.

engines operate very successfully with nothing more than a few modifications to the stock oiling system.

Conversely, when horsepower levels top 500 and normal operating speed exceeds 6000 rpm—or when severe g-forces lead to oil starvation—special components must be installed to ensure an adequate flow of oil. The best engine insurance you can buy is a top notch lubrication system filled with "SG" or "SH" grade oil. However, as an oiling system becomes more exotic, it also becomes

more costly, so it's necessary to strike a happy medium between cost and capabilities.

Oiling systems for internal combustion engines fall within one of two categories—wet sump or dry sump. The sump is traditionally the lowest part of a lubrication system—the place to which oil will ultimately return after making a tour through the engine. If the oil reservoir is maintained in the sump—or oil pan—the system is described as a "wet" sump. On the other hand, if the reservoir is held in a remotely located

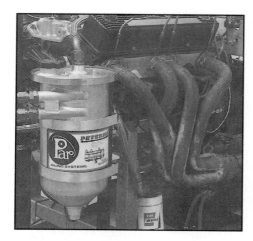

In a dry sump system, oil is held in a remotely mounted tank, not in the oil pan. In addition to serving as a reservoir, a properly designed tank also separates air from oil. Aside from improved lubrication, a dry sump system contributes to the production of horsepower because it minimizes oil windage related power losses.

tank, the system is called a "dry" sump. Each design offers particular advantages and disadvantages.

Dry Sump Systems

In a dry sump system, oil is sucked out of the pan by the scavenge stages of the oil pump; consequently the tank doesn't need to be at the lowest point of the system. Dry sump systems are more sophisticated than their wet sump brethren so naturally, they're more expensive. They also move a lot more oil, which means the power required to drive them is greater. On the plus side of the ledger, with an adequate supply of oil in the tank, even the highest g-forces (encountered during acceleration, braking and cornering) will not pull oil away from the pump pickup so momentary oil starvation is avoided—unless the drive belt breaks. Although a dry sump system is de rigeur on most types of race cars, it isn't an absolute necessity in all instances. According to Randy Dorton of Hendrick Motorsports' Winston Cup teams:

"There's no doubt a dry sump system is the best way to go, but you also have to think about whether you really need one. If you run high rpm's for hours at a time, you need a dry sump system. But if you're running short features, and competing for a $250 purse, it doesn't make much sense to buy a $1,000 oil pump versus a $40 oil pump. You have to win an awful lot of races to pay for that oil pump. Now a lot of guys think that just because every Winston Cup car has a dry sump system that they need one. That may not be true. It all depends on how hard you run the engine and for how long."

Operation—Dry sump systems are not without drawbacks, but obviously, they offer several notable advantages as justification for their increased cost. The primary among these is consistency of operation. Most dry sump systems contain three stages—two scavenge stages to pull oil out of the pan and one pressure stage to keep oil flowing to vital parts (four and five stage pumps are sometimes used in road and oval track racing). Oil drawn out by the scavenge stages is returned to an external tank which is constructed to separate any air drawn in with the oil before it can reach the inlet to the pressure pump.

Multiple scavenge stages ensure that little if any oil will remain inside the pan and deaeration of the oil in the tank prevents momentary losses of lubrication. But some engine builders feel that the advantages of a dry sump are too costly when weighed against the power required to drive them. On the other hand, keeping oil away from the crankshaft allows more power to be delivered to the flywheel and this offsets the power lost driving the pump.

To put things in perspective, consider what happens when you're driving a car and hit a puddle. The car momentarily slows down and the same thing happens when a crankshaft hits a puddle of oil. If you can keep a pan dry, you'll have more usable power. Certainly, it takes more power to turn a three-stage pump compared to a single stage model, but in a dry sump system, the two scavenge stages are sucking air much of the time so it really isn't costing that much power.

Wet Sumps

In a wet sump system, the oil is returned to the oil pan after circulation via gravity. Automakers in Detroit and overseas have found that a well designed wet sump oiling system is more than adequate for the average passenger-car engine. It's also relatively inexpensive to produce and

In some racing classes, use of a wet sump oiling system is mandatory. Operation is improved through installation of a large capacity oil pan with special baffling. In many cases, evacuation systems are included to keep blowby gasses out of the crankcase. With these systems, breathers in the valve covers are connected to the header collectors. The exiting exhaust draws vapors out of the engine.

The standard small block-oil pump utilizes two spur gears, each with seven teeth, inside a cast iron housing. Standard volume pumps have gears measuring 1.20" long; high volume pumps have 1.50" gears.

that brings something to the faces of corporate bean counters that is rarely seen—a smile. And although not as glamorous as a dry sump system, stock wet sump arrangements are the only choice for some classes of drag race and oval track competition—so say the rules. However, any wet sump system installed in a race engine should contain an oil pan with special baffling to prevent oil starvation during hard acceleration or cornering. For details, go to the section on Oil Pans.

OIL PUMPS

Wet or dry, a pump is needed to drive oil through the oiling system. The most commonly found oil pump is the gear type in which two spur gears mesh within a cast-iron housing. Power to drive the pump is supplied by the camshaft, through the distributor. An oil pump driveshaft transmits power from the distributor to the oil pump. Being driven by the camshaft, the oil pump turns at half engine speed. As the gears rotate, oil is drawn in through the pickup to the pump inlet and carried around the outside of each gear in the space

BLUEPRINTING YOUR PUMP

It would seem that if you purchase a high quality oil pump, all you have to do is make sure it's clean and install it in your engine. If you do, you may be in for a big surprise. Unquestionably, it's best to start with a performance type pump that has the gear pinned to the shaft. But don't take anything for granted. Pull the cover off and inspect it, paying particular attention to the end clearance between the gears and pump housing. It should be .002" to .0025", but just as importantly, it must be uniform front to rear. In all too many instances, particularly with off-brand pumps, the housings aren't machined square, resulting in excessive clearance on one end of the pump. High spots on the gears, burrs and dings are also likely to rear their ugly heads when a pump is pulled apart for inspection. It may be possible to dress the offending areas, but if a lot of clean-up work is required, you may be better off swapping for another pump. Excessive end clearance or wide front-to-rear clearance variations will reduce pump efficiency and can lead to oil starvation.

In standard pumps, the drive gear is simply pressed on the shaft. Press fits have been known to loosen and if it does, the oil pump won't move any oil. Not a good situation for engine health.

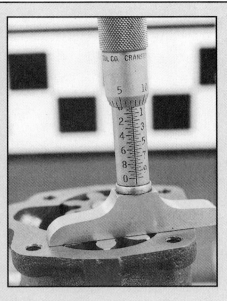

This brand new name brand oil pump was disassembled for routine inspection which turned out to be fortunate. Rotor-to-housing clearance was .007" at the front...

But only .0025" at the rear. That may not seem like much of a difference, but it's enough to compromise the flow of oil through the engine.

between the teeth and housing. When the gears mesh in the center, oil is forced out from between the teeth into an outlet passage, producing oil pressure. The stock Chevy pump and all direct replacements are gear pumps.

Rotor Pump—A second type of pump is the gerotor or rotor-and-scroll type. This type of pump is available for small-block Chevys only as an external wet or dry sump pump. A gerotor oil pump employs a lobe-shaped inner gear meshing with a lobe shaped outer rotor to build oil pressure. The gear (which is driven, while the rotor goes along for the ride) has more lobes than the rotor so as it turns, it moves into and out of each rotor lobe. As the lobes separate, a slight vacuum is created, drawing oil in through the pump pickup. Continued rotation not only causes successive gear lobes to move back into a rotor lobe, but also turns the rotor so that the rejoining takes place on the outlet side of the pump housing. Thus, as the lobes mesh, they push oil through the outlet passage and into the engine.

High Volume Wet Pumps

Even though a number of manufacturers offer high volume oil pumps for the small-block Chevy, in most cases these are a waste of money. There's nothing wrong with a high volume pump but all too frequently, one is installed in an engine that doesn't warrant it. What results is excessive oil flow at all engine speeds, and that doesn't do much but consume excess horsepower and increase the possibility of spark scatter. Since the distributor drives the oil pump (in stock, internally mounted

Special internal wet sump oil pumps are available from a variety of manufacturers. Unique features include pressure adjustment, oversized pick-up tube hole (3/4" instead of 5/8") and anti-cavitation slots machined in the bottom cover.

wet sump systems), varying resistance within the pump affects distributor shaft rotation. As the pump gears rotate, they cause a loading/unloading cycle which can cause spark timing to jump around or "scatter." Higher oil pressures and volumes are associated with a higher degree of spark scatter with distributor-driven oil pumps. Rapid distributor gear wear is another possibility of too much oil pressure.

All stock small-block Chevy oil pumps have two gears, each with seven teeth. Standard pumps, including the Z/28 model (Chevrolet part no. 3848907) have gears measuring 1.20" long. High-volume small-block pumps contain gears measuring 1.50" long. Note that the Z/28 pump is nothing more than a standard production pump with a high tension bypass spring (part no. 3848911).

Adding Washers—The same effect can be achieved by placing one or more small washers between the spring and the pin that keeps it in place. Unfortunately, unless you have "calibrated" washers, you won't know how much you've bumped pressure. If too many washers are used, the piston will not uncover the relief port

completely, which can lead to excessive pressure when the engine is started and the oil is cold. Even when a standard spring is used, some engine builders drill the bypass channel to a larger diameter to prevent excessive cold start oil pressures. Pressure can be so high that the oil filter will split or the gasket will be pushed out. Excessive distributor gear wear can also result from the high load. On the other hand, the Z/28 spring, which has a white stripe on it, will usually peg oil pressure at 60-70 psi, depending on oil viscosity and bearing clearances.

Big-Block Pumps—Most small-block oil pumps have a 5/8" diameter pickup tube hole engine, but some race pumps are drilled to accept a 3/4" tube—the same size as found in a big-block pump. That fact is relevant because a big-block oil pump can be bolted into a small block with no modifications except for the windage tray, which may have to be trimmed to clear, and a special length oil pump driveshaft. Big-block pumps have

A big-block pump will bolt right into place on a small block. Five, rather than four bolts attaching the bottom cover to the housing identify big block pumps. Irrespective of the pump type used, the pickup should be positively attached to the housing.

An external wet sump pump is actually a single stage from a dry sump pump. An external line connects the inlet side to the oil pan and another line route oil from the pump into the block.

In this installation, oil is brought into the block through an adapter that bolts to the oil filter mounting pad. The small line is attached to an oil temperature probe used during dyno testing.

One of the advantages of an external oil pump, be it of the wet or dry sump variety, is that a full-length windage tray can be used. This custom built tray is the handiwork of Harold Elliot.

gears with 12 teeth and can be easily identified by the five, rather than four bolts that attach the bottom cover.

One of the advantages of the big-block pump is that the 12 teeth on its gears make for smoother operation and reduced spark scatter. However, bigger isn't always better; in terms of oil delivery, a big-block oil pump amounts to overkill when installed in a small block with reasonable bearing clearances.

Even with a small-block high-volume pump, so much oil can be put through the engine that the pump can literally suck the pan dry. All it takes is for the oil level to be about a quart low, or for centrifugal force to pull a bit too much oil away from the pickup. To guard against such possibilities, any type of high-volume wet-sump pump should be accompanied by a large capacity pan in which the oil level is scrupulously maintained.

External Wet Pump

Until fairly recently, wet sump systems always used an oil pump mounted in the stock location. Competition modifications typically involved nothing more than installation of a deeper-than-stock oil

pan, a high pressure or high volume pump and an extended pump pickup. But where dry sump systems are unavailable, prohibited or too expensive, an externally mounted wet sump arrangement can be advantageous.

First of all, it allows the use of a full length windage tray because there's no pump hanging down in the pan. Other benefits are that ignition timing is more accurate because the distributor isn't driving the pump. Also, pressure can be adjusted very easily and the external mounting makes it much easier to prime an engine prior to initial start-up. It is often possible to run a lower oil level in the pan when an external wet sump pump is used because the pick-up is a fitting in the bottom of the oil pan.

Gerotor pumps are generally more efficient at moving oil which means you can get the volume you need without having to use super high pressures. Aside from providing better insurance against oil starvation, gerotor pumps are reputed to require less horsepower to drive them.

Proponents of gear pumps dispute the claims made on the gerotor's behalf, but my personal experience

with them has been very positive. In a series of dyno tests with a 355 small block, and a Peterson external wet sump, pressure was set at 55 psi. It never exceeded that figure, and never varied more than three psi from 1,750 to 6,000 rpm.

Dry Sump Pumps

As is the case with wet sump pumps, two types of multi-stage dry sump pumps are available—gear or rotor. Once again, the superiority of each type is a matter of opinion. Weaver Brothers are the largest suppliers of dry sump oil pumps and

A dry sump pump consists of three or four pumps bolted together to form a single unit. Each stage is simply a single pump with a specific purpose. The scavenge stages draw oil and air out of the pan, the pressure stage pushes oil through the block just as it does in a wet sump system. This is a gerotor type pump.

they manufacture a gear type. On the other hand, many of the engine builders who use a gerotor type swear by them.

One of the considerations relative to pump type has nothing to do with efficiency—it has to do with digestion. Dry sump pumps have aluminum housings and when a piece of debris gets caught between the gear teeth and housing, the latter is generally destroyed. Conversely, with a rotor type pump, debris passes between the gear and rotor, both of which are steel, so the pump has a better chance of digesting it and remaining intact; damage isn't as great and it can be repaired by replacing a few components instead of the whole pump.

One of the major disadvantages to any system using an externally mounted oil pump is that the drive belt can break, or be thrown off, in which case oil pressure becomes a thing of the past. Such occurrences are rare, but they do happen, so some type of safety measure is required to avoid running an engine with no oil pressure.

Pickups

The weakest link of a small block's oiling system is the oil pump pickup. In its stock form, the pickup tube is simply pressed into the oil pump's bottom cover. Although this arrangement may seem adequate, it isn't. Some form of positive retention is required. The most common method is to braze or tack-weld the pickup tube in place. To avoid heat generated during welding from warping critical components, it's advisable to remove the cover from the pump and to pull out the relief piston and spring before welding. It's

Regardless of the type of oil pump installed, make sure the pickup tube is securely retained. In a stock-type pump/pickup assembly, the pickup tube is simply pressed into a hole machined in the pump body. Vibration has been known to cause the pickup to move around, so it should be welded or brazed in place. If the thought of welding a pickup to the pump housing isn't particularly appetizing, a special bolt-on pickup can be used. Be sure to match pickup position to pan depth.

also advisable to add a bracket from the pickup to the pump to provide extra support. The easiest type of bracket to fabricate is one that is attached by the same bolt that holds the pump to the block, or one that is held in place by one of the bottom cover bolts.

Construction—Regarding actual construction of the pickup, the most important consideration is controlling the vortex that develops as the pump draws oil out of the pan. If the pickup screen were simply a round, unbaffled affair, the incoming oil would "whirlpool" and leave the pump sucking air. Consequently, all stock shaped pickups contain a baffle to prevent this occurrence. Many high performance baffles are square or rectangular in shape for the same reason.

When a special deep sump oil pan is installed, it's necessary to either use an extended pickup or to space the pump

down from the block. If a pump spacer is used, the standard oil pump driveshaft will be too short, so a lengthened shaft must be installed. Spacer kits, such as those marketed by Moroso, include the necessary driveshaft and attaching hardware.

Whichever method is used, the end result should be the same—the pickup should be 1/4" to 3/8" from the pan's bottom surface. If it's too high, it may not be able to pick up sufficient oil; if it's too close to the pan, flow will be restricted.

Position—Another consideration is pickup position. For street and road race engines, the standard location is adequate. However, engines installed in drag race cars should have the pickup located toward the rear of the pan; oval track racing requires pickup placement towards the right side of the pan. In both applications, the philosophy is the same—place the pickup in the area of greatest potential

Bearing clearance, oil viscosity and crankshaft preparation play a role in determining the oil pressure and volume required to adequately lubricate an engine. This Winston Cup crankshaft is mated to polymer coated bearings and is run at a relatively tight clearance. The crank counterweights have also been coated to shed oil, thereby reducing windage related power losses.

oil supply. That area is largely influenced by the g-forces generated during competition.

Clearance, Viscosity & Pressure

As applied to racing and high performance engines, the rule of thumb is that 10 psi of oil pressure should be maintained for each 1000 rpm. This is especially important in an engine with wide bearing clearances because there is so much internal hemorrhaging. Harold Elliot, who was been Rusty Wallace's engine builder for several years (including 1989, when Wallace won the NASCAR Winston Cup championship) states:

"Our race engine bearing clearances are right at street car clearances. When some of our engine assemblers started a few years ago and saw that we fit main bearings up at .002" to .0025" and the rods at .0018" to .0022", they couldn't believe it because they didn't even fit street engines up that tight. But that's how

efficient our oiling system is—we can run them that tight. The tighter the better so long as you don't touch the bearings to the crank. People call me all the time and ask me what we fit our bearings at and I know they think I'm lyin', but our tightest is .0018" and our loosest is .0022". We don't throw off that much oil, so our recovery system doesn't have to work that hard. Generally, most of our stuff only passes 4-1/2 to 5 gallons per minute, so we don't have to recover that much and our scavenge stages don't have to work that hard."

In combination with tight bearing clearances, Elliot uses polymer coated bearings and 5W-30 synthetic motor oil. As with most automotive engine subsystems, a complete combination of parts and procedures must be developed to optimize performance. Use of lighter viscosity oil goes hand-in-hand with tighter bearing clearances. But just a few years ago, 5W-30 oils suitable for racing simply weren't available. In fact, it wasn't that long ago that straight 50 weight was considered mandatory in virtually any type of race engine. Tight bearing

clearances wouldn't have been suitable back then because oil flow would have been too restricted. On the other hand, when tight clearances are employed, there's no need for an oil pump with the capacity to fill an Olympic swimming pool in two hours.

However, all this oiling system philosophizing neglects one thing—the driver. In order for a finely tuned oiling system to function properly, the oil must be brought to temperature before the engine is put under maximum load. And the oil and filter must be changed regularly. Some engine builders have found it necessary to set relatively wide bearing clearances because they know that the driver will do nothing more than unload the car at the track and hammer the throttle.

OIL PANS

Confusion and controversy surround this subject because a number of conflicting theories exist, yet each has merit. A configuration that provides superior performance in one application may severely

Whether it's part of a wet or dry sump system, an oil pans should be designed to keep oil away from the crankshaft. A scraper, or wiper, and windage tray are included in most race pans to accomplish this. In this dry sump pan, both the scraper and windage tray run the whole length. The shallow depth of dry sump pans provides increased ground and chassis clearance.

Wet sump pans are available in a variety of shapes, depending upon application. This Moroso pan, with its winged bottom offers increased capacity with no loss in ground clearance. It's suitable for high performance street and road race engines.

compromise power in another. Therefore, one must subscribe to an open-minded approach because as application changes, so does the ultimate oil pan design.

On a stock engine, an oil pan serves the perfunctory purpose of a holding tank. Oil is pumped out of the reservoir residing within, through the engine and returned. The shape of the pan is therefore dictated by engine skirt contour and the placement of chassis members. So long as a pan fits the engine in question, doesn't leak, doesn't contact any chassis parts and is reasonably efficient at preventing oil from scooting away from the pump pickup, it is deemed satisfactory.

Dry Sump Pans

Obviously, if there is no oil in the pan, it can't interfere with the crankshaft. That's the philosophy behind a dry sump system. Two or three scavenge stages effectively vacuum out oil draining back to the pan (after having circulated through the engine) into an external reservoir.

That would seem to imply that any type of pan is acceptable. But you know better than that—nothing is ever that simple.

As the crankshaft rotates, it moves the air around it much in the manner of a fan. The resulting envelope of swirling air carries quite a bit of force with it (the amount of which is partially determined by rpm) and it can literally draw oil up from the surface of a pan floor or windage tray and whip it into an air/oil emulsion. A dry sump pan must therefore be constructed to cause oil to flow rapidly to a collection area that is not affected by crank-generated whirlwinds. To do this with maximum effectiveness, a windage tray or baffle must be used with a complementary wiper.

Properly arranged inside the pan, the wiper/tray assembly will pull oil from the crankshaft and route it to an area below the tray. This prevents oil leaving the crankshaft from being drawn back into the whirling airstream before it can reach a scavenge port. The kick-out seen on

some dry sump pans is also part of the anti-windage equation. The scraper and tray create a channel through which oil wiped from the reciprocating assembly flows. However, if the oil pan wall were not moved outward, flow into the collection area would be restricted and much of the oil scraped from the crank would remain on the tray surface and be swept up by the air whirling around the crank—precisely the condition that the pan/scraper/tray assembly was designed to minimize or eliminate.

Ideally, a full depth "kick-out" should run the entire length of a pan. However, use of a pan with full kick-out requires relocation of the starter and in some applications, this is difficult or impossible. Pans with stepped kick-outs are a viable alternative as they are either compatible with a standard starter or require only a minor relocation of the starter.

Wet Sump Pans

In terms of windage treatment, the philosophies governing construction of dry sump oil pans apply to those in the wet sump category. The primary difference is that oil is much more troublesome when it's left in the pan rather than being removed to a remote storage tank. Typically, even though a wet sump and dry sump oil pan makes the same horsepower on an engine dyno, a dry sump pan shows superior power on the race track

The reason for this is quite simple. When a vehicle accelerates, decelerates or turns, the resulting g-forces imparted to the oil push it up a wall of the pan. Given sufficient force, the oil will actually find its way into a crankshaft's path. Obviously,

A crankshaft with a large flange on the rear is designed for use with the one-piece rear main oil seal introduced in 1986. Adapters are available (Chevrolet part no. 10051118) to allow installation of old style crankshafts in blocks machined for the new style seal.

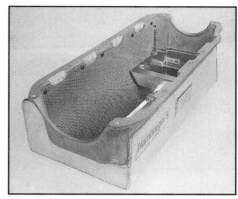

Lightweight oil pans fabricated from sheet aluminum are popular for drag racing. They'd be popular in other forms of motorsports too, if they weren't so prone to damage. Aluminum just doesn't resist rocks, debris other flying objects as well as steel.

with several quarts of oil in a wet sump pan, the problem is much more acute than with a dry sump arrangement. However, irrespective of the sump configuration, as pan depth is increased, oil-induced power losses tend to be minimized as the oil must travel further to reach and interfere with the reciprocating assembly.

In addition to minimizing power losses related to windage, a wet sump pan must also ensure that oil stays in the area of the pump pickup under all operating conditions. It is for precisely this reason that the leading pan manufacturers offer oil pans for specific applications. Typically, a drag race pan has no provision to prevent side-to-side oil slosh because a car generates no lateral g-forces traveling in a straight line. Baffling is therefore designed to prevent oil from climbing the rear pan wall (during acceleration) and from shooting forward away from the pickup (during braking). The latter consideration is especially important for cars competing in categories with a break-out rule. Even though the engine may not be under power when the brakes are applied, it is still rotating at an elevated rpm. If the oil isn't effectively contained around the pickup, starvation can easily result.

Use of an oil pan designed only for drag racing, on a car that is street driven, may therefore be somewhat like signing a death warrant for the engine in question. Oil starvation will occur if the pan is so constructed that oil can easily migrate away from the pickup when lateral forces are applied (as in a turn). Many drag race type pans can be used successfully on a street/strip car but rather than risk lunching an engine, it is best to check the pan is okay for such use before making a purchase.

Other specialized applications include oval track, road racing and marine. Pans intended for oval track use aren't suitable for anything else because their baffling is effective only when a car is turning left. Conversely, road race pans are applicable to cars that turn both left and right and most are quite suitable for street/strip use. However, they are typically more expensive than oil pans designed for high performance street or dual-purpose cars and offer comparatively little advantage in anything other than a full-on racing environment. Marine-style oil pans would be fine in a car except that they are full depth over their entire length and won't fit within most automotive frames.

Recommendations

With the myriad of styles and shapes in which oil pans are produced, deciding upon a particular model can be exasperating. However, there are several practical considerations that cut through the jungle of confusion:

• **Rules:** In many classes, dry sump systems are not allowed. But even if the rules do allow a dry sump system, if your competitors race successfully with wet sump systems, you should be able to as well. The prize money has to be pretty good to justify the added expense.

• **Budget:** The more exotic the oil pan, the higher its cost. There's no sense considering a $1,500 dry sump system if the budget won't allow an expenditure of more than $500.

• **Practicality:** An oil pan must not only fit engine and chassis, it must afford a few inches of ground clearance. Some deep pans may be unacceptable because their proximity to the ground will make them a target for road debris or the pavement itself.

• **Operating Range:** The greatest benefits from reduced windage related power losses accrue at engine speeds in excess of 6000 rpm. If an engine is never taken beyond 6500-7000 rpm, benefits derived from a super exotic pan/tray/scraper assembly (compared to a deep pan with a simple tray) may be barely measurable.

For most applications, a dry sump system offers the best lubrication

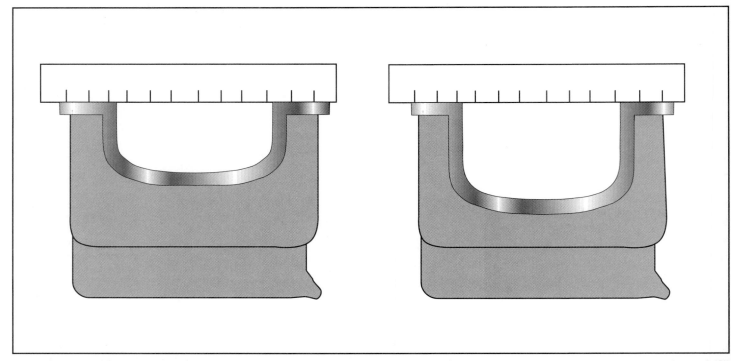

Oil pans used on 1974 and earlier engines accept a front seal that's 1/4" thick. Beginning in 1975, oil pans were built to accommodate a 3/8" thick front seal. To identify which seal a pan is designed to accept, place a straight edge across the pan rails and measure down to the seal surface. A dimension of 2-1/4" indicates an early pan and a thin seal; if the measurement is 2-3/8", it's a late pan which accepts the thick seal. Either seal can be installed with either pan, but if the wrong seal is used, it will become obvious very quickly.

capabilities and minimal windage related power loss. However, the expense of such systems ($1,000-$2,000 depending upon equipment selected and prevailing pricing) puts it out of reach for many racers, which isn't all bad. In many instances, a good wet sump system is more than adequate. And, of course, there's always the debate over the additional power required to operate a multi-stage dry sump pump more than offsetting the reduction in windage related horsepower losses.

Winged Pans—With the idea behind a high performance wet sump pan being to keep the oil reservoir as far from the crankshaft as practical, recommendations usually lead to the deepest pan that will fit. In instances where additional depth cannot be accommodated, a "wing-bottom" pan

is a viable alternative. Rather than being exceptionally deep, this type of pan flares out at the base, hence oil level is still lowered. In general, a deeper or larger capacity pan always helps whether you're running on a dyno or a race track because anything you can do to lower the oil level without reducing capacity is beneficial. While it isn't recommended, running a wet sump system one or two quarts low will usually produce a measurable power increase. However, a much safer way to accomplish the same thing is to install a deep or wing-bottom oil pan.

Windage Tray—Even though expenses aren't always justified by the amount of performance improvement, any engine will benefit from a properly designed windage tray. The major power improvements occur at

6000 rpm and above, but there is something to be gained at lower engine speeds. For a number of years, the need for a windage tray was largely debated because some Chrysler racers used to run without a tray—but that was because they had special pans that were designed to

If you want to build or modify your own oil pan, just add a universal windage tray and scraper kit to take advantage of the latest in oil control technology. Both parts must be custom fit to the crankshaft for maximum effectiveness.

OIL PAN/GASKET BLOCK COMPATIBILITY

YEAR	DIPSTICK	FRONT SEAL	REAR MAIN SEAL
1955-74	Left	Thin	Two-Piece
1975-79	Left	Thick	Two-Piece
1980-85	Right	Thick	Two-Piece
1986-97	Right	Thick	One-Piece

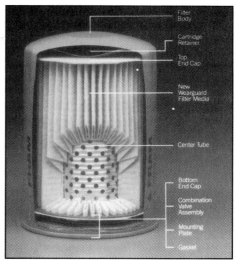

Oil filters contain more internal parts than you might think. This cut-away of a Fram Wearguard filter shows what it takes to keep oil clean without pressure drop and restriction. Racing filters like those offered by K&N have heavy-duty cases with a higher burst strength than a standard filter. The filtering medium is also specifically designed for high performance applications.

serve as a tray. Lately, the trend is towards a semi-circular, Teflon-coated windage tray which minimizes oil puddling. Another school of thought holds that a screen-style tray is superior because oil can't puddle on it; with a screen or louvered tray, oil drains through it instead of laying on top of it.

With no definitive test results available, it is impossible to say whether a screen or solid windage tray is most effective. The primary difference in operating theory is that with a solid, semi-circular tray, the air mass rotating with and around the crankshaft is used to blow oil along the tray surface into a collection channel. Conversely, with a screen tray, oil immediately moves out of the crankshaft's path upon contacting the mesh. However, it has been argued that once the screening is saturated, the tray effectively becomes solid, allowing oil to puddle on its surface.

Z/28 Combo—For most street and street/bracket engines, a Z/28 pan and windage tray combination is right on target. Oil pan number 465220 (four-quart capacity) and curved windage tray number 3927136 are relatively low in price and have been used quite successfully in a variety of high performance and race engines. Also available is a five-quart Corvette oil pan (part no. 359942) which mates

with a flat windage tray (part no. 14071077). Both the curved and flat trays mount with five special main cap bolts which also serve as mounting studs. For 1968 and later blocks (which accept crankshafts with 2.45" diameter main journals) five of part no. 14087508 main cap bolts are required; 1967 and earlier blocks (which house crankshafts with 2.30" diameter journals) call for part no. 3972718 bolts.

The H.O. Pan—Another oil pan suitable for performance is listed as part number 10110837. This pan is supplied on the High Output 5.7-liter engine that's sold by Chevrolet and GM Performance Parts dealers. It features internal baffling and a right-hand (passenger side) dipstick relief and can be installed on 1986 and later engines which have a one-piece rear main seal.

High performance parts manufacturers like Milodon and Moroso also offer a variety of economically priced high performance oil pans that are suitable for street engines. These manufacturers also offer a wide selection of specialized oil pans and matching windage trays.

While there may be considerable controversy as the best method of reducing windage related power losses, the fact that such losses do exist is irrefutable. And that means

there just may be some free horsepower hiding in your oil pan. All you have to do is claim it.

OIL FILTERS

There are oil filters and there are oil filters. For most engines, it's hard to go wrong with a brand-name filter like Fram, AC, Lee, Motorcraft or Purolator. In fact, some off-brand or private brand filters are actually produced by these manufacturers. In some cases, they're just as good, but lower in price because of reduced advertising and packaging costs. But as is the case with motor oil, individual brand preferences tend to be strong—even though documented evidence concerning performance differences is hard to find.

Racing Filters
Racing oil filters, marketed by companies like Fram and Moroso, are

With a dry sump system, a remote filter is usually incorporated and the inlet and outlet holes in the block plugged. This block has also been treated to some machine work which removed unnecessary weight in and around the filter pad.

similar to standard filters in construction with one major exception—burst strength. Standard spin-on filters have a burst strength of 200 psi or less; racing filters are typically rated at over 400 psi. Racing filters also feature a thicker flange plate for improved gasket retention and a low restriction filtering medium with superior fuel resistance.

Screen Type—Another type of racing filter uses a mesh screen rather than a paper or fabric filtering element. Most engine builders prefer this type of filter, manufactured by System One and Oberg, because the screen is reusable and can be easily removed for inspection.

Bypass Valve

Although it may seem ludicrous that an oiling system would develop sufficient pressure to burst a standard filter, it does happen. Race engines are particularly adept at blowing up oil filters because the bypass valve is normally plugged to assure full filtration. Although the Chevy small block is supposed to be equipped with a "full flow" oil filter, much of the oil is normally bypassed. The stock filter

adapter (part no. 3952301) that bolts to the block, and to which the filter attaches, contains a bypass valve that opens under relatively low pressure. Theoretically, this valve serves to relieve excess pressure. But in real life, it's open almost all the time, and whatever oil flows through it bypasses the filter. Most race engine builders block the valve opening with an Allen plug so that all the oil must flow through the filter.

This arrangement is a double-edged sword. Although it assures maximum filtration, it also builds higher than normal pressures in the filter. However, pressure usually reaches the critical point only if an engine is run at high speed while the oil is still cold. If the crankcase is filled with a multi-viscosity oil, and common sense is used, pressure will never reach a level that will threaten oil filter integrity.

Remote Installation

In some instances, it may be desirable to install the oil filter remotely. This is commonly accomplished with an adapter that mounts in the oil filter cavity. A remote filter mount can then be plumbed to the adapter with flexible line. Some filter mounts do not accept a standard small block, so you may end up having to use a Ford (the horror!) filter on your Chevy. There's no particular advantage to remote mounting except that it may make filter changing easier. However, some remote mounts have provisions for two filters, making for a quick and easy way to increase filtering capacity. Unfortunately, some dual-filter mounts accept only filters with internal bypass valves which means that much of the oil will circulate through without being filtered. If you

plan to install a remote filter, look for a mount that does not have a bypass and accepts a non-bypassing type filter. AC's number 832 Chevy truck filter has been popular as a remote racing filter for many years.

OTHER CONSIDERATIONS

No, we're not done talking about the engine's lubrication system just yet. There are still several other items or factors you need to consider when designing or modifying your oiling system.

Temperature

When an engine runs under load, it generates a tremendous amount of heat. One of the most important functions of the oil is to remove this heat. But without a "radiator" the only component that can pull any amount of heat out of the oil is the pan. That's acceptable in many street cars because the engine rarely runs under full load, and when it does, it's only for brief periods. But any time a vehicle is used for towing, or operated continuously at wide open throttle, engine oil can easily exceed the maximum desirable operating temperature (270 deg.). Consequently, any type of competition engine, except for those used in drag racing, can benefit from an oil cooler.

Most coolers can be plumbed to the engine with the same type of adapter that's used for connecting a remote oil filter. But if you race during cold weather, be sure that the oil doesn't stay too cool. The key is to make sure the oil is within the desired temperature range—not too hot and not too cool. In cold weather, it may be necessary to partially block airflow through the oil cooler to maintain adequate oil temperature. Ideally, oil temperature should not exceed 220° during normal operation. If it does, an oil cooler should be installed. But don't be wooed into installing an oil cooler just because Winston Cup, Grand National, ARCA and other race cars of that ilk are so equipped. If your engine's oil temperature stays within the recommended range, an oil cooler is nothing more than excess weight. Of course, you'll never know if an oil cooler is required unless you install an oil temperature gauge.

Oil Accumulators

On occasion, even the most carefully designed wet sump lubrication system can momentarily lose pressure. All it takes is for g-forces to pull the oil away from the pickup a few seconds and the pump winds up pumping air instead of oil. One safeguard against such an occurrence is an oil accumulator such as the Accusump which was introduced by Mecca Industries. An Accusump system is essentially a sealed tube with a floating piston inside. It is connected to the pressure side of the oil pump so that whenever the engine is running, oil is pumped into one end of the tube which forces the piston toward the tube's other end. However, the chamber on the piston's back side is filled with air, so oil being pumped in compresses that air. With normal oil pressure on one side, and compressed air on the other, the piston remains stationary. However, should oil pressure drop below normal operating level, the compressed air behind the piston forces oil held in the Accusump cylinder into the engine, thereby preventing momentary oil starvation. By installing a manual valve in the line between the engine

and accumulator cylinder, an Accusump can also be used to pressurize the oiling system immediately prior to start-up.

Oil

What's the best oil? That's an eternal question without an answer. Many people have very definite preferences and wouldn't be caught dead with anything other than their favorite brand of oil in their engine's crankcase. But the fact of life is that small-block Chevys have been raced successfully with just about any brand of oil you can think of in their respective crankcases.

Viscosity and applicability are of far more importance than brand identification. Motor oils have been improved dramatically in recent years, largely through the formulation of the additive package that's added to the base stock. The additive packages blended into racing oils offer superior performance under severe service operation. Specifically, they are more resistant to deterioration caused by extreme heat and pressure.

Viscosity—Then there's the matter of viscosity. For years, it was standard procedure to run SAE 40W or 50W oil in any type of race engine. But the additive packages developed in recent years have eliminated the need for "thick" oils. Even in the most demanding forms of competition, 20W-50 is about the heaviest weight oil now being used. 10W-30 mineral based and 5W-30 synthetic oils are also routinely used in all types of racing engines.

With the quality of oils now available, the hot tip is to run the lightest viscosity oil possible so long as adequate oil pressure can be maintained—the lighter the oil, the

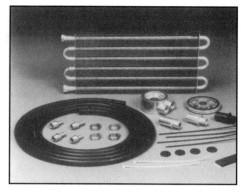

Aftermarket oil coolers are designed for easy installation and frequently include an adapter that mounts to the oil filter pad. Oil exits the adapter, flows through the oil cooler then returns to the adapter whereupon it exits into the oil filter which attaches to the bottom of the adapter. From the filter, it return to the block.

less power required to drive the oil pump. Old time racers will disagree with that statement, but several Winston Cup teams race week after week with 5W-30 synthetic oil— and qualify with 0W-20 oil.

Synthetic vs. Conventional—There's absolutely no question that synthetic motor oils are far superior to their mineral oil-based counterparts. There's also no question that it's more expensive. What you get for your money is superior lubrication, reduced friction and longer oil life. Of course, those benefits are largely dependent upon the additive package that's blended in with the base oil stock. Some of the problems associated with early synthetics arose form over-enthusiasm about synthetic oil's lubricating qualities and the resultant erroneous thinking that additives were required only in small amounts. Now that the additive packages have been perfected, the superiority of synthetic oils has become a matter of record.

Rather than merely being refined goo from beneath the ground (or on top of it if you live near an oil spill), synthetic oils are created by molecular

The lateral acceleration encountered in autocrossing requires an adequate oil supply and proper pan baffling. While a stock pan may be adequate, it doesn't leave much margin for error--especially in high speed autocrossing.

engineering. The advantage of this process is that all the molecules (and the hydrocarbon chains they form) are the same size. In regular mineral oil, molecules that are extremely small burn off (which translates into oil consumption) while molecules at the other end of the size spectrum lead to oil thickening and sludge build-up.

Mineral oils have over 300 molecular structures; synthetics have one. Synthetics also contain no wax (paraffin) so they have better low temperature properties. And since they're lighter and more fluid than conventional oils, they allow greater engine efficiency and horsepower output and also run cooler.

Although the term "synthetic oil" may bring images of mad scientists creating bizarre new compounds from thin air, the technology is much more ground based. Synthetics begin as either crude oil or natural gas. During refining, ethylene, which is created as a byproduct, is extracted and brought into contact with a catalyst which transforms it into linear alpha olefins. This compound is then hydro-treated to convert it to poly alpha olefins which is synthetic base oil.

As is the case with mineral-based oils, synthetics vary according to manufacturer. However, the differences tend to be much less dramatic than with mineral oils because most synthetics meet 'SG' or 'SH' standards. It's hard to go wrong with a name brand synthetic.

The biggest question in most inquiring minds is, "What do I get with synthetic oil that justifies the increased price?" The answer to that is summed up rather well by Tim Kerrigan of Red Line Synthetic Oil Company. According to Kerrigan, "Just about any synthetic will deliver improved horsepower, fuel economy and engine life. I can only speak for our oils in terms of specific numbers because there are differences from one brand to another. For openers, I'd say that with Red Line, you can easily go 12,000 to 15,000 miles between oil changes. It's not a bad idea to change the filter and add a quart (to replace what's lost in the filter change) at the halfway point. Now the change interval depends on the vehicle and operating conditions, but 12,000 to 15,000 miles should be no problem for a vehicle that's driven normally—

back and forth to work with some "spirited" driving on the weekends.

"Some people are stuck on the 3,000 mile interval, but that's ridiculous. That's largely a result of the 'quickie' oil change places trying to increase sales. With the way the motors in newer cars are sealed up combined with fuel injection and unleaded fuels, you just don't get the solids in the oil like you used to. In addition to saving money from longer oil change intervals, you're also helping the environment. New oil isn't an environmental problem, dirty oil is. If we do nothing more than double the change interval—from 3,000 to 6,000 miles, think of all the waste that's eliminated."

Synthetics are also changing the way racers view oil changes. In the past, it was almost a rule that the oil in an 800+ horsepower alcohol-burning sprint car engine was changed after every race. Kerrigan reports that racers are now going three or four races between oil changes. In drag racing, alcohol-burning 8.90 and 9.90 cars are now making 35 passes before an oil change. Gasoline-fired engine can run even longer between changes because dilution tends to be less severe.

Horsepower and fuel economy are also typically increased as a result of a switch to synthetics. In some cases, increases of up to 4 mpg have been documented. Increases of three to five horsepower have also been demonstrated. Obviously, these types of improvements aren't seen on every vehicle, but there's enough substantiated evidence to expect measurable performance increases when a small-block Chevy is switched from mineral oil to synthetic oil lubrication. ■

EXTERNAL COMPONENTS

12

COOLING SYSTEM

If your small block maintains its cool under all conditions, a water pump is little more than an appendage stuck to the front of the engine. But if high coolant temperatures and overheating are common problems, a water pump, like every other part of the cooling system, takes on new significance.

Overheating is rarely caused by a water pump. However, it can be a contributor in a marginal cooling system. Typically, overheating is brought on by insufficient airflow through the radiator, a collapsed radiator hose, a blocked radiator, a defective or inadequate pressure cap, a failed fan clutch or too little coolant capacity. While a killer water pump won't cure any of these problems, it can mean the difference between normal operating temperatures and overheating if cooling capacity is marginal.

Of course, if a water pump is to do its job properly, it must be spun at the correct speed. Stock pulleys are adequate in virtually all street applications, and underdrive pulleys (which slow down water pump and alternator speeds as a means of gaining horsepower) are also acceptable in most cases.

Power may be produced inside an engine, but if the external components aren't up to snuff, the power won't last long. That means the cooling system, vibration damper and fuel pump must be up to the task at hand.

Thermostat

Depending upon ambient air temperature, either a 160°, 180° or 195° thermostat is usually installed in a small block. Although it is possible to operate an engine with no thermostat, such a practice is ill advised because the coolant will take too long to reach normal operating temperature, if it does at all. In some racing applications, it may be possible to install a 5/8" or 11/16" diameter restrictor in place of a thermostat, but for the majority of street and race engines, use of a thermostat is highly recommended.

Bypassing—However, reworking a small block's bypass system can pay off with improved cooling. Under normal circumstances, when an engine is cold, a bypass in the water pump housing allows coolant to circulate enough to avoid a pressure build up when the thermostat is closed, and to allow the thermostat to open properly. Some engine builders have found that improved cooling efficiency results when this bypass hole is plugged (with either silicone or a standard plug) and four holes are

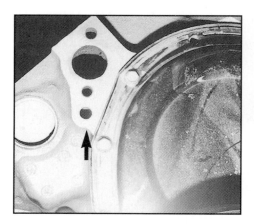

The bypass hole in a small block is located beneath the lower bolt hole on the passenger side of the block. When the thermostat is closed flow through this hole is the only thing that keeps coolant moving through the engine.

From left to right are a pre-1969 short pump, a 1971-82 Corvette pump and a 1969 and later long pump. Lengths are 5.545", 5.795" and 6.900" respectively.

drilled in the thermostat (see photo). Typically, four 1/8" diameter holes are adequate. However, Myron Cottrell of TPI Specialties recommends four .200" holes in a 160° thermostat for summer operation and four .080" holes in a 180° thermostat for winter operation. This may seem like splitting hairs, but an engine that's overcooled produces less horsepower. The thermostat modification also improves block filling since air in the waterjackets has an escape path.

Even if everything in the cooling system is operating properly, drilling holes in the thermostat and plugging the internal bypass usually results in a measurable drop in coolant temperature. And it may cure an overheating problem if the "wrong" parts have been installed. Some race water pumps and aftermarket cylinder heads (a passage in the bypass circuit leads from the block to the heads) do not have provisions for the internal bypass. If the circuit is already blocked, the thermostat modification will cool things down.

1992 and later LT1 engines and 1996 truck small blocks employ a different type of coolant temperature control system. When the engine is cold, coolant flows throughout the block and heads, but is essentially cut off from the radiator. Only when temperature rises sufficiently for the thermostat to open is coolant routed to the radiator.

Water Pumps

Many people, even some small-block Chevy experts, don't realize that there are three different water pump configurations. Engines built prior to 1969, as well as 1969 and 1970 Corvette engines, were equipped with a "short" pump that's 5.545" long (measured from the face of the fan hub to block mating surface); 1971-1982 Corvette water pumps measure 5.795" in length; 1969 and later passenger car and truck engines use a "long" pump that's 6.900" long. 1984 and later Corvette water pumps (which are aluminum) are the same length as the earlier models but are not interchangeable because they're designed for reverse rotation because they're driven by a serpentine drive belt. Because of high production volumes, Corvette aluminum water pumps are relatively low priced, but more than one person has found out the hard way that price isn't the only consideration. When driven by conventional V-belts, a Corvette aluminum pump just won't cool an engine because it's spinning in the wrong direction.

The water pump used on the 1992 and later LT1 engine is unique in a number of aspects. Not only does it serve as a thermostat housing, it is also driven by the cam gear so there's no provision for a pulley–or a fan.

This cutaway shows the water pump drive mechanism and thermostat mounting in the LT1. Note that coolant does not flow to the radiator until the thermostat opens.

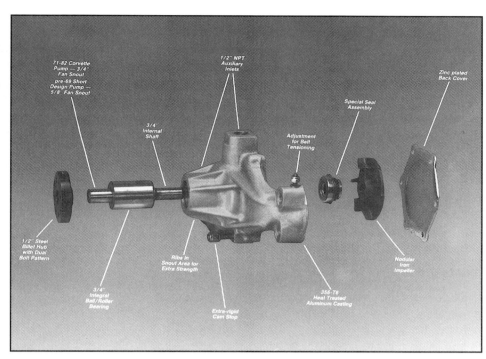

Exploded view of a Stewart Components Stage III water pump illustrates the features that are beneficial for high performance operation. Premium quality components are used throughout.

Aside from the length differences, shaft diameters also vary. Corvette and heavy-duty pumps have a 3/4" diameter shaft, standard passenger car pumps are fitted with a 5/8" shaft. Shaft size would be of no consequence aside from strength except that it's difficult to install a pulley or fan clutch with a 5/8" hole on a 3/4" shaft. Also, the bearing that's used with a 3/4" shaft cannot be installed in a standard "short" pump unless special components are used.

Internally, either a cast-iron or stamped-steel impeller is used. The cast iron version is stronger and moves more water, so it is typically found in race-type water pumps. Some companies offer a steel plate that can be riveted to the vanes of a stamped-steel impeller. Although great claims of increased cooling efficiency are made, testing has shown that this device has virtually no effect.

Bearings and seals can also differ from pump to pump. Standard pumps have two roller bearings whereas race pumps, such as those produced by Stewart Components (High Point, NC, 910/889-8789) utilize a ball/roller bearing combination that has approximately five times the load

carrying capability of the standard bearings. The ball/roller assembly is used in conjunction with a special seal which is compatible with both water and anti-freeze. The seals in standard pumps will usually fail if only water is used in the cooling system; water doesn't lubricate as well as anti-freeze.

Cooling System Operation

Selecting the right water pump is one step in the quest for a trouble-free cooling system. But understanding system operation is even more important if you want your engine to keep its cool.

Howard Stewart of Stewart Components manufactures racing water pumps and although the Stage III Stewart pump is superior to any other type, Howard was convinced that something better could be built. The biggest problem was that there

was no reliable means of testing water pumps. So he designed a water pump dyno.

Water Flow—His test results proved to be very enlightening and served to dispel a number of cooling system myths that have existed for years. One long-standing myth that frequently leads people to the wrong conclusions concerns water flow. A common belief is that if water flow is too high, an engine will overheat because it isn't in the block long enough to carry heat away. This dates back to the days of the '55-'57 Chevys—when the thermostat was removed on these cars, overheating would invariably result. The (incorrect) conclusion that most people came to was that removal of the thermostat allowed water flow to increase so much that it moved through the engine too quickly to provide adequate cooling.

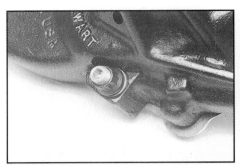

Although not necessary for most street engines, an adjustable cam stop is a definite asset on a race engine. The stop contacts the timing cover and stabilizes it so any cam thrust forces are better controlled.

Some race pumps are adjustable so belt tension can be maintained without an idler. This arrangement is typically used in conjunction with a short belt that runs only around the crank and water pump pulleys.

In fact, what actually happens is that when the thermostat is removed from a cooling system with a vertical radiator, the point of highest pressure in the system moves to the radiator tank. Consequently, normal operating pressure exceeds the capacity of the radiator cap spring, so the cap opens and allows coolant to escape—even though the engine is not overheating. But it doesn't take long for coolant loss to reach the point where there isn't enough left in the system to provide sufficient cooling. So it appears that unrestricted flow leads to overheating, which causes coolant to escape. However, what really occurs is that normal pressure causes the cap to lift, which allows coolant to escape, which leads to overheating.

Winston Cup Secrets

Stewart isn't alone in his belief. According to John Wilson, the engine builder in charge of the small-block Chevys at Joe Gibbs Racing Winston Cup operation:

"In the past, with some body styles, we've had a real problem because of the grille location. We wound up with all kinds of debris accumulating in the grille and blocking airflow. If there's one plastic bag anywhere near the track, it will wind up on the grille. With that situation, we found that when we ran high pressures, we could run longer without overheating when we got junk in the grille."

Wilson runs a Stant cap rated at 22 psi, and checks every one to make sure its rating is accurate. More often than not, the pressure cap is installed on a large capacity aluminum radiator. The aluminum radiator helps keep nose weight down and does a real good job—sometimes they have to tape it off because the engine runs too cool. Since adequate cooling is such a critical issue, Wilson also uses a Stewart Stage III water pump.

Most of the engine builders working with dirt track late models have also found that increasing pump speed eliminates cooling problems. The 430 cid small blocks used in these cars used to be alcohol fueled and cooling wasn't a problem. But after a rules change made it necessary to run gasoline, overheating became common. Changing from 30% underdrive to a 1:1 water pump drive ratio solved the overheating problems.

These engines run 8000 rpm, which means the water pumps are also turning 8000 rpm, so cavitation is obviously not a problem.

Pressure

This brings up the subject of pulling water. Cavitation is largely blamed for all manner of cooling system inadequacies, but according to Stewart, it's simply not a factor in cooling, so long as the system is pressurized. On Stewart's water pump dyno, the effects of system pressure are readily apparent—higher pressure translates directly to increased flow. Another factor that affects flow is the impeller clearance. One of the "secrets" of Stewart Components water pumps is that impeller clearance is precisely set in every pump. With most water pumps, production tolerances may exist, but judging by the end product, no one knows what they are. Howard Stewart tested three-vane impellers (stock impellers with every other vane removed), six-vane impellers, with curved and straight vanes, and did not record any increase in flow. The same results occurred when he pop-riveted the plate to the back of the impeller. But when he set the clearance proper on a stock pump, Stewart noticed a measurable increase in flow.

Horsepower Loss

But there's always a question about the horsepower cost incurred in the name of cooling efficiency. While there is a correlation between the volume of water pumped and the horsepower consumed doing it, the overall power loss is relatively insignificant. Besides measuring water flow, Stewart's water pump dyno also monitors power consumed

One of the factors controlling water pump efficiency is the clearance between the impeller and housing. It should be less than .100". On most standard water pumps, itŌs greater than that which frequently leads to cooling system problems that are almost impossible to solve.

driving the pump. Depending on the model, spinning a water pump at 8000 rpm (pump speed) requires between 6 and 11 horsepower. That's not much of a penalty to pay especially when you consider that most water pumps are underdriven (by at least 30%), so power consumption would be less.

The water pump dyno is set up to measure total flow, as well as flow through the left side or right side only. This configuration allowed Stewart to confirm what only a handful of engine builders have known; in a small-block Chevy, one side of the engine frequently runs hotter than the other. In fact, the left side of a small block may have 30% less water pumped through it than the right side. The ramifications of this difference are far reaching. Not only in terms of tuning, but also in evaluating cooling system modifications. For example, when every other vane was removed from a Stewart Components Stage III pump, not only did total flow decline, but the left-to-right bias was skewed in the wrong direction. Although Stewart's Stage III pump (with a 43% left/57% right ratio) is more than adequate for the cooling demands of the majority

of small blocks, a Stage IV pump has been introduced for maximum output endurance competition like Winston Cup. This pump includes a unique internal configuration, delivers equal flow to both sides of the engines and requires only 5.3 horsepower to drive at 8000 rpm pump speed.

Cooling Considerations

Due to operating environment, street and drag race engines place considerably fewer demands on the cooling system. However, in all cases, the highest rated pressure cap available should be installed (assuming the radiator is in good condition). A pressure cap is merely a safety valve and has no function if the system is operating properly. Increased cap pressure assures optimum water flow through the engine.

This is especially true in vehicles with upright radiators because the cap is exposed to maximum system pressure. Outlet restrictors can be used to concentrate pressure in the engine, rather than the radiator, but a cross-flow radiator is a much better arrangement as the pressure cap is on the suction side of the system.

Electric Motors—In the name of horsepower conservation, drag race engines typically do not drive the water pump off the crankshaft pulley. Instead, a small electric motor is used to spin the pump. Sharp racers have recently discovered that this system is like jumping over dollar bills to pick up pennies. The few horsepower saved by this arrangement is more than offset by the power lost due to the tuning requirements of an engine that isn't being cooled properly. The electric motor doesn't spin the water pump fast enough to pressurize the block. Consequently water flow to the cylinder heads, particularly at the rear, is inadequate for proper cooling. In turn, ignition timing and air/fuel ratio must be adjusted to compensate. Even though drag race engines run for a relatively short time, they still develop

For years, it has been fashionable to equip drag race engines with a small electric motor to turn the water pump. While this arrangement definitely reduces power losses compared to an engine-driven water pump, it doesn't move enough coolant to pressurize the block. Many drag racers have recently gone back to driving the water pump off the crankshaft for improved cooling and more tuning latitude.

One of the latest developments in small block water pumps is the Stewart Components DRV8 impeller that's incorporated in Stage IV pumps. The unique shape is made possible by computer aided design and CNC machining. This impeller almost doubles coolant flow while consuming less horsepower than conventional impellers.

enough heat to warrant a fully operational cooling system with a water pump spinning fast enough to pressurize the block.

Reverse Flow—Then there's the question of flow direction. Reverse flow cooling systems made a big splash a few years ago and while the theory may seem to have some validity, in practice, it seems to cause more problems than it cures. Stewart takes exception to the whole concept.

"You don't really need a reverse flow cooling system because the block is a water manifold. You don't need to do much cooling down around the bottom of the cylinders. The holes in the head gasket are orifices or restrictions so when the coolant in the block is pressurized (by the water pump) cooling is uniform from front to back. About the only thing wrong with a standard system is that coolant has to flow from the back of the cylinder head to the front, and that leads to higher temperatures at the front of the

head. External water manifolds cure that problem. Look at it this way—an unrestricted Winston Cup engine puts out over 650 horsepower, runs at maximum rpm for three hours, and under normal conditions never overheats. How bad can conventional cooling system design be? With a street car, the situation might be a little different because of engine speed. If a car is built that way fine, but otherwise, the expense of converting to a reverse flow cooling system just doesn't seem justified."

Fans

Driving down the road at a speed of 30 mph or faster, an engine doesn't need a fan to keep it cool. But when traffic brings forward movement to a halt, even the coolest running small block will overheat. A fan hanging on the end of the water pump, or mounted to the radiator and driven electrically, is clearly necessary.

Much has been made of the power-robbing effect of engine driven fans. While that's definitely a consideration, it's hard to beat an original equipment fan mounted on a thermal fan clutch. Up to approximately 5000 rpm, this arrangement requires less than five horsepower to keep it spinning. Flex fans eat up considerably more horsepower.

The one problem with a stock-type fan and a clutch is that they are heavy. If an engine regularly sees more than 4000 rpm—even for short bursts—water pump bearing failure will result in relatively short order.

By far, the best arrangement is to install an electric fan and completely remove the mechanically driven one. In some cases, if a large diameter fan (17" or 18") can't be obtained, two smaller diameter units (12" to 14")

The advent of a single serpentine belt to drive all front mounted accessories has made it easy to switch to underdrive pulleys. Underdrive pulleys for serpentine systems are most frequently installed on the crankshaft and water pump. Alternator pulleys are also available. Pulleys are available in both aluminum and steel; steel is preferable for durability. Underdrive pulleys are also available for conventional v-belt accessory drives. The least expensive models are made of cast aluminum. Machined billet pulleys shown here are also offered by a number of manufacturers.

may be required. In all cases, special shielding may be required to direct airflow through the radiator.

Pulleys

For years, stock pulleys were deemed sufficient for race as well as street engines. Then, some enterprising individual noticed that the diameters selected by the factory for use on plain vanilla passenger cars weren't the hot tip for performance.

Underdrive pulleys have been around for years, but it wasn't until the

Comparing the size of a stock crankshaft pulley (right) to an underdrive version makes it easy to see why the latter delivers a measurable performance improvement. In addition to slowing the speed of crank-driven accessories, the smaller diameter pulley also reduces the mass that must be accelerated by the engine.

The water pump on this Winston Cup engine is underdriven a good bit, but that's not always the case. Depending upon the race track and time of year, it may be driven at any ratio up to 1:1. Water pumps on street engines are typically over-driven because they have to deliver adequate coolant flow at comparatively low engine speeds.

advent of the single serpentine belt systems that they achieved widespread popularity. With a single belt system, the effects of a pulley drive ratio change are more readily apparent because the speed at which all accessories are driven is changed at one time. Switching to underdrive pulleys can improve quarter-mile times by up to .2 seconds. The most effective approach is to change the crankshaft, water pump and alternator pulleys. Many three-pulley kits allow the original belt to be retained.

VIBRATION DAMPERS

When the sanctioning bodies that govern organized drag racing outlawed stock vibration dampers (also called harmonic balancers) in most classes, they did so out of concern for safety. That raises concerns over the use of a stock vibration damper on a street car—

especially one with a high performance engine. Do the safety considerations that apply to race engines also pertain to street powerplants? As it turns out, they do. Therefore it makes sense to consider installing a high performance damper on a street engine. However, safety is only one reason. More power and improved engine life are other potential advantages.

Stock Dampers

There's really nothing wrong with a stock vibration damper—except that it's designed for the engine in Aunt Martha's luxobarge which will never see daylight above 4000 rpm. At higher engine speeds, stock dampers have been known to fracture and ultimately explode. While such occurrences are rare on a street-driven vehicle, they do happen.

Cast-iron flywheels have the same tendency which is why they are forbidden on high revving (race) engines. On a stock damper, the inertia ring is constructed of cast iron, hence the concern. Although acceptable for low rpm applications (where a change in materials would do little besides increase costs) cast iron has a nasty habit of fracturing when subjected to the high levels of centrifugal force generated by elevated engine speeds. Once the ring begins fracturing, pieces break off and are hurled outward. As you might imagine, when a few ounces of iron being spun at 6500 rpm break free, they hit like a blast from Dirty Harry's favorite handgun. A half-pound of iron on the outer ring of an 8" damper generates a force of 3182 pounds when spun at 7000 rpm. Although the probability of a stock inertia ring fracturing is remote, it's not out of the

question.

Elastomer Strip—Of course, there are other considerations. Another weak point of a stock damper is the elastomer strip between the hub and inertia ring. This strip functions in the manner of a tightly wound spring. Vibrations are damped because the inertia ring, which seems to be solidly mounted to the inner hub, actually rotates forward and back on the hub in response to crankshaft vibrations. As the inertia ring works to and fro on the elastomer strip, it creates heat. All dampers function by converting vibration energy to heat.

Because it is rubber and therefore does not take kindly to heat, elastomer deteriorates when repeatedly exposed to high temperatures. Before long, the elastomer loses its grip and allows the inertia ring to slide forward or rearward, to rotate freely around the hub, or to fall off. Many times, ignition timing is found to be off

Stock vibration dampers have been used on high performance engines for many years, but the inertia ring tends to slip, or come off entirely when the elastomer strip between it and the hub deteriorates. Viscous dampers seem to be the preferred design with professional engine builders. This cutaway photo shows the inertia ring which resides inside a hermetically sealed housing. The silicon fluid that surrounds it knots up in response to crankshaft vibration. Viscous high performance dampers are available from independent suppliers and Mr. Goodwrench (GM Performance Parts).

Engines using a 3-3/4" stroke crankshaft from a 400 cid small block are externally balanced and require a damper with a counterweight. The term "externally balanced" simply means that some amount of counterweight is contained by the damper and/or flywheel. In an internally balanced engine, all the counterweight needed to offset the mass of the pistons and connecting rods is located on the crankshaft. Internal components of both types of engines must be individually balanced when an engine is built.

because the inertia ring has moved from its original position. These types of damper failures do occur on high performance street engines with some amount of regularity; they occur more frequently on race engines. The harder an engine is run, and the higher the rpm, the more prone a stock damper is to failure.

Many of the high performance dampers that meet race organization specifications are actually nothing more than a stock-type damper with a steel rather than cast-iron inertia ring. Some brands of elastomer dampers are a bit cheaper than either friction or viscous types, and while they do eliminate the potential for inertia ring explosion, they are subject to the same heat-induced elastomer deterioration that plagues stock

dampers. When the elastomer deteriorates, the damper must be scrapped. Some elastomer dampers are supposed to be rebuildable, but the jury is still out on the feasibility of replacing the elastomer strip.

Viscous Dampers

Diesel engines have horrendous vibration problems and the viscous damper was developed specifically for this application. A number of years ago, Vibratech Performance, Alden, NY, (716/937-3603) the world's largest manufacturer of diesel vibration dampers, began producing Fluidampr viscous dampers for high performance street and race engines. With their superior damping capability, viscous dampers have mushroomed in popularity. In fact, they are now available through the Chevrolet and Goodwrench high performance parts programs.

The concept behind a viscous damper is actually quite simple. Thick silicone fluid is pressure-fed into the narrow gaps between the inertia ring and its hermetically sealed housing. The inertia ring is not physically attached to the housing, and the silicone fluid provides a connection in much the same manner as transmission fluid is the link between the input and output sides of a torque converter. To carry the analogy a bit further, the silicone fluid's consistency determines its 'stall speed'—the point at which the fluid shears. The shearing action provides vibration damping.

During normal engine acceleration, the fluid offers enough resistance to keep the inertia ring spinning just slightly slower than crankshaft rpm. However, crankshaft vibration occurs in the range of 300 cycles per second,

and when these high amplitude forces attempt to make the damper housing vibrate, the fluid "knots up" or wedges itself between the inertia ring and the housing. When this occurs, the mass of the inertia ring actively resists crankshaft vibration because of fluid action in the housing. But when vibration-induced crank movement subsides, the inertia ring does not have to rebound to its original position. This allows the viscous damper to control vibrations at all engine speeds, which is advantageous.

Conversely, elastomer type dampers are frequency sensitive which means they offer maximum vibration damping only at a particular engine speed (where vibration frequency is within the range that the damper is tuned to control). Consequently, if the mass of the reciprocating assembly is changed (such as when aftermarket pistons, or connecting rods are installed or when crankshaft stroke is changed), the damper's effectiveness will be diminished. By comparison, the intensity (amplitude) of the vibration, not its frequency, is the controlling factor with amplitude sensitive dampers. An amplitude sensitive damper will therefore offer

Fluidampr offers this chrome damper for show and marine engines. Measuring only 6-1/4" in diameter, it's lighter than a stock damper yet provides better vibration control.

A wheels-up launch is accompanied by a heavy g-force load. That presents unique problems for the fuel delivery system. Typically, an electric fuel pump, mounted at the rear is required to ensure adequate fuel delivery.

One of Holley's Volumax fuel pumps will handle the fuel delivery needs of most small blocks. These pumps are available in two flow rates—160 and 250 gallons per hour. Larger pumps. up to 400 gallons per hour are also available, but generally present an overkill situation.

maximum vibration damping at all engine speeds.

Do you need a high performance vibration damper? That depends upon how your small block will be used. If you do any type of racing, or routinely run your engine at high speeds, or have added a blower or nitrous oxide, the answer is an unqualified yes. If you just drive your street engine hard on occasion, you can slide by with a stock damper—just be sure to inspect it occasionally.

While a high performance damper may seem like overkill for most street engines, sometimes it's more of a necessity than a luxury.

Now that high performance dampers have been on the market for several years, evidence is mounting that they do indeed provide superior vibration damping capability. And in many cases, they'll actually deliver a slight power improvement because reduced crankshaft vibration provides greater cam and ignition timing accuracy. The problem is that a

damper's effect on power output isn't consistent from one engine to another. Sometimes a damper change will produce a noticeable power increase, other times it won't. However, in all cases, a high performance damper that controls crank vibration over the widest range of engine speeds always shows a reduction in bearing and crank wear. Consistency usually improves as well.

FUEL PUMPS

Much ado is made about fuel pumps on race engines, and for good reason. Fuel starvation is one of the most frequent causes of poor performance. Starvation means the carburetor doesn't receive, under some circumstances, enough fuel to keep the fuel bowls full. It doesn't mean the carb runs dry. Fuel starvation is rarely a problem with fuel-injected engines because the high pressure fuel pumps that are required usually have sufficient capacity to handle an

engine's needs.

Capacity—In drag racing, the rule of thumb is that an electric fuel pump should be able to output one gallon of gasoline (measured at the carburetor inlet) in 20 seconds or less. Mechanical fuel pumps are not usually adequate for serious drag engines—even though they can pump enough fuel to supply the demands of a 700-horsepower NASCAR Winston Cup engine.

The g-forces working against the fuel pump constitute a major difference between drag racing and oval track fuel systems. With a mechanical pump located on the engine, it must pull fuel from the rear of the car; g-forces push fuel away from the pump inlet. On the other hand, an electric fuel pump is mounted at the rear of the car adjacent to the fuel tank. It therefore pushes fuel under pressure all the way to the carburetor.

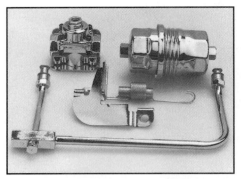

A high performance fuel pump can overpower a carburetor's inlet needles at low rpm when the engine needs relatively little fuel. Consequently, an adjustable pressure regulator (top left) is required. A fuel filter isn't a bad idea either, provided it has enough capacity and doesn't lead to fuel starvation. The chrome parts shown here (fuel line, throttle cable bracket, return spring in addition to the regulator and filter) are designed for applications where show is as important as go.

High Capacity Pumps

High capacity fuel pumps are available from a variety of sources. For carbureted engines, a Holley or Carter high-volume mechanical fuel pump is usually more than adequate for street and oval track race engines. These pumps are frequently offered as Super Speedway models by carburetor specialists. Internally, they're the same as a standard high-volume pump, but they have oversized fittings heli-arc welded into place. Six-valve pumps rated at 130 gallons per hour (gph), and either 7 or 15 psi, are also available.

A variation on the mechanical pump is the belt-driven type that is frequently used with super high horsepower gasoline and most alcohol-fired small blocks. Driven by a belt off the crankshaft, these pumps can deliver over 350 gallons per hour. They are usually plumbed to a bypass and fuel pressure varies with engine speed.

High capacity electric pumps vary widely in capacity; some street models are rated at 97 gph while maximum output race versions carry a 400+ gph rating. While some of the larger models constitute overkill for most small blocks, their capacity does offer some amount of insurance against fuel starvation.

Although race-type electric fuel pumps put out all kinds of volume, they don't have enough pressure for most types of fuel injection. Consequently, special pumps capable of producing over 50 psi are used with all TPI engines. Throttle body injection systems use lower pressures, but are still above the pressure ratings of electric pumps designed for carbureted engines.

Fuel Lines—Irrespective of the type of pump selected, it must be connected to adequately sized fuel lines. On a high performance street car, 3/8" or -6 line is generally adequate. Race cars call for 3/8" or 1/2" hard lines or -8 or -10 braided hose, depending on the application. In routing fuel lines, the important point to remember is that they should be kept away from all exhaust system components and any bends in rubber hoses should have a large radius. Many fuel starvation problems are caused by nothing more than a sharply bent rubber fuel line sucking closed.

Regulating Pressure—Although adequate volume is the key to avoiding fuel starvation, pressure is typically used to monitor fuel flow. That's because pressure is far easier to measure, and if a given amount of pressure is maintained within a fuel line of a specific diameter, adequate flow is usually assured. Any fuel system that can maintain at least 4 psi

of fuel pressure through 3/8" lines—at maximum engine speed and maximum load—is probably capable of keeping up with the demands of most small blocks. This assumes that there are no restrictions in the line. If a car is plumbed with adequately sized lines, but an undersized fitting is used at the carburetor, or in a fuel block, or a low capacity fuel filter is included, fuel starvation is a very real possibility. Also keep in mind that most pressure regulators are restrictive—which is the reason that some race cars are equipped with two or more pressure regulators.

That doesn't mean that a system should be run without a regulator. If it is, excessive fuel pressure at idle may literally blow the carburetor inlet needles of their seats and fuel may come pouring out the booster nozzles. Similarly, the fact that a fuel filter is a potential restriction doesn't mean it should be left out. Low restriction fuel filters are available from a variety of sources and should be included on any vehicle. ■

For oval track racing and street driving, a high performance mechanical fuel pump is the weapon of choice. Several versions of this type of pump are available; this is a six-valve model.

ENGINE ASSEMBLY

13

The subject of assembling a small block Chevy short block, or any other type, for that matter, is like asking for instructions for driving on a road filled with pot holes. Irrespective of the knowledge or skill level of the person giving advice, you stand a good chance of sticking one or more wheels in a hole. On the other side of the coin, one person's pot hole is another's surface irregularity. The severity of the bump is dependent on personal point of view.

Therefore, it's perfectly understandable that some engine builders will agree with the information to follow, others won't. If you're planning to have a particular shop do the machine work on your engine, assemble it or both, you're well advised not to tell that person how to do a particular job (if you feel you have to, find another machinist). If you talk candidly with most high performance or race-oriented engine builders, you'll find that they all have the same complaint—some of their customers read too much. The common scenario is that someone reads a magazine article or book and determines that he or she has become an expert capable of determining precisely how an engine should be machined.

What they fail to realize is that many practices that apply to a race

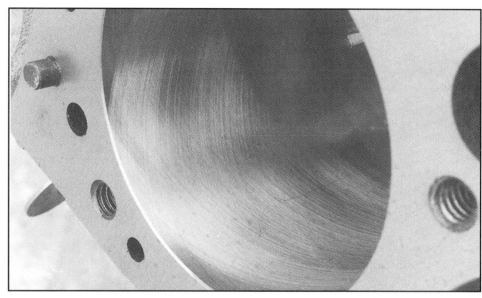

1. When you pick your block up from the machine shop, the cylinder walls should have a textbook cross-hatch pattern like this. Each type of ring material requires a different finish smoothness, but in all cases, a cross-hatch pattern should be evident.

engine don't apply to a street engine and vice versa. Also, some machining practices are required because a particular type of component is being used. If you demand a particular cylinder wall finish, but don't use the type of rings that are compatible with that finish, ring seal will be poor—but you'll blame whoever honed the block when your engine smokes like a mosquito control sprayer.

If you've never built a small-block Chevy before, or haven't been turning wrenches for a few years, find a machinist or engine builder with whom you can discuss your engine project. Ask for recommendations—if

they don't sound reasonable, or if you're not comfortable with the advice you're being given, look elsewhere. Just remember, there are any number of correct ways to build an engine and an equal number of incorrect methods. One engine builder may build race-winning engines using parts and procedures that another equally successful engine builder considers junk. So don't go trying to combine ideas from different people because they may be incompatible.

If all the machine work is done accurately, assembling an engine isn't difficult and can be completed in a few hours.

2. After you've completed all the cylinder block machine work, a thorough washing is in order. To ensure cleanliness, you'll need to use hot, soapy water and scrub all surfaces with rags or brushes. Use a special cylinder-scrubbing brush mounted in an electric drill to lean all machining oil and metal chips off the bore surfaces.

3. It's also vital to thoroughly clean all oil galley passages. A special engine-cleaning brush kit is available from Powerhouse Products. After you've cleaned the block, coat all machined surfaces except the cylinder bores with WD-40 or a similar lubricant; coat the bores with motor oil. Once the block is thoroughly cleaned, move it to as clean an area as possible. The importance of cleanliness can't be over-emphasized.

4. As a double check to ensure that bearing diameter is correct and that the main bearing saddles are machined to the proper dimension, it's advisable to insert at least one main bearing and measure the inside diameter after the cap bolts have been tightened.

5. If the bearings measure the proper diameter, remove those that have been measured, wipe the saddles and bearings clean and insert the bearings and rear main seal. Lubricate the bearing surfaces and set the crankshaft in place.

6. Note the position of the rear main seal. By rotating it slightly, so that its parting line is offset from the main cap-to-block parting line, the potential for oil leakage is reduced. A little dab of white lube on the seal surface helps break-in and improves the long term seal performance. Also note that when inserting the seal, some amount of material will usually be peeled off the back. Fel-Pro supplies a plastic "shoehorn" to prevent this.

7. Once the bearing halves are inserted in the main caps, set the caps in place and torque the bolts to specifications. As with head bolts, the main cap bolts should be tightened in steps and in sequence. Start with the center cap and torque the bolts to 30 ft-lbs. Then move sequentially to number 4, 2, 5 and 1 mains and repeat the process. Next, repeat the sequence with all bolts tightened to 50 ft-lbs. Finally, run through the sequence a final time and pull the bolts to 70 ft-lbs. On four-bolt main blocks, the outer bolts are tightened to 65 ft-lbs.

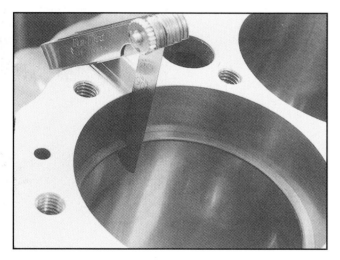

8. To ensure proper end gap, each ring is fit to the cylinder in which it will be installed. End gap is measured and then filed until the desired measurement is obtained. If rings are to be file fit to the cylinders, diameter should be .005" larger than finished bore dimension to allow for filing. (A 4.035" ring set is used in a 4.030" diameter bore.)

9. End gap can be adjusted with a regular flat file, but filing is faster and more accurate when a proper ring filer is used. Irrespective of the tool used, the file should always move from the outside of the ring towards the inside to prevent burrs from cropping up along the edges that contact the cylinder walls.

10. The piston and rod assemblies should be lined up in order so that after all the rings are filed, they can easily be matched with and installed on the proper pistons. Each connecting rod should have a number stamped on it corresponding to the cylinder in which it is to be installed.

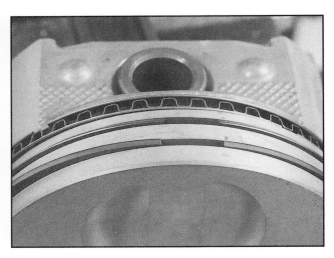

11. Use a ring expander to install the rings in their respective grooves. After all rings are in position, rotate the end gaps so they're positioned approximately 180 degrees from each other.

12. Keeping the rings properly positioned, and with a lubricated bearing half inserted in the connecting rod, place a short length of rubber hose over each rod bolt. Then put a ring compressor in place and lower the piston and rod assembly carefully into a cylinder. (Make sure the rod journal for the cylinder on which you're working is properly positioned, down out of the way.) Guide the lower end of the rod with one hand and tap the piston into the cylinder (using the handle end of a hammer) with the other.

13. As the rod approaches the crank pin, guide it so that it's centered over the journal and keep tapping on the piston until the rod bearing is seated on the crank.

14. With a lubricated bearing in place, slip the rod cap over the bolts and seat it. Then thread the nuts into place by hand.

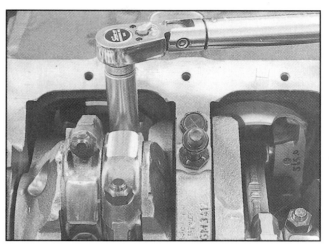

15. The rod nuts should be tightened to 40 ft-lbs. Bring them up gradually, working side to side. It's best to tighten the nuts for each rod immediately after putting the cap in place. It was done that way with this engine, but the photographer was sleeping on the job.

16. Connecting rod side clearance should be .019" to .025" to minimize internal oil hemorrhaging. There's not much you can do about it at this point, you if you have any question, trial fit a few rods and check side clearance before final assembly. Precise setting of side clearance is one of the features distinguishing a high performance engine from a garden variety rebuild.

17. Deck clearance is another critical dimension affecting performance. Many race engines are assembled with zero deck clearance—with a compressed thickness of .037" to .038", a composition gasket is thick enough to prevent the piston from hitting the head. Minimum deck clearances obviously boost compression ratio and in so doing, power is increased and the tendency to detonate is reduced. If deck clearance is in doubt, check it before you begin final assembly.

18. The camshaft can be installed just about any time, but if you wait until all the pistons and rods are in place, you reduce the "opportunities" to damage a lobe with a connecting rod. Each lobe should be liberally coated with assembly lube before sliding the cam into place.

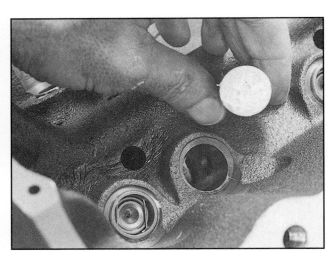

19. Before each lifter is inserted in a bore, its bottom should coated with assembly lube. Thorough application of assembly lube to the cam lobes and lifter bottoms is vital to proper cam break-in.

20. Since the crankshaft drives the cam, it needs a sprocket. No fancy tools are required, just a hammer and an "adapter" to fit over the crank snout.

21. Line up the marks on the cam and crank sprockets and with the chain in place, slip the cam sprocket onto the cam. Install a single bolt to keep the sprocket in place and rotate the crankshaft a few degrees in either direction, then back to its original position. The marks on the gears should once again be properly aligned.

22. Now you're ready to degree-in the camshaft. First you have to locate true Top Dead Center. This is accomplished by first bolting a positive stop to the top of the block, over cylinder number 1, as shown.

23. Install a degree wheel on the crankshaft and a pointer on the block. To find TDC, rotate the crank in one direction until the piston contacts the stop. Note the reading on the degree wheel, then rotate the crankshaft in the opposite direction until the piston once again contacts the stop. Note the reading once again, then split the difference. In this case, the readings were 21° before TDC (BTDC) and 17° after. That meant the pointer was off by two degrees. It was reset to 19° BTDC.

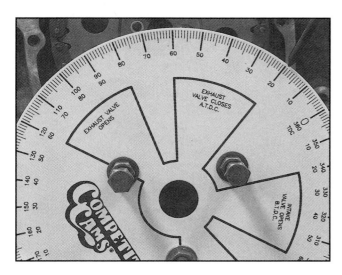

24. Once the pointer has been reset, rotate the crank in the opposite direction until the piston again hits the stop. In this case, the pointer indicated 19° after TDC. Since it indicated the same reading in both directions, 19° BTDC in one direction and 19° ATDC in the other, the degree wheel was properly positioned.

25. Next mount a dial indicator on the block and set it to zero with the lifter on the base circle of the cam. Cam timing is verified by turning the crankshaft in its normal direction of rotation (clockwise as viewed from the front). When the dial indicator registers the specified amount of lift (as the valve opens), the degree wheel reading is noted. Then the crank is rotated clockwise until the dial indicator shows the same amount of lift on the closing side of the lobe. These figures should match the opening and closing specifications included on the cam card.

26. Installation of the cylinder heads isn't a particularly difficult task, but it must be done properly. Start with top quality head gaskets such as Fel-Pro part number 1003 for cast-iron heads and 1010 for aluminum heads.

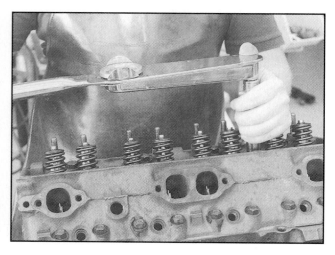

27. Set each head on the block, lightly coat the head bolt threads and the underside of the bolt heads with a sealant and install them in sequence. Thread each bolt in until its head just contacts the cylinder head. Then tighten the bolts.

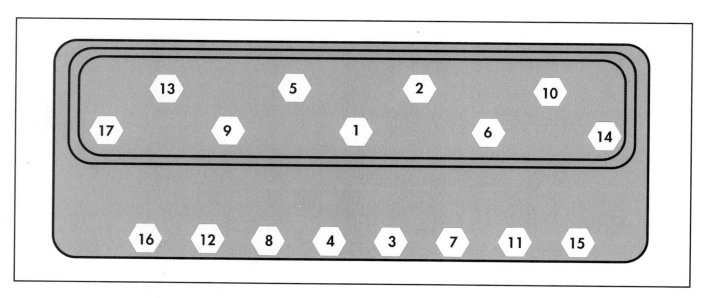

28. Tighten head bolts progressively in the sequence shown. After all bolts have been fully threaded into place, start with number one and tighten them all to 25 ft-lbs. Then run through the sequence again tightening them all to 45 ft-lbs. Make your last pass through the sequence by tightening all bolts to 65 ft-lbs. Be sure to use a sealer/lubricant on the threads and beneath the bolt heads to assure proper torque readings and no leaks.

29. After the heads are installed and all bolts properly torqued, set the intake manifold in place to prevent unwanted objects from falling into the valley. Then install the rocker arms. After they're all in place, remove the intake manifold and adjust lifter preload to .030" to .045". This can be accomplished most easily by rotating the crankshaft until the number 1 piston is at TDC at the end of the compression stroke. Then adjust cylinder number 1 intake and exhaust valves. Tighten each rocker nut while twirling the pushrod between your fingers. When you feel resistance, all clearance has been taken up. Tighten each nut an additional half turn and preload will be set correctly. Work through the firing order (1-8-4-3-6-5-7-2), and rotate the crankshaft 90° before proceeding to the next pair of rockers.

30. If you're using stock type rockers with pivot balls, coat the balls and the portion of the rocker that they contact, as well as the tips with assembly lube. With roller rockers, use motor oil on the trunion bearings and tips.

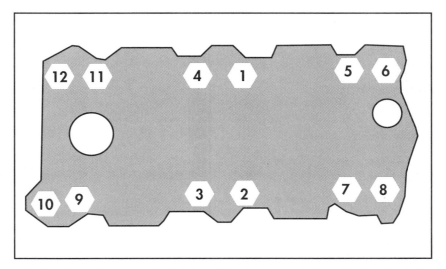

31. After the rockers are adjusted, install the intake manifold and tighten the bolts in sequence to 30 ft-lbs. Use a thread sealant and tighten the bolts in steps—snug, 15 ft-lbs. and then 30 ft-lbs.

32. Now you're ready to flip the engine upside down and finish up the bottom end. Install the oil pump drive rod by simply slipping it into place as shown.

33. Set the oil pump in place, making sure it properly engages the drive rod, but don't tighten the attaching bolt at this point.

34. The distance between the pickup and the pan is critical—if it's too close, oil flow can be choked off, if it's too far, the pickup can end up sucking air instead of oil. Engine builder Garry Grimes takes a very pragmatic approach to setting height. He places a 3/8" diameter rod over the end of the pickup, sets the oil pan in place and taps it until it's firmly seated against the block. The pickup position is automatically set precisely 3/8" from the pan. Pickups have been known to fall out of an oil pump, so after setting the pickup position, remove the pump and weld the pickup to the housing.

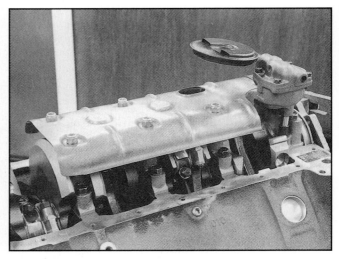

35. Before putting the oil pan in place, it's a good idea to install a windage tray. Hopefully, you already thought of this because special main cap bolts are required for tray installation and they should already be installed.

36. With the timing chain and oil pump in place, the sheetmetal (timing cover and oil pan) can be installed. The Z/28 pan requires use of the thicker (3/8" rather than 1/4"). Be sure to install the correct one.

37. There's a trick to installing a vibration damper—coat the inside of the hub and the crank snout with anti-seize.

38. Then use a proper installation tool—NOT a hammer to pull the damper into place. After this operation, the only things left are installation of the fuel pump, water pump, valve covers, carburetor and distributor.

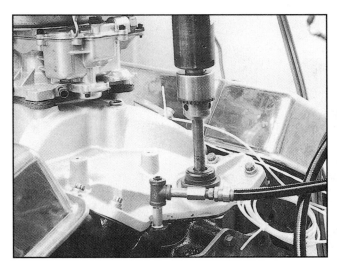

39. But before the distributor is put into place, it's advisable to prime the oiling system. It's advisable to connect an oil pressure gauge and keep the primer spinning until at least 20 pounds of oil pressure is recorded. Priming tools are available from several suppliers. Once the oiling system is primed, you're ready to fire the engine, break it in, and enjoy the fruits of your labor.

ENGINE COMBINATIONS

14

Small-block Chevy engines can be built in an almost limitless number of configurations. The most popular small block is the 350 cid combination because it has the greatest performance potential for the widest variety of applications and all internal components are readily available and attractively priced. The following engine combinations are representative of the power levels that can be extracted from a 350 engine that is suitable for street driving. A stock engine is included to provide a baseline against which the performance engines can be compared. Although all tests were run on SuperFlow 901 dynamometers, they cannot all be directly compared because testing was done at different dyno facilities. However, comparisons between the results from tests A, B, and C can be made.

Comparisons can also be made between tests I, J, K, L, M, and N which were all conducted using the same Camaro LT1 engine. These tests, in which results range from 293 to 412 horsepower, reveal a good deal about the power-producing capabilitiy of the LT1 engine and the need to take an overall "systems" approach. In all charts, an asterisk (*) indicates the maximum readings obtained in that particular test.

TEST A

Engine: Stock 350.
Maximum Horsepower: 280 @ 5000 rpm.
Maximum Torque: 375 @ 3500 rpm.
Specifications: 1.94" intake, 1.50" exhaust valves, 76cc combustion chambers, 9.5:1 compression ratio, cast-iron intake manifold, QuadraJet carburetor, 1-5/8" diameter headers, MSD distributor, 38° total mechanical spark advance.
Camshaft: Chevrolet 3896929. Advertised duration: 280/288. Duration at .004" lift (lift point at which SAE duration is computed): 258/268. Duration at .050" lift: 194/202. Lift: .390/.410".

SPEED (rpm)	CBTrq (lb-ft.)	CBPwr (hp)
1750	343	114
2000	345	131
2250	354	152
2500	349	166
2750	365	191
3000	359	205
3250	360	223
3500	375*	250
3750	370	264
4000	361	275
4250	342	277
4500	324	277
4750	308	279
5000	294	280*
5250	273	273
5500	248	259

Notes: A "typical" standard performance 350 equipped with a single four-barrel. Strong low-speed torque is to be expected from a stock engine, as is moderate horsepower. Short cam duraton restricts breathing, which limits horsepower above 4000 rpm. Note that the horsepower curve is virtually flat from 4000 to 5000 rpm, rising from 275 to 280, an increase of only 5 horsepower.

TEST B

Engine: Baseline 350 with camshaft and intake system modifications.
Maximum Horsepower: 317 @ 5000 rpm.
Maximum Torque: 392 @ 3750 rpm.
Specifications: 1.94" intake, 1.50" exhaust valves, 76cc combustion chambers, 9.5:1 compression ratio, Edelbrock Performer intake manifold, Holley 650cfm carburetor, 1-5/8" diameter headers, MSD distributor, 38° total mechanical spark advance.
Camshaft: Competition Cams 255DEH. Advertised Duration: 255/261. Duration at .050" lift: 203/212. Lift: .421/.451".

SPEED (rpm)	CBTrq (lb-ft.)	CBPwr (hp)
1750	347	116
2000	347	132
2250	361	155
2500	369	176
2750	380	199
3000	382	218
3250	384	238
3500	386	257
3750	390*	279
4000	385	294
4250	376	304
4500	362	311
4750	345	312
5000	332	316*
5250	315	315
5500	288	302
5750	278	304

Notes: The manifold, carburetor and camshaft added 37 horsepower and 17 lbs-ft. of torque over the stock 350 in Test A. Note that the torque peak only increased 250 rpm, from 3500 to 3750. More significantly, torque increased at all test points, so the boost in horsepower did not come at the expense of low-speed torque. The increase in torque is largely due to the earlier intake valve closing which traps more air and builds more cylinder pressure than the stock cam. This combination would be excellent for just about any street type car or truck, and is equally suitable for off-roading and marine use. However, while the cam does have a smooth idle, it's not smooth enough for some car owners. Also, as with any high performance cam, this one might not provide 100,000-plus mile durability, which is the goal of a stock camshaft.

TEST C

Engine: Baseline 350 w/camshaft & intake system modifications.

Maximum Horsepower: 337 @ 5250 rpm.

Maximum Torque: 388 @ 3750 rpm.

Specifications: 1.94" intake, 1.50" exhaust valves, 76cc combustion chambers, 9.5:1 C.R., Edelbrock Performer manifold, Holley 650cfm carburetor, 1-5/8" dia. headers, MSD distributor, 38° mechanical spark advance.

Camshaft: Competition Cams 265 DEH. Adv. Duration: 265/279. Duration at .050" lift: 211/221°. Lift: .442/.465".

SPEED (rpm)	CBTrq (lb-ft.)	CBPwr (hp)
1750	337	112
2000	320	122
2250	343	147
2500	360	171
2750	372	195
3000	374	214
3250	380	235
3500	384	256
3750	388*	277
4000	385	293
4250	378	306
4500	370	317
4750	360	326
5000	347	330
5250	337	337*
5500	319	334
5750	301	329
6000	285	325

Notes: Increasing cam duration brought the horsepower curve up higher and kept it there longer—but at the expense of low-speed torque. The trade-off is only 4 lbs-ft. for 20 horsepower at the peak. But at 2000 rpm, there's a 28 lbs-ft. loss compared to the shorter duration cam and that a sizable torque loss continues up through 3500 rpm. At the other end, horsepower is up by 33 at 5500 rpm and by 25 at 5750. Compared to Test B, this combination is better suited to vehicles that are driven aggressively. The engine must be revved higher to take advantage of the top-end power increases. This engine would do well in a relatively lightweight street or street/strip car. However, if compression ratio were bumped 1/2 to 1 point (to compensate for loss cylinder pressure loss due to increased cam duration) a lot of the torque would come back.

TEST D

Engine: Modified 350

Maximum Horsepower: 403 @ 6500 rpm.

Maximum Torque: 392 lbs-ft. @ 4000 rpm.

Specifications: 492 head castings with 2.02" intake, 1.60" exhaust valves, 64cc combustion chambers, porting in valve pockets and three-angle valve job, 11:1 compression ratio, Holley 300-36 intake manifold, Holley 750cfm carburetor, 1-5/8" diameter headers, MSD distributor, 38° total mechanical spark advance.

Camshaft: Comp Cams Magnum 292H. Advertised Duration: 292/292. Duration at .050" lift: 244/244. Lift: .501/.501".

SPEED (rpm)	CBTrq (lb-ft.)	CBPwr (hp)
2000	289	110
2250	304	130
2500	321	153
2750	330	173
3000	356	203
3250	366	226
3500	378	252
3750	385	275
4000	391*	298
4250	390	315
4500	380	326
4750	381	344
5000	366	348
5250	354	354
5500	368	385
5750	360	395
6000	348	397
6250	331	394
6500	326	403*

Notes: A killer street engine that's also suitable for street/strip or bracket race use or a ski boat. Note that the increased compression ratio led to a much quicker recovery of mid-range torque. With the cam's relatively long duration (at least for a street cam) torque takes a heavy hit below 3250 rpm, but by 3750 rpm, it has reached a reasonable level. The cam really comes into its own above 5000 rpm. A single-plane intake manifold would further increase power above 5000 rpm, so it would be a better choice if racing is the top priority. However, the dual-plane manifold is a better choice for general street driving. This cam is a definite fender-shaker in a 350 cid or larger engine, and idle would be rougher yet in a 300-327 cid powerplant. A cam like this definitely requires a high stall converter in cars equipped with automatic transmission.

TEST E

Engine: Modified 350 with Tuned Port Injection.
Maximum Horsepower: 356 @ 4750 rpm.
Maximum Torque: 420 lbs-ft. @ 4250 rpm.
Specifications: 492 head castings with 2.02" intake, 1.60" exhaust valves, 64cc combustion chambers, porting in valve pockets and three-angle valve job, 10:1 compression ratio, TPIS-modified manifold, runners and plenum, stock throttle body with air foil screens removed from mass airflow sensor, Magnum PROM, 1-3/4" diameter headers.
Camshaft TPI Specialties hydraulic. Advertised Duration: 278/286. Duration at .050" lift: 228/236. Lift: .490/.510".

SPEED (rpm)	CBTrq (lb-ft.)	CBHpw (hp)
2000	321	122
2250	330	142
2500	346	165
2750	374	196
3000	397	227
3250	405	250
3500	405	270
3750	410	293
4000	416	317
4250	420	340
4500	403	346
4750	394	356
5000	361	344

Notes: This power curve is fairly typical of a modified TPI engine--buckets of torque, but not much horsepower. The long runners of a TPI manifold—even if oversized—just don't flow enough air to support a horsepower curve that extends much beyond 4750-5000 rpm. On the other hand, with all that torque from idle to 4750 rpm, you can give up a little at the top end. This type of engine is ideal for the street or for marine use because all the power is down in the part of the rpm range where it can be used most easily. Throttle response is also excellent, adding even more to suitablility for street operation.

TEST F

Engine: Modified 350 with TPIS Mini Ram.
Maximum Horsepower: 400 @ 5750 rpm.
Maximum Torque: 380 lbs-ft. @ 4750 rpm.
Specifications: 492 head castings with 2.02" intake, 1.60" exhaust valves, 64cc combustion chambers, porting in valve pockets and three-angle valve job, 10:1 compression ratio, TPIS Mini Ram stock throttle body, screens removed from mass airflow sensor, TPIS Magnum PROM, 1-3/4" diameter headers.
Camshaft: TPI Specialties hydraulic. Advertised Duration: 278/286. Duration at .050" lift: 228/236. Lift: .490/.510".

SPEED (rpm)	CBTrq (lb-ft.)	CBPwr (hp)
2000	339	129
2250	329	141
2500	337	161
2750	352	184
3000	359	205
3250	354	219
3500	352	234
3750	357	255
4000	364	277
4250	374	302
4500	378	324
4750	380*	344
5000	375	357
5250	374	374
5500	367	384
5750	366	400*
6000	336	384

Notes: Proof once again that there's no free lunch. TPI Specialties developed the Mini Ram specifically to weave TPI fuel management technology into an induction system that supports high rpm operation. the switch from TPI to Mini Ram added 44 horsepower and increased usable rpm by over 1000. But peak torque dropped by 40 lbs-ft. If you like an engine that revs like there's no such thing as a redline, and pulls like a demon right up to valve float, this is it. If low rpm stump-pulling is your game, a stock TPI system is what you need.

TEST G

Engine: 383
Maximum Horsepower: 431 @ 5500 rpm.
Maximum Torque: 452 @ 4000 rpm.
Specifications: Brodix -8 cylinder heads with 2.02" intake, 1.60" exhaust valves, 68cc combustion chambers, Manley pistons (part no. 49453), 5.7" connecting rods, Edelbrock Performer manifold, Holley 750 cfm carburetor, 1-3/4" diameter headers, MSD distributor, 36 degrees total mechanical advance.
Camshaft: Competition Cams special hydraulic roller. Advertised duration: 280/286. Duration at .050-in lift: 224/230. Lift: .525/.560".

SPEED (rpm)	CBTrq (lb-ft.)	CBPwr (hp)
2000	343.7	130.9
2250	367.5	157.4
2500	374.8	178.4
2750	410.8	215.1
3000	422.5	241.3
3250	436.5	270.1
3500	444.7	296.4
3750	451.1	322.1
4000	451.8*	344.1
4250	450.4	364.5
4500	445.5	381.7
4750	432.0	390.7
5000	429.4	430.8*
5250	422.5	422.3
5500	411.4	430.8
5750	371.5	406.7
6000	319.1	364.5
6250	269.2	320.4

Notes: Much has been written about the torque prowess of the 383 and these test results show why—452 lbs-ft. torque at the peak and over 400 lbs-ft. from 2750 to 5500 rpm. The additional 1/4" stroke (compared to the stock 350) works wonders, and with a decent pair of heads, horsepower doesn't do too badly either. The advantage of the roller cam is that the relatively quick valve opening and closing velocities provide excellent airflow potential with comparatively short total duration. That adds up to a fairly smooth idle—in spite of all the power. Obviously, hydraulic roller cams pay the same type of dividends when installed in smaller displacement engines.

TEST H

Engine: Supercharged 350
Maximum Horsepower: 626 @ 6000 rpm.
Maximum Torque: 575 @ 5200 rpm.
Specifications: Dart II cast-iron Sportsman heads with TRW 2.02" intake, 1.60" exhaust valves, ported and modified by Oddy's Automotive, 68cc combustion chambers, TRW L2441F-30 supercharger pistons, Weiand 6-71 Supercharger and drive assembly, two Holley 600 cfm vacuum secondary carburetors, 1-3/4" diameter headers, MSD distributor, 32° total mechanical advance, 9% blower overdirve, 10 lbs. boost.
Camshaft: Competition Cams hydraulic roller. Advertised duration: 286/286. Duration at .050" lift: 230/230. Lift: .560/.560".

SPEED (rpm)	CBTrq (lb-ft.)	CBPwr (hp)
3600	511.3	350.5
3800	528.7	382.5
4000	534.2	406.9
4200	541.3	432.9
4400	551.2	461.8
4600	564.3	494.2
4800	569.1	520.1
5000	572.9	545.4
5200	574.8*	569.1
5400	572.3	588.4
5600	569.9	607.7
5800	564.4	623.3
6000	547.6	625.6*
6200	527.4	622.6
6400	504.7	615.0

Notes: For brute power, it's hard to beat a 6-71 blower and a pair of Holley four-barrels. Talk about drive-in appeal—the combination of blower whine and staccato idle lets everyone know your serious about horsepower. Of course, those are relatively subtle indicators when you consider that the blower and carbs are poking through the hood. For Pro Street, street/strip, bracket racing and marine applications, this combination has a lot to make you smile—575 lbs-ft. torque and 626 horsepower. Although not shown here, a separate low-rpm test revealed over 400 lbs-ft. torque at just 2000 rpm. Talk about low-end grunt! On the negative side, all of this exotic hardware doesn't come cheaply. When installing an engine of this power capacity, everything from the flywheel back should be heavy-duty as well.

Test I

Engine: 350 LT1.
Maximum Horsepower: 293@ 5200 rpm.
Maximum Torque: 331 @ 3900 rpm.
Specifications: Stock LT1 aluminum cylinder heads with 1.94" intake, 1.50" exhaust valves, stock 52cc combustion chambers, stock Camaro exhaust manifolds and exhaust system, 48mm throttle body
Camshaft: Stock LT1 hydraulic roller. Advertised duration: 268/270. Duration at .050" lift: 203/208. Lift: .450/.460".

SPEED (rpm)	CBTrq (lb-ft.)	CBPwr (hp)
3000	328	187
3200	328	200
3400	331	214
3600	330	226
3800	328	238
3900	331*	245
4000	331	252
4200	330	264
4400	327	274
4500	326	279
4600	322	282
4700	321	287
4800	315	288
4900	311	290
5000	307	292
5100	300	291
5200	295	293*
5300	287	289
5400	282	290
5500	276	289
5600	271	289
5700	264	286
5800	257	283

Notes: This stock Camaro LT1 engine is rated at 275 SAE net horsepower. With SAE net correction factors, it produced 278 horsepower, which says something for the accuracy of this series of dyno tests. The 293-horsepower figure was arrived at by using the standard correction factor. This baseline run provides an excellent basis for comparisons with test results achieved after modifications. Notice the flatness of both the torque and horsepower curves. This is a characteristic of the LT1.

Test J

Engine: 350 LT1.
Maximum Horsepower: 320@ 5500 rpm.
Maximum Torque: 339@ 4300 rpm.
Specifications: CNC-ported LT1 aluminum cylinder heads with 1.94" intake, 1.50" exhaust valves, 52cc combustion chambers, stock Camaro exhaust manifolds and exhaust system, 48mm throttle body
Camshaft: Stock LT1 hydraulic roller. Advertised duration: 268/270. Duration at .050" lift: 203/208. Lift: .450/.460".

SPEED (rpm)	CBTrq (lb-ft.)	CBPwr (hp)
3000	333	190
3200	330	201
3400	330	214
3600	333	229
3800	333	241
4000	335	255
4100	336	263
4200	338	271
4300	339*	278
4400	339	284
4500	336	288
4600	338	296
4700	336	301
4800	334	305
4900	329	307
5000	327	311
5100	323	313
5200	318	315
5300	314	317
5400	308	317
5500	305	320*
5600	299	319
5700	294	319
5800	286	316

Notes: The only change made for this test was a pair of cylinder heads ported by CNC Cylinder Heads of Pinellas Park, FL. The head swap increased torque by 8 lbs-ft. and horsepower by 27. That's an impressive increase considering that the camshaft, air filter and Camaro intake ducting are significant restrictions. Note the flat torque and horsepower curves remain.

Test K

Engine: 350 LT1.

Maximum Horsepower: 327 @ 5700 rpm.

Maximum Torque: 342 @ 4400 rpm.

Specifications: CNC-ported LT1 aluminum cylinder heads with 1.94" intake, 1.50" exhaust valves, stock 52cc combustion chambers, stock Camaro exhaust manifolds and exhaust system, high flow intake ducting to stock mass air sensor, 48mm throttle body.

Camshaft: Stock LT1 hydraulic roller. Advertised duration: 268/270. Duration at .050" lift: 203/208. Lift: .450/.460".

SPEED (rpm)	CBTrq (lb-ft.)	CBPwr (hp)
3000	330	188
3200	329	200
3400	331	214
3600	335	230
3800	335	242
4000	336	256
4100	337	263
4200	341	272
4300	339	278
4400	342*	286
4500	341	292
4600	340	298
4700	340	304
4800	340	311
4900	337	314
5000	331	315
5100	326	317
5200	323	320
5300	319	322
5400	316	325
5500	310	324
5600	306	326
5700	301	327*
5800	296	327

Notes: Simply eliminating the restrictive Camaro intake ducting produced increases of 3 lbs-ft and 7 horsepower. This demonstrates the reasons for the popularity and effectiveness of systems like Random Technology's RamMax ram air system.

Test L

Engine: 350 LT1.

Maximum Horsepower: 339 @ 5800 rpm.

Maximum Torque: 348 @ 4500 rpm.

Specifications: CNC-ported LT1 aluminum cylinder heads with 1.94" intake, 1.50" exhaust valves, 52cc combustion chambers, stock Camaro exhaust manifolds and exhaust system, 52mm TPIS throttle body.

Camshaft: Stock LT1 hydraulic roller. Advertised duration: 268/270. Duration at .050" lift: 203/208. Lift: .450/.460".

SPEED (rpm)	CBTrq (lb-ft.)	CBPwr (hp)
3000	333	190
3200	331	202
3400	334	216
3600	336	230
3800	339	245
4000	336	265
4100	339	264
4200	342	274
4300	344	282
4400	345	289
4500	348*	298
4600	347	304
4700	347	310
4800	345	316
4900	344	321
5000	342	326
5100	338	328
5200	337	333
5300	337	333
5400	327	336
5500	320	335
5600	315	336
5700	312	338
5800	307	339*

Notes: LT1s like to breathe, especially after they've been treated to a pair of ported cylinder heads. Switching from the stock 48mm to a TPI Specialites 52mm throttle body added 6 lbs./ft. and 12 horsepower. The increases wouldn't be this impressive with stock cylinder heads, but would still be significant.

Test M

Engine: 350 LT1.
Maximum Horsepower: 382 @ 5500 rpm.
Maximum Torque: 384 @ 4700 rpm.
Specifications: CNC-ported LT1 aluminum cylinder heads with 1.94" intake, 1.50" exhaust valves, 52cc combustion chambers, Arizona Speed & Marine 1-3/4" headers, Random Technology exhaust system, 52mm TPIS throttle body.
Camshaft: TPIS ZZ9 hydraulic roller. Advertised duration: 282/287 Duration at .050" lift: 212/226 Lift: .483/.520".

SPEED (rpm)	CBTrq (lb-ft.)	CBPwr (hp)
3200	358	218
3400	360	233
3600	364	250
3800	368	267
4000	379	289
4200	379	303
4400	378	317
4600	381	334
4700	384*	344
4800	384	351
4900	380	354
5000	375	357
5100	369	359
5200	368	364
5300	372	376
5400	369	380
5500	365	382*
5600	357	380
5700	340	369
5800	333	368

Notes: Installation of a TPI specialties ZZ9 camshaft and Arizona Speed & Marine 1-3/4" headers and Random Technology exhaust system really bring the LT1 to life. In combination, the cam and headers add 43 horsepower and 36 lbs-ft. of torque. Note that these power increases are all within the engine's normal operating rpm range and that the power peak occurs at 5500 rpm. At this point, the stock exhaust system is imposing flow restriction that are definitely hindering power. Note also that increases would not be as great had the heads not been modified. The LT1 is a very well coordinated engine package and requires that modifications be equally well-coordinated for maximum effectiveness.

Test N

Engine: 350 LT1.
Maximum Horsepower: 412 @ 5800 rpm.
Maximum Torque: 405 @ 4700 rpm.
Specifications: CNC-ported LT1 aluminum cylinder heads with 1.94" intake, 1.50" exhaust valves, 52cc combustion chambers, Arizona Speed & Marine 1-3/4" headers, Random Technology experimental dual catalytic converter exhaust system, 52mm TPIS throttle body.
Camshaft: Stock LT1 hydraulic roller. Advertised duration: 268/270. Duration at .050" lift: 203/208. Lift: .450/.460".

SPEED (rpm)	CBTrq (lb-ft.)	CBPwr (hp)
3200	387	236
3400	387	250
3600	384	263
3700	383	270
3800	380	275
3900	383	284
4000	384	292
4100	386	301
4200	389	311
4300	390	320
4400	399	334
4500	399	342
4600	403	353
4700	405*	363
4800	405	370
4900	402	375
5000	399	380
5100	396	385
5200	396	392
5300	392	396
5400	389	400
5500	386	404
5600	379	404
5700	375	407
5800	373	412*

Notes: The standard Camaro exhaust system is definitely restrictive, which is no surprise. GM even acknowledged it by equipping the Camaro with dual catalytic converters for the 1996 model year. That change increased horsepower from 275 to 285. In this case, installation of dual converters increased torque by 21 lbs-ft. and horsepower by 30.

INDEX

FEL-PRO INTAKE MANIFOLD GASKET SPECIFICATIONS

Fel-Pro Gasket No.	Port Dimensions (inches)
For Standard Port Configurations	
1204*	1.23 x 1.99 (stock size)
1205	1.28 x 2.09
1206	1.34 x 2.21
1207	1.38 x 2.28
1209	1.38 x 2.38
For Special Port Configurations	
1263 Raised runner & Pontiac 867	1.31 x 2.02
1277 High Port 18-degree	1.25 x 2.15
1296 Splayed Valve head	1.60 x 2.00
1237 SB2	1.40 x 1.90

*Gasket number 1256 has the same port opening size but has an open rather than a blocked heat-riser opening.

EXHAUST HEADER GASKET SPECIFICATIONS

Fel-Pro Gasket No.	Port Dimensions (inches)
1444	1.38 x 1.38 stock square opening
1404	1.50 x 1.50 square
1405	1.55 x 1.55 square
1406	1.55 x 1.63 D-shape
1426	1.59 diameter round
1407	1.81 diameter round
1408	2.19 diameter round
1409	1.81 diameter round Brodix spread port
1482	1.74 x 1.60- 18-degree head
1483	2.00 round 18-degree adapter plate
1484	1.94- diameter splayed valve head

NOTES

ABOUT THE AUTHOR

Photo by Jim Monteith, Country House Studios.

Dave Emanuel began his career in automotive journalism in 1970 when his first article was published in *Car Craft* magazine. Since then, his byline has appeared on over 1,500 feature articles in magazines such as *Hot Rod, Super Chevy, Stock Car Racing, Super Stock, Popular Hot Rodding, Road & Track, Motor Trend, Corvette Fever, Muscle Car Review, Home Mechanix, 4-Wheel & Off-Road*, and *Automobile Quarterly*. He has also written six books and has appeared on the television program *Road Test Magazine* which airs on The Nashville Network (TNN).

A thorough knowledge of a subject is required before an author can write authoritatively about it and Dave gained his knowledge about automobiles the old-fashioned way—he broke them. It wasn't long after he began driving legally that Dave made his first visits to a drag strip, initially as a spectator, then as a competitor. After several years of racing experience, the marriage of journalism and automobiles came about when Dave set a track record and decided to chronicle his efforts. After dabbling in journalism on a part-time basis for several years, Dave decided to abandon his job as a computer systems analyst and began writing full-time.

In a relatively short time, he established himself as one of the country's leading automotive journalists. Although he has done road tests, product reviews, personality profiles and features, he is best known for his technical articles and books. He brings a unique perspective to these through a combination of personal relationships with a number of the most successful race engine builders in the nation, and extensive hands-on experience. ■